A Quick Steep Climb
Up Linear Algebra

version 1.0

Stephen Davies, Ph.D.
Computer Science Department
University of Mary Washington

Copyright © 2021 Stephen Davies.

University of Mary Washington
Department of Computer Science
James Farmer Hall
1301 College Avenue
Fredericksburg, VA 22401

Permission is granted to copy, distribute, transmit and adapt this work under a Creative Commons Attribution-ShareAlike 4.0 International License:

http://creativecommons.org/licenses/by-sa/4.0/

The accompanying materials at `www.allthemath.org` are also under this license.

If you are interested in distributing a commercial version of this work, please contact the author at `stephen@umw.edu`.

The LaTeX source for this book is available from: `https://github.com/rockladyeagles/quick-steep-climb`.

Cover art copyright © 2015 Elizabeth M. Davies. Images courtesy `pinterest.com/laerpearce` and `serpmedia.org` (p. 212), `https://commons.wikimedia.org/wiki/User:Roger_McLassus_1951` and `pxhere.com` (p. 213), `https://commons.wikimedia.org/wiki/User:Andrey_Korzun` (p. 229), and `https://unsplash.com/@sjcbrn` (p. 242).

Contents at a glance

	Contents at a glance	i
1	Stretching our legs	1
2	Vectors	11
3	Linear independence	53
4	Matrices	83
5	Linear transformations	113
6	Matrix multiplication	143
7	Applications	177
8	Eigenanalysis	211
9	Eigenapplications	233

Also be sure to check out the forever-free-and-open-source instructional videos that accompany this series, at www.allthemath.org!

Chapter 1

Stretching our legs

We've got a steep climb up ahead of us. What exactly are we up against? And what will we see from the summit that will be worth all the effort to get there?

As we did in the opening chapter of A Cool, Brisk Walk, let's take the two words of our subject – "Linear Algebra" – one at a time, and talk about what they mean. And just like we did for "Discrete Mathematics," we'll consider the words in reverse order.

1.1 "Algebra"

When most people hear the word "algebra," they flash back to middle school, to that subject where they first learned to work with letters (like x) instead of just numbers (like 5) in a math class. They remember the quadratic formula, collecting like terms, factoring expressions, and so on.

That middle school class is indeed related to the subject of our book, but more distantly than you might imagine. Properly speaking, that middle school subject is a *proper* noun: "Algebra" with a capital 'A.' It's actually a special case of the *common* noun that mathematicians deal with: an "algebra" with a lower-case 'a.' Okay. So what's *an* algebra," then?

An algebra is any system of mathematical objects together with operations that can be used to combine them. The middle school Algebra is an example: the "objects" are numbers (or letters that stand for numbers) and the operations are things like addition, multiplication, powers, roots, and the like. We can take numbers (or stand-ins) like:

$$5, x, 3, y, q, 17, 14, z, 9$$

and combine them to build up a complex expression like:

$$\frac{\frac{(5+x)^3}{y} - q \cdot 17}{\sqrt{(14+x)^z + 9 + y}}.$$

It looks kinda gross, but I think you'll agree that if you knew what numbers each letter stood for, you could laboriously crank out the answer with a calculator.

Another example was the algebra of sets we learned about in *Cool, Brisk Walk* chapter 2. We could take the sets $A, B, \mathbb{N}$, and $\mathbb{Q}$ and combine them with set operations to get:

$$((A \cap \mathbb{N}) \cup \overline{B}) \times A - \overline{(\mathbb{Q} \cup B)}.$$

Or, from chapter 8 of *Cool, Brisk Walk*, we could combine the logical propositions P, Q, R, and S to get a compound proposition like:

$$(\neg P \vee Q \wedge \neg(R \oplus P)) \Leftrightarrow (\neg S \Rightarrow P).$$

Any system of mathematical objects and operations like this is an "algebra." The subject of this book is *linear* algebra in which the "mathematical objects," instead of being numbers or sets or propositions, are **vectors** and **matrices**.

Closure

Key to the notion of an algebra, by the way, is the notion of **closure**. Closure means that when we combine two or more of the

1.2. "LINEAR"

mathematical objects in question, we get back another object *of the same type*. For instance, whether or not you can simplify $\frac{227}{45}$ in your head, you *do* know that when you divide 227 by 45 you will get *a number*. Similarly, if you take the union of two sets $D \cup M$, you will get *a set*. And if you take the exclusive-or of two propositions $L \oplus A$, you will get *a proposition*.

This is important because without this guarantee, we couldn't build up complex expressions and be certain they would mean anything. Take the expression $12 + \frac{227}{45}$. Even without a calculator, you know these operations can in principle be done, because whatever exact value $\frac{227}{45}$ turns out to be, it's guaranteed to be *a number*, and therefore it can be meaningfully added to 12. If, when dividing one number by another, the result might wind up being a *set* (or a proposition, or a porcupine), then the whole expression would become meaningless: you can't add a number to a porcupine.

In this book we'll combine vectors and matrices in a myriad of different ways, and we will always get vectors and matrices back. That's why they constitute "an algebra."

1.2 "Linear"

The word *linear* is related to the word *line*: this is because a function that is linear looks like a line when it's plotted.[1] Suppose I make $11.75/hour at my part-time job, and I want to figure out my take-home pay for last week's work. Obviously, my paycheck (before taxes and what-not) will be 11.75 times the number of hours I

---

[1] Now there's one confusing detail I want to clear up right away. You'll recall that in high school, you learned that the equation for a straight line was "$y = mx + b$". Would it surprise you if I told you that this is *not* considered a linear function, according to the worldview of this book? Yep. :\ Sorry for the surprise. That high school thing is actually called an **affine** function rather than a linear function. The reason is the b, also called the y-intercept. If b is anything other than zero, then neither of the two "linear expectations" that we'll see on p. 5 will be true. For example, if $f(x) = 3x + 7$, then $f(2)$ (which is 13) won't be $2 \cdot f(1)$ (which is 20), as our linearity definition requires. For us in this book, the only functions considered "linear" are those lines that *pass through the origin*, and thus have a y-intercept of 0.

work. The left side of Figure 1.1 shows my hours vs. my pay, which is, not surprisingly, a line.

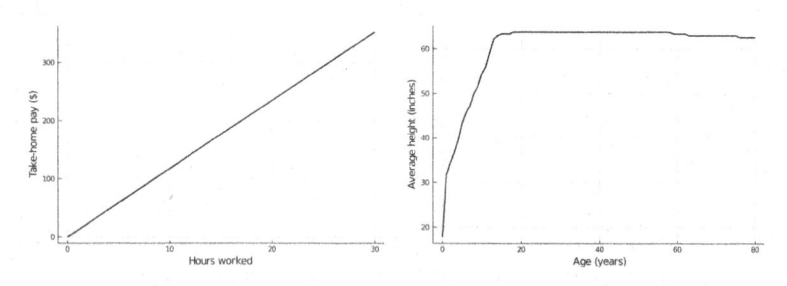

Figure 1.1: Linear and non-linear functions.

By contrast, suppose I wanted to predict how tall a typical American human female would be based on her age. While it's true that for most age ranges the two variables increase together (just as more hours-worked implies more take-home pay, so does more years-on-earth implies more inches-off-the-ground), the plot is no longer a straight line (see the right side of Figure 1.1).

It's worth lingering for a moment on what linear *means* and how it colors our assumptions about what to expect. Imagine this conversation:

YOU: Hey boss, I know I'm normally only scheduled to work for 12 hours a week, and I get 120 bucks for that. But I need to start saving up for a plane ticket to see my grandparents, so I'd like to work 15 hours next week. That okay?

BOSS: Sure, you can do 15 next week. That'll make your take-home pay an even $5,000 for the week.

YOU: [*Jaw drops open*] Whoa, five *grand*?! Heck, in that case, push me up to 20 – I can make some headway on my fall tuition!

BOSS: Twenty hours it is – you'll earn a total of 75¢ for that.

YOU: *D'oh!!*

1.2. "LINEAR"

The above dialogue is absurd. But exactly *why* is it absurd? Answer: because we expect weekly-pay-vs.-hours-worked to be linear, and the values given in the dialogue violate our linear assumptions.

The following scene, by contrast, *isn't* absurd:

YOU: It's now been 12 months since I bought it, and my Blackberry stock is currently worth $120. Dear Crystal Ball, how much will it be worth three months from now (at the 15-month point)?

CRYSTAL BALL: Blackberry will skyrocket in the public's imagination three months from now, so at the 15-month mark your stock will be valued at $5,000.

YOU: Woo-hoo! And how about at the 20-month mark?

CRYSTAL BALL: Unfortunately for shareholders, Blackberry Inc. will make some bad business decisions and crash. The stock will be nearly worthless – just 75¢.

YOU: Yikes – glad I asked! Please sell it in three months, okay?

This scenario doesn't seem out of the question because we have no expectations about stock prices being linear in time.

So what exactly are those linear expectations? If you work it out, they come down to two:

If a function $f(x)$ is linear, then:
- $f(a \cdot x)$ is always simply $a \cdot f(x)$.
- $f(x + y)$ is always simply $f(x) + f(y)$.

Take the first one. Let's say Wawa is selling a King Size Kit Kat bar for $1.50. How much would four bars cost? The answer's got to be $6.00. It would be weird to be anything else. In this example, x is the number of Kit Kat bars, and $f(x)$ is the total cost. $f(x) = 1.5x$, and predictably, $f(4 \cdot 1) = 4 \cdot f(1) = 4 \cdot 1.5 = 6$.

For the second rule, let's say we bought two Kit Kat bars today and three more tomorrow. How much for the total? If the universe is working normally, buying two today and three tomorrow would be the same price as buying five altogether. And it's true: $f(2+3) = f(2) + f(3) = 3 + 4.5 = 7.5 = f(5)$. It would be weird to work any other way.

When we have non-linear functions, we don't expect these things to be true. If my nine-year old daughter is 4 feet tall, I don't expect her to be 8 feet tall when she turns eighteen. $f(a \cdot x) \neq a \cdot f(x)$. And if my Blackberry stock is worth $5,000 after sixteen months and $100 after the company's disastrous seventeenth, we don't count on it being worth $5,100 after 33 months. $f(x+y) \neq f(x) + f(y)$.

For the rest of this entire book, the two assumptions above will always be true. It may seem limiting, but as we've seen, there are lots of cases where it simply doesn't make any sense for our function *not* to be linear.

1.3 This book contains only elephants

The great mathematician and computational scientist Stanisław Ulam once quipped that dividing functions into linear and non-linear is like dividing zoology into "elephant" and "non-elephant." In a way it's true, because there are certainly far more functions that *don't* obey the above two properties than there are those that do. By the same token, though, there are far more pay schemes we could invent than just "a regular hourly rate." But hourly rates come up very, very often, and when they do, there's a lot of amazingly useful things we can do with them. Join us on our hike and you'll see.

🐍 *Appendix: Python*

Each chapter of this book comes equipped with an appendix showing how to carry out the various linear algebra calculations in a programming language called Python. Here's the first one!

Most readers will have done at least a little bit of computer programming before making it to this book. If you haven't, don't worry about it. We're not really going to be programming *per se*, but rather using the Python language as a glorified calculator.

Python is of course a fully-functional, feature-rich programming language that can be used for just about any program you want to write, whether that's a PC or smartphone app, a data analysis program, or a dynamic website. It's a great and very readable language, and I highly recommend adding it to your quiver as you assimilate various high-tech tools.

Installing and navigating Python

For this book, all you'll need to do is download a Python IDE[2] and the "package" (bundle of software) called "**numpy**." NumPy[3] stands for "numerical Python," and has the various cogs and gears to create vectors and matrices, the mainstays of this book. The easiest way I know of to do this is to download the **Anaconda** Python distribution from www.anaconda.com, and then start the **Spyder** application that automatically comes with it.

Whether you use Spyder or a different IDE (Eclipse, IDLE, and PyCharm are some other popular ones), the main thing to focus on – and the only thing I'll describe in this book – is the Python code itself, which you'll type in an **editor** window that sorta resembles Microsoft Word or Google Docs.

---

[2]IDE stands for "Integrated Development Environment" and just means "a point-and-click interface that lets you write programs, edit them, run them, and debug (find and remove errors) them."

[3]NumPy can be pronounced either "NUM-PIE" or "NUM-pee." I've heard both.

After you type in some code and want to try running it, you'll execute whatever the "run/execute" operation is in your IDE (in Spyder it's a little green "run" arrow). The output of the code will then appear in some kind of **console** window (normally another pane on the screen; in Spyder it's on the lower-right by default). Just think of this like a calculator: you first type in something like "258 × 312" and then when you press the equals sign ("=") the answer 80496 appears.

That's more or less all we'll be doing in this book. The code you write in the editor window will be like the "258 × 312" part (except it will involve vectors and matrices), and the 80496 is what Python will print to the console window. Our "programs" won't even really deserve the name.

From now on, whenever I give example Python code in this book, I'll write it in a box like this:

```python
# Our first code example!
from numpy import *

founding = 1776
usa_age = 2021 - founding
print("Our country is {} years old!".format(usa_age))
```

That box means "this stuff goes in the editor window."

When I write the corresponding output (*i.e.*, what gets printed to the console when you run the code) I'll write it like this:

```
Our country is 245 years old!
```

That vertical bar means "this stuff is the printed result of executing that code."

First steps

And actually, before we end this first appendix, let's talk briefly about the code in that very first box and what it means.

1.3. THIS BOOK CONTAINS ONLY ELEPHANTS

First off, you'll see that the first line of that code snippet begins with a hashtag ("#"). This tells Python to *ignore* that line entirely. It doesn't contain Python code, after all, but English text, which Python can't understand. This is called a **comment**. Comments are used quite often as "notes to oneself," to organize a program, or to narrate non-obvious sections of code.

Another use of the hashtag (perhaps even more common) is to temporarily "comment out" lines of code that you don't want to run for the time being. Instead of outright deleting things you want Python to ignore for the moment, it's convenient to stick hashtags on the far-left of such lines, since you can easily remove the hashtags whenever you want to get Python to recognize those lines again.

Moving on, the very first (non-commented) line of code you'll put in every Python program is this one:

```
from numpy import *
```

which just means "I'd like to use the NumPy package, please."[4]

The next two lines of code create **variable**s, which are named containers that hold values. In this case, the values in question are simply integers, although later in the book we'll be using variables to store vectors and matrices and other goodies.

To create a new variable (or change the current value of an existing variable), you simply give the variable a name (with no spaces or funky characters) and use the equals sign to **assign** that variable a value, as in "`founding = 1776`". Unlike in math, a program variable's value can change throughout the program any time the code assigns it a new value.

---

[4]You may see other ways of importing NumPy, particularly this one:

```
import numpy as np
```

This is actually slightly better practice, but it also means that any time you'd want to use NumPy stuff – like the `array()` function we'll talk about in Chapter 2 – you'd have to prefix it with "`np.`" It's slightly more convenient to avoid that for our Python-as-quick-calculator approach.

The following line is only slightly more complicated: it performs a subtraction operation to **calculate** a value for the usa_age variable.[5] Some of the symbols used for common mathematical operations are obvious, and some are not:

        `+` – addition
        `-` – subtraction
        `*` – multiplication
        `/` – division
        `%` – modulus ("remainder when dividing by")
        `**` – exponentiation ("to the power of")
`sqrt(`*value*`)` – square root

Finally, the last line of that code (with `print()`) is used for displaying output to the console. Inside the parentheses, you put a quoted piece of text that you want to display. You put a pair of back-to-back curly braces ("`{}`") to create a placeholder for a variable's value to be inserted.[6] Then, following the final quotation mark, you put "`.format()`" (notice the leading dot) and inside *its* parens you list the variables (in order and separated by commas if there's more than one) that you want Python to substitute in the placeholders. Make sure you get the syntax right, character-for-character, because like most programming things it's unforgiving.

Code in a Python program executes line-by-line, top-to-bottom. So after the NumPy library is imported, and the `founding` variable is given the value 1776, the next line subtracts 1776 from 2021 and sets `usa_age` to 245. The print statement then sticks that value in for the placeholder in its message, and outputs the complete message to the screen: "Our country is 245 years old!"

That's it! After you've typed this example program into Spyder's (or your IDE's) editor, and run it to see the output shown above in the console, I hereby declare you Python-ready for the rest of the book.

---

[5]Underscores are commonly used in variable names to split up multiple words. Underscores are *not* considered "funky."

[6]There are other ways, too, of combining text and numbers in a message without using curly-brace placeholders and the `.format()` function.

Chapter 2

Vectors

As I stated on p. 1, every "algebra" is comprised of a set of mathematical objects which you can combine with various operations. In linear algebra, those building blocks are **vectors** and **matrices** (singular: matrix). Buried within them are many mysteries. We'll cover them in considerable detail in this chapter and the next.

2.1   Vector vs. scalar quantities

The first thing we should do is perhaps distinguish between a vector quantity and a **scalar quantity**, which probably had the spotlight in most of your previous math classes. A scalar value is simply a *single* number, like 5, or -3.2, or π, or even $9 + 2i$ if you're into imaginary numbers. The word *scalar* is related to the word *scale*, as in a "scale of measure." Think of stepping on a scale to weigh yourself in the morning: your scale gives you back a single number (which you may or may not like; I won't judge).

We'll call scalars **one-dimensional** values. That might seem odd, since we haven't really talked about "dimensions," yet. But think of the plain-old **number line** you learned about back in elementary school. Zero's drawn in the middle, positive numbers to the right and negative numbers to the left, and the whole thing extends infinitely in just one direction[1].

Examples are so ubiquitous they're hardly worth mentioning. A person's weight in the morning is a scalar. A company's stock price on a given day is a scalar. So is the net *movement* (up or down) of a stock's price from one day to the next. So is a respondent's answer to the survey question "on a 1-to-10 scale, how much do you enjoy tuna fish?" You can think of countless others.

We of course often use variables to represent scalar quantities, and in this book we'll put a variable in italics (like "*x*" or "*price*") to signify that its underlying value is a scalar quantity.

A vector: a multi-dimensional quantity

Now a vector quantity is kind of the same thing, except that it represents *more than one* value. Suppose we wanted to represent not just a stock's price on a given day, but an entire year's worth of prices on consecutive days. Then, we would need a vector quantity. Instead of a survey respondent's answer to just one question, we might want to store her entire set of answers to all twenty questions on the survey. Instead of tracking just my weight, I might want to record my weight, height, BMI (body-mass index), and pulse, all at a given moment.

Vectors are **multi-dimensional** quantities. And they can't be represented on a number line. Let's say my weight is 210 lbs. and my height is 6'2", or 74 inches. (This is not theoretical.) I could of course draw a number line and put a dot at 74 and another dot at 210, but this wouldn't fully represent the fact that my weight was 210 and my height was 74. For one thing, the numbers are on completely different scales. (There's that word "scale" again.) For another, it's not clear which is which – is the right-most point supposed to be my height, or my weight? Trying to squeeze a two-dimensional quantity into a one-dimensional number line would

---

[1] It might seem like "two directions," since the number line goes both to the left and to the right. But since left-ness is the exact opposite of right-ness, these are considered "the same direction"; it's just a matter of how far you go back or forth you go along that one straight path.

2.1. VECTOR VS. SCALAR QUANTITIES

lose information. We need a representation scheme that can accommodate the complexity of our quantity.

For a two-dimensional quantity like weight-and-height, the obvious choice is the two-dimensional Cartesian plane. I've drawn the vector with my height and weight on the left side of Figure 2.1. You'll see that there's an *arrow* from the origin to the point (210,74), rather than just a circular dot at that point, as you might have expected. This is because sometimes, it turns out, we want to treat a vector as "a net movement in a particular direction for a particular distance."

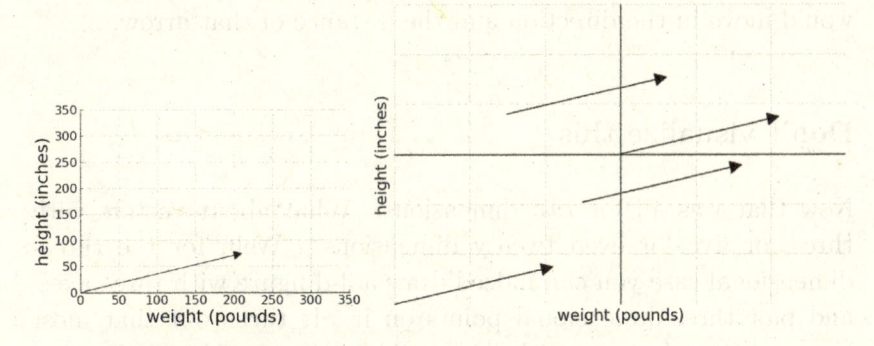

Figure 2.1: Left: a two-dimensional vector, depicted in a Cartesian plane. Right: several copies of *the same vector*, shown originating at various points. They're considered "the same" vector because they all go in the same direction and have the same length; the point they start at is irrelevant.

You can see this illustrated on the right-hand side figure, where I've drawn several copies of *the same vector*. This may seem weird, but in terms of pictures, here's how you want to think of it: **a vector has a direction and a magnitude, but not a starting point**. The direction is the specific angle in which it points, and (for now) we use the word **"magnitude"** to mean how long the vector is from its **tail** to its **tip**. (As Arya Stark would say, the tip is the "pointy end" with the arrowhead.) Curiously, there are alternative ways of judging the length, or magnitude, of a vector, which we'll revisit in section 2.6.

In the case of Stephen's biometric vector, its direction is east-by-northeast-ish (about 19.4° counter-clockwise from the x-axis) and its magnitude is 222.6. But it doesn't have any intrinsic "point of origin"; it's just an arrow pointing this-a-way and yea-far, no matter where it might be anchored.

Interestingly, the word *vector* comes from a root meaning "to carry." You may have heard people describe mosquitoes as being "vectors" for a particular disease – this means that they carry that disease. By thinking of a vector as an arrow like in Figure 2.1, the "carry" interpretation might start to make sense. A vector can represent a transposition from one point to another. If I grew 74 inches taller and gained 210 more pounds, my point on the Cartesian plane would move in the direction and the distance of that arrow.

Don't visualize this

Now that was all for *two* dimensions. What about vectors with three, or five, or even twenty dimensions? Well, for the three-dimensional case you can indeed draw a 3-d figure with three axes, and plot three-dimensional points on it. It turns out that most humans, though, are positively horrible at interpreting such plots. And when you move beyond three dimensions, it's utterly hopeless. (A friend of mine in fourth grade claimed he could visualize four dimensions in his head, but I didn't believe him and still don't.)

But importantly, that doesn't mean we won't ever deal with higher-dimensional vectors. In fact, vectors with lots and lots of dimensions will come up constantly for us in this book – believe it or not, we'll do an example where the vectors have 50,000 dimensions! :-O

Don't worry; this won't make your head explode. In fact, it's a lot easier than you might think to work with very high-dimensional vectors. Consider the example I gave above about tracking a company's stock price every day for a year. That's just a list of 365 numbers, all in a row. How hard is that to imagine?

To work with vectors of more than three dimensions, you only have to do one thing: give up trying to visualize them in a geometric space. As I'll describe in the next section, it only occasionally

2.2. FIVE WAYS TO THINK ABOUT VECTORS

makes sense to think about vectors geometrically anyway; much of the time, we'll simply think of them as quantities that have more than one component, unlike their simple brethren the scalars.

Finally, the notation we'll use for vector variables. Instead of putting the variable name in italics, we'll put it in bold-face with an arrow on the top of it, like this: $\vec{\mathbf{x}}$. The individual components of the vector will be listed in boxies (square-brackets) like this: [−2 5.9 17 −3]. So, if we define $\vec{\mathbf{stephen}}$ as the vector with my height and weight in it, we would write:

$$\vec{\mathbf{stephen}} = [\ 210\ \ 74\ ].$$

2.2 Five ways to think about vectors

abstract

5. just a "thing" which satisfies certain properties

4. a collection of non-numeric elements
[red red blue purple]
  jezebel filbert biff betty lou

3. a collection with non-numeric indices
[89 93 70 133]
 jezebel filbert biff betty lou

2. a sequence of more than two coordinates
[89 93 70 133]
  0   1   2   3

concrete

1. a sequence of two coordinates
[89 93]
 0   1

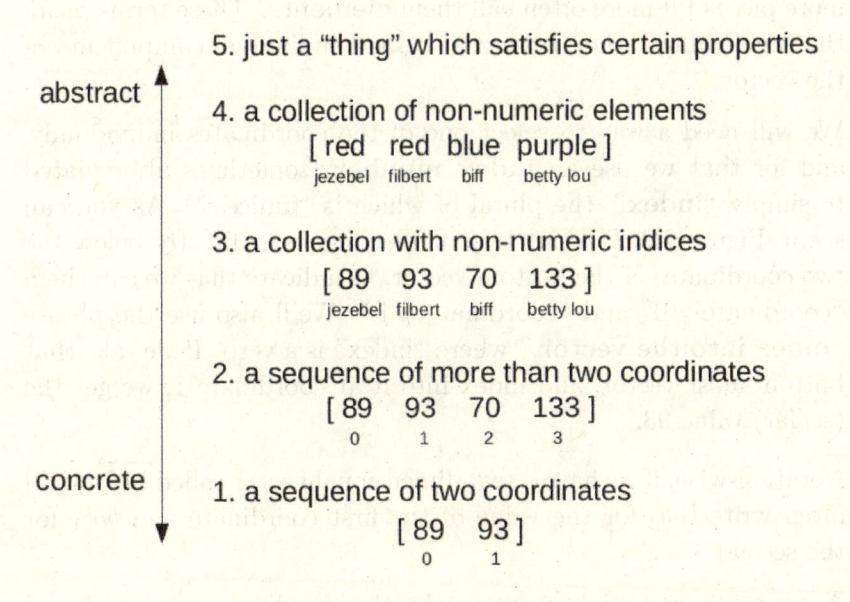

Figure 2.2: Five ways to think about a vector.

In the mathematical writings you'll encounter, computer scientists use the word "vector" in a variety of ways. They're all ultimately compatible with each other, but they can seem disorientingly different at first. Really, it's a tribute to how powerful the vector concept is that people use them in so many ways for so many different things.

I'm going to suggest that there are *five* different ways to think about a vector, and I'm going to arrange these ways on a continuum from "concrete" to "abstract." This spectrum is depicted in Figure 2.2.

Let's take it from the bottom.

1. A sequence of two coordinates

This is the height-weight example, in which something like $\overrightarrow{\text{stephen}}$ is an ordered pair that can easily be visualized on a two-dimensional Cartesian plane. Because of this plotting aspect, I'll often call the two parts of the vector **coordinates**, but as we create vectors with more pieces I'll more often call them **elements**. These terms mean the same thing – they both refer to the individual components of the vector.

We will need a way to select one of the coordinates individually, and for that we use an **index number** (sometimes abbreviated to simply "**index**," the plural of which is "indices.") As you can see in Figure 2.2, I've put two smaller numbers directly below the two coordinates of the bottom vector, to indicate that we call them "coordinate #0" and "coordinate #1." We'll also use the phrase "**index into the vector**," where "index" is a verb. If we take that bottom-most vector, and index into it at coordinate 1, we get the (scalar) value 93.

Notation-wise, if we have a two-dimensional vector called $\overrightarrow{\text{bob}}$, we'll often write bob_0 for the value of the first coordinate and bob_1 for the second.

As an aside, you might wonder why the coordinates are numbered 0 and 1 instead of 1 and 2. The answer has to do with the fact that we'll be using Python in this book. Every programming language has a way of indexing into its vector-like objects, and Python, Java,

2.2. FIVE WAYS TO THINK ABOUT VECTORS

and C++ all begin indexing with the number 0. There are actually some good reasons for this, which I won't get into. It's not universally embraced, however; languages like R and Julia start their indexing at 1. Go figure.

Geometrically, we can compute a vector's direction and magnitude using trigonometry. Figure 2.3 shows a vector $\vec{v}$ = [9 21] pictorially. Its 0th coordinate (a.k.a. v_0) is 9, measured on the x-axis, and v_1 is 21. Traditionally, a two-dimensional vector's magnitude is called r (for "radius," I believe, although don't think about that too hard) and its direction is called θ ("theta"). The magnitude is just the crow-flies distance from the vector's **tail** to its **tip** (computed using the Pythagorean Theorem) and the direction is the arctangent of the rise-over-run. In equations:

$$r = \sqrt{v_0^2 + v_1^2}$$
$$\theta = \tan^{-1} \frac{v_1}{v_0}$$

In this case, r works out to 22.8 and θ is 66.8°. Think about this, too: if, instead of giving you the values of v_0 and v_1, I instead gave you the values of r and θ, you'd still have *all the information about the vector*, just in a different form. We sometimes call r and θ the **polar coordinates** of a vector, and v_0 and v_1 the **Cartesian coordinates**. The polar coordinates are usually written as "22.8∡66.8°," which is the same vector as [9 21], just written in a different way.

Anyway, I put this way of thinking about vectors at the extreme "concrete" end of the spectrum, because it's so nuts-and-bolts and easy to visualize. As we ascend up the hierarchy, things will get less and less visualizable.

2. A sequence of more than two coordinates

As I mentioned earlier in this chapter, having more than two coordinates in a vector isn't really all that weird...you simply have to give up any hope of visualizing it geometrically. But it's easy enough to do: a list of four numbers – 89, 93, 70, and 133 – is

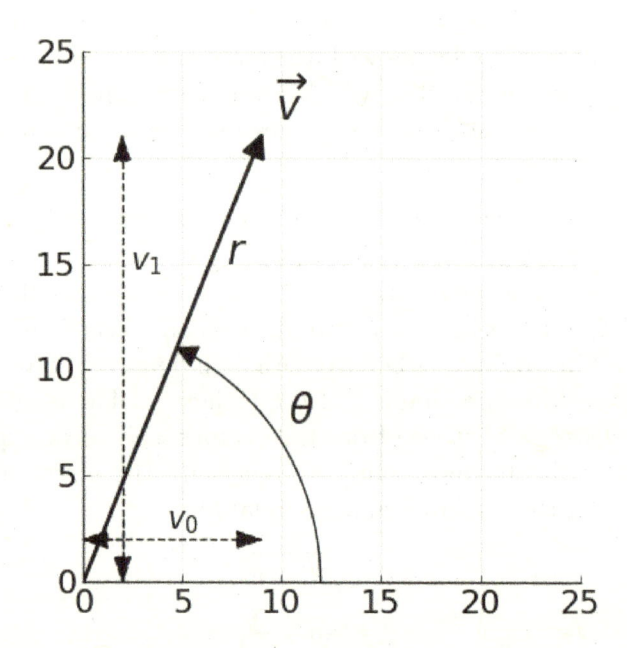

Figure 2.3: The direction (θ) and magnitude (r) of the vector $\vec{v}$ = [9 21]. The direction θ is the angle that $\vec{v}$ makes counter-clockwise with the x-axis, and the magnitude is the length of the line.

the most natural thing in the world. One could imagine finding the sum of the elements, the maximum element, the number of negative elements, or other more exotic things.

Again, our indexing starts at 0, and this time goes up to 3. Note what this implies: if we have a vector with four elements, there is no element #4! This is a common pitfall for newcomers to the subject and to languages like Python. If I have a vector with n coordinates, those coordinates are numbered 0 up to $n-1$, but *not* up to n.

Also note that the number of elements/coordinates is also the **dimensionality** (number of dimensions) of the vector. Simply put, a vector that has nine elements in it is called "a 9-dimensional vector."

2.2. FIVE WAYS TO THINK ABOUT VECTORS

3. A collection with non-numeric indices

At this point of the hierarchy, I change my nomenclature from "sequence" to "collection." That's because here, we don't *number* the elements of our vector anymore but instead *name* them. Thus there isn't any meaningful order to the elements anymore – instead of "IQ #0," "IQ #1," and so forth, we have "Jezebel's IQ," "Filbert's IQ," and the like. Nothing super weird here, but things may be starting to look less and less math-y to you.

I'll sometimes call the names of the elements **labels**.

4. A collection with non-numeric elements

And heck, if the indices don't have to be numbers, why would the elements need to be? And indeed we will often have cause to work with vectors like the one in step 4 of the hierarchy (Figure 2.2, p. 15), in which there's not a number in sight. This example holds the favorite colors for each of our four friends, which are of course non-numeric.

5. Just a "thing"

Finally, you won't see this usage of vectors until you get to some more advanced math, but I'd be doing you a disservice if I didn't point it out here. I remember the first time I read some research in which the author was going on and on about "vectors," and I was dreadfully confused because none of his "vectors" seemed to have any elements in them! I was like, "what do you mean *vectors*, dude? Did your word processor auto-correct a different word?"

This computer scientist was treating "vectors" as whole objects, not even considering what their elements were (or whether they even *had* any elements). He was working with an abstract notion called a **vector space** which we'll touch on next chapter; for now I'll just tell you that it's closely related to the notion of an algebra that we discussed in Chapter 1. He was taking advantage of some of the elegant results presented later in this book, which are guaranteed to hold for whatever mathematical objects you care to define, as long as you obey certain ground rules – whether those objects have any "elements" to them or not. I mention this mostly to anchor your future self in solid ground the first time you inevitably come across the use of "vector" as a very un-list-like thing. You'll remember reading this, say to yourself "ah yes – Stephen warned me once that the extreme abstract end of the continuum works like this," and proceed with confidence. I won't say anything more about it in this book.

2.3 And a vector is also a function

Oh, and yet another way to think of vectors: as **functions**. We'll talk about vectors as inputs to functions later in this book. But it's worth recognizing at this point that a vector itself essentially *is* a function.

You'll remember from Chapter 3 of *Cool, Brisk Walk* that a function is a mapping from a set of inputs to a set of outputs. Each member of the input set (a.k.a. the "domain") is assigned a member of the output set ("codomain") as its value. (No member of the domain can be assigned to more than one member of the codomain, but the reverse is not a constraint: multiple members of the domain *can* be assigned to the same member of the codomain.)

Now consider this vector:

$$\vec{x} = [\ \underset{0}{45}\ \ \underset{1}{-12}\ \ \underset{2}{9}\ \ \underset{3}{45}\ \ \underset{4}{0}\ ]$$

It's a sequence of numbered elements, sure. But couldn't it just as easily be interpreted as a function from index numbers to values? (See Figure 2.4.)

In function syntax, $\vec{x}(0) = 45$, $\vec{x}(1) = -12$, $\vec{x}(3) = 45$, and so on. It makes even more sense with a non-numeric vector like the "favorite color" example (Fig. 2.2), where **faveColor**(Biff) = blue

2.4. VECTOR OPERATIONS

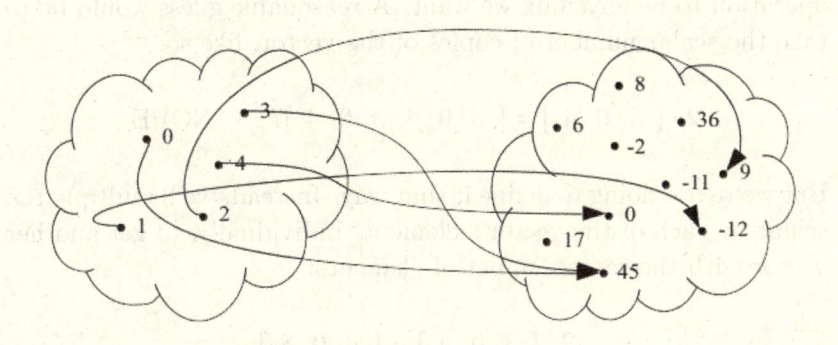

Figure 2.4: The vector $\vec{x}$, interpreted as a function.

and $\overrightarrow{\textbf{faveColor}}$(Betty Lou) = purple. Instead of index numbers, the function's domain is comprised of the vector's labels.

I remember having a real "ah-ha!" moment the day I first realized that vectors (called "arrays" or "lists" in some programming languages) were really the same as key/value-pair-based associative arrays (also called "dictionaries" or "hash tables") with *an index number as the key*. Later, I had another "ah-ha!" and realized that both were equivalent to functions as well, if you viewed the keys/indices as the function's domain and the elements as the codomain. Wow. Sometimes it seems like the universe is really all just one thing.

2.4 Vector operations

We're going to be combining scalars/vectors to yield other scalars/vectors like literally all the time. The following three operations must be mastered until you can do them in your sleep.

Operation #1: Scalar-vector multiplication

What do you think you'd get if you multiplied a scalar like 2 by a vector like [3 0 4]? As with all mathematics, we can define this operation to be anything we want. A reasonable guess would be to take the scalar number of copies of the vector, like so:

$$2 \cdot [\ 3\ 0\ 4\ ] = [\ 3\ 0\ 4\ 3\ 0\ 4\ ]? \quad \text{NOPE}$$

But we're not doing to define it that way. Instead, we'll multiply the scalar by each of the vector's elements individually, to get another vector with the same number of elements:

$$2 \cdot [\ 3\ 0\ 4\ ] = [\ 6\ 0\ 8\ ]$$

This turns out to be more useful. So in general, a scalar a times a vector $\vec{v}$ will be:

Scalar-vector multiplication:

$$a\vec{v} = a[\ v_0\ v_1\ \ldots\ v_{n-1}\ ] = [\ a \cdot v_0\ \ a \cdot v_1\ \ \ldots\ \ a \cdot v_{n-1}\ ],$$

where n is the number of elements in the vector.

Interestingly, there's no such thing (in common use) as "scalar-vector *addition*." In other words, if someone tried to do this:

$$2 + [\ 3\ 0\ 4\ ] = ??$$

we're simply going to say "no can do."

By the way, some programming languages (including Python) do give the programmer a convenient shorthand by allowing them to type $2 + [\ 3\ 0\ 4\ ]$ and get the value $[\ 5\ 2\ 6\ ]$. This isn't considered a bona fide mathematical operation, though; just a notational convenience.

Operation #2: Vector addition

Adding two vectors together, though, is a perfectly acceptable enterprise, provided that the vectors have the same number of elements. The way we do it is to add each pair of elements together

2.4. VECTOR OPERATIONS

and produce another vector of the same number of dimensions. In other words, adding [2 9] to [4 − 2] gives us:

$$[\ 2\ \ 9\ ] + [\ 4\ \ -2\ ] = [\ 6\ \ 7\ ],$$

and in general:

Vector addition:

$$\vec{x} + \vec{y} = [\ x_0\ \ x_1\ \ \ldots\ \ x_{n-1}\ ] + [\ y_0\ \ y_1\ \ \ldots\ \ y_{n-1}\ ]$$
$$= [\ x_0 + y_0\ \ x_1 + y_1\ \ \ldots\ \ x_{n-1} + y_{n-1}\ ],$$

where n is the number of elements in each vector.

An important issue arises in level 3 of our Figure 2.2 hierarchy (p. 15). How do we add two vectors that aren't indexed by number? Answer: we add the elements from each vector that correspond to the same *label*. And yes, the vectors must *have* exactly the same labels in order to be legitimately added in this way; otherwise, we call the whole thing off. So:

$$[\ \underset{\text{peacock}}{3}\ \ \underset{\text{green}}{5}\ \ \underset{\text{plum}}{8}\ ] + [\ \underset{\text{peacock}}{1}\ \ \underset{\text{green}}{-6}\ \ \underset{\text{plum}}{4}\ ] =$$

$$[\ \underset{\text{peacock}}{4}\ \ \underset{\text{green}}{-1}\ \ \underset{\text{plum}}{12}\ ],$$

and

$$[\ \underset{\text{scarlet}}{2}\ \ \underset{\text{mustard}}{1}\ \ \underset{\text{green}}{4}\ ] + [\ \underset{\text{scarlet}}{3}\ \ \underset{\text{white}}{3}\ \ \underset{\text{plum}}{0}\ ] =$$

"no can do."

You can probably tell that vector addition is **commutative**, meaning that whether we add $\vec{x} + \vec{y}$ or $\vec{y} + \vec{x}$, we get the same answer. It's also true that vector addition, combined with scalar-vector multiplication, is **distributive**. This means:

$$a(\vec{x} + \vec{y}) = a\vec{x} + a\vec{y}$$

and

$$(a + b)\vec{x} = a\vec{x} + b\vec{x}$$

for any scalars a and b and vectors $\vec{x}$ and $\vec{y}$. This is a useful fact to know, which we'll sometimes rely on.

By the way, you might wonder whether vector subtraction is a thing, and it is: in fact it turns out to just use scalar multiplication by -1. So:

$$\vec{x} - \vec{y} = \vec{x} + (-1\vec{y}) =$$
$$[\; x_0 - y_0 \quad x_1 - y_1 \quad \ldots \quad x_{n-1} - y_{n-1} \;].$$

For example, $[\;5\;\;2\;\;7\;] - [\;1\;\;4\;\;7\;]$ is just $[\;4\;\;-2\;\;0\;]$.

Operation #3: Vector multiplication (dot product)

Our third and final vector operation is the least intuitive of the three; at least, it doesn't work the way I expected it to when I first learned it. It's most commonly called the **dot product**.[2]

The first thing you have to wrap your head around is the fact that *two vectors multiplied together give you a scalar.* Yeah, no cap: if you multiply an 18-dimensional vector by another 18-dimensional vector, you get back a single lonely number.

Operationally, what happens is that you *multiply* the corresponding elements of the two vectors together, and then *add* the result. So:

---

[2] There is at least one other type of vector multiplication in common use, which we won't need in this book. It's called the **cross product**, and is designated by a × instead of a ·. Interestingly, although the dot product is defined for vectors of any number of dimensions, the cross product is only defined for vectors of exactly three dimensions. (Not 2. Not 4. Only exactly 3.) Another curious fact is that the cross product between two vectors gives you a vector back, not a scalar like the dot product does.

2.4. VECTOR OPERATIONS

$$[\ 7\ \ 8\ ] \cdot [\ 5\ \ 1\ ] = 7 \cdot 5 + 8 \cdot 1 = 43$$

As with vector addition, we disallow taking the dot product of two vectors with differing numbers of elements. Also, in the case of vectors with labels instead of index numbers, we insist that the vectors have identical labels in order to meaningfully dot-product them.

Vector multiplication (dot product):

$$\vec{x} \cdot \vec{y} = [\ x_0\ \ x_1\ \ \ldots\ \ x_{n-1}\ ] \cdot [\ y_0\ \ y_1\ \ \ldots\ \ y_{n-1}\ ]$$
$$= x_0 \cdot y_0 + x_1 \cdot y_1 + \cdots + x_{n-1} \cdot y_{n-1},$$

where n is the number of elements in each vector.

It should be obvious to you that the dot product operation is commutative: $\vec{x} \cdot \vec{y}$ always gives the same result as $\vec{y} \cdot \vec{x}$.

Why?

Okay, now to address the elephant in the living room: *why* would mathematicians define vector multiplication in this way? What's the matter with just multiplying corresponding elements and yielding a vector answer, like we did with vector addition?

The answer is that the dot product as defined above is incredibly useful, much more so than pairwise-multiplication will turn out to be. In fact, it's possibly the single most important calculation in linear algebra: all kinds of applications and more advanced computations use it as a building block.

To see this, consider the following question. What needs to be true about two vectors in order for them to have a large dot product?

Your first inclination might be to answer "the individual vector entries need to be large." This is sort of true...but only sort of. Consider the following two vectors:

$$\vec{a} = [\ 95\ \ 0\ \ 381\ ]$$
$$\vec{b} = [\ 0\ \ 1056\ \ 0\ ]$$

Thar's som' mighty big entries in them vectors. Surely multiplying them together would give a large result, right? No:

$$[\ 95\ \ 0\ \ 381\ ] \cdot [\ 0\ \ 1056\ \ 0\ ] =$$
$$95 \cdot 0 + 0 \cdot 1056 + 381 \cdot 0 = 0.$$

We get zilch. By contrast, these two wimpy-looking vectors:

$$\vec{c} = [\ 1\ \ 2\ \ 5\ ]$$
$$\vec{d} = [\ 0\ \ 2\ \ 7\ ]$$

do give a fairly hefty result:

$$[\ 1\ \ 2\ \ 5\ ] \cdot [\ 0\ \ 2\ \ 7\ ] =$$
$$1 \cdot 0 + 2 \cdot 2 + 5 \cdot 7 = 39.$$

What's going on here?

If you stare at the above calculations, you'll hit on a deep truth which is worth pondering at length. And that is that in order for the dot product to be large, the vectors must not only have large entries, but be large *in the same places*.

The reason that $\vec{a}$ and $\vec{b}$ had such a stunningly low dot product is that although they had large entries, they were completely out of sync with each other. $\vec{a}$ had high values precisely where $\vec{b}$ had low ones, and vice versa. On the other hand, even though the individual

2.4. VECTOR OPERATIONS

elements of $\vec{c}$ and $\vec{d}$ were pretty small, they fit together nicely: for example, $\vec{c}$'s largest entry and $\vec{d}$'s largest entry were in the same place (element #2), which led to a kind of synergy.

Consider how the dot product would change if we altered $\vec{d}$ to be [7 2 0] instead of [0 2 7]:

$$[\ 1\ \ 2\ \ 5\ ] \cdot [\ 7\ \ 2\ \ 0\ ] =$$
$$1 \cdot 7 + 2 \cdot 2 + 5 \cdot 0 = 11.$$

Dang, we dropped from 39 all the way to 11 just by reordering the entries.

This ability to judge roughly "how aligned" two vectors are comes up all the time. Consider a dating website. Let's say that Jezebel, a heterosexual female, signs up for a dating service and answers the questions on a compatibility survey. She's asked, "on a scale of 1 to 10, how much do you like action movies? Outdoor hikes? Candlelight dinners? Reading mystery novels?" Suppose her answers are the following:

$$\vec{\text{jezebel}} = [\ \underset{\text{action}}{5}\ \ \underset{\text{hiking}}{2}\ \ \underset{\text{candlelight}}{10}\ \ \underset{\text{mystery}}{2}\ ]$$

Now there are three eligible heterosexual bachelors on this site: Biff, Filbert, and Wendell. They also took the survey, and came up with these responses:

$$\vec{\text{biff}}\ \ =\ [\ \underset{\text{action}}{10}\ \ \underset{\text{hiking}}{10}\ \ \underset{\text{candlelight}}{1}\ \ \underset{\text{mystery}}{1}\ ]$$

$$\vec{\text{filbert}}\ =\ [\ \underset{\text{action}}{6}\ \ \underset{\text{hiking}}{2}\ \ \underset{\text{candlelight}}{8}\ \ \underset{\text{mystery}}{4}\ ]$$

$$\vec{\text{wendell}} = [\ \underset{\text{action}}{1}\ \ \underset{\text{hiking}}{3}\ \ \underset{\text{candlelight}}{3}\ \ \underset{\text{mystery}}{10}\ ]$$

The central question that `matchmaker.com` must ask is: which of these three young gentlemen should be recommended to Jezebel?

The answer lies in the dot product. Just by eyeballing the survey results, you can probably tell that Filbert is Jezebel's best match: he has high values in roughly the same place that she does. If we compute the dot product of Jezebel with each of the three guys, we see that the math bears that out:

$$\overrightarrow{\text{jezebel}} \cdot \overrightarrow{\text{biff}} = 5 \cdot 10 + 2 \cdot 10 + 10 \cdot 1 + 2 \cdot 1 = 82$$

$$\overrightarrow{\text{jezebel}} \cdot \overrightarrow{\text{filbert}} = 5 \cdot 6 + 2 \cdot 2 + 10 \cdot 8 + 2 \cdot 4 = 122$$

$$\overrightarrow{\text{jezebel}} \cdot \overrightarrow{\text{wendell}} = 5 \cdot 1 + 2 \cdot 3 + 10 \cdot 3 + 2 \cdot 10 = 61$$

Since Filbert has the highest dot product with Jezebel, Filbert's vector is in some sense "more closely aligned" with hers, reflecting their similar interests. So our website will show Filbert's pic and profile to Jezebel.

It might occur to you that someone could "beat the system" here by answering 10 on all their survey questions. After all, increasing the individual entries in a vector can't *hurt* its dot product with another vector; the worst it could do is not help matters, if the second vector has a zero there. So let's say the insidious Mr. Right (?) creates an account on the system, and answers:

$$\overrightarrow{\text{mrright}} = [\;\; \underset{\text{action}}{10} \quad \underset{\text{hiking}}{10} \quad \underset{\text{candlelight}}{10} \quad \underset{\text{mystery}}{10} \;\;]$$

Pairing him with Jezebel yields:

$$\overrightarrow{\text{jezebel}} \cdot \overrightarrow{\text{mrright}} = 5 \cdot 10 + 2 \cdot 10 + 10 \cdot 10 + 2 \cdot 10 = 190$$

2.4. VECTOR OPERATIONS

which blows away the competition. Mr. Right can have any girl he wants, whether or not he and she are truly compatible. There's a way to fix this, which we'll see later in this chapter (section 2.7, p. 43). For now, just grasp the main point that two vectors having large entries in the same places tends to magnify their dot product.

Geometric interpretation

Now let's build some *geometric* intuition about the dot product. Consider the two vectors $\vec{a}$ and $\vec{b}$ in Figure 2.5. $\vec{a}$ is the vector [2 0] and $\vec{b}$ is [0 3]. What is their dot product? $2 \cdot 0 + 0 \cdot 3 =$ a big fat zero.

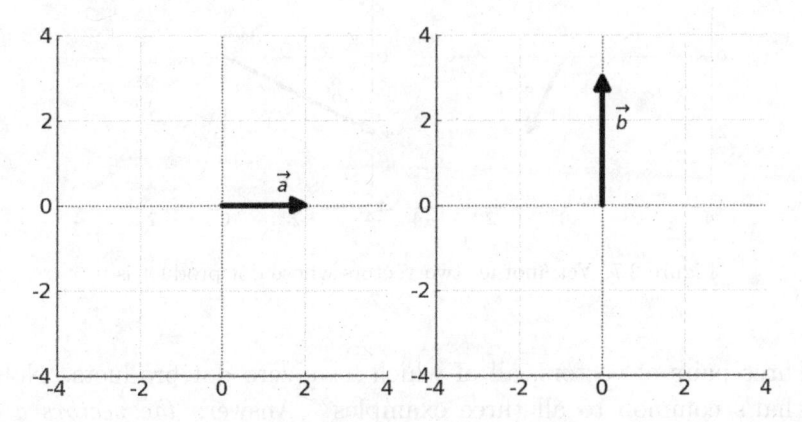

Figure 2.5: Two vectors whose dot product is 0.

Okay, same exercise, but now in Figure 2.6. Now we have the vectors $\vec{a}$ = [3 3] and $\vec{b}$ = [−2 2]. What is their dot product? Once more, zero: $3 \cdot -2 + 3 \cdot 2 = 0$.

One more chorus. Figure 2.7 shows the vectors $\vec{a}$ = [1 − 2] and $\vec{b}$ = [−4 − 2]. What is their dot product? Yet again, exactly zero: $1 \cdot -4 + -2 \cdot -2 = 0$.

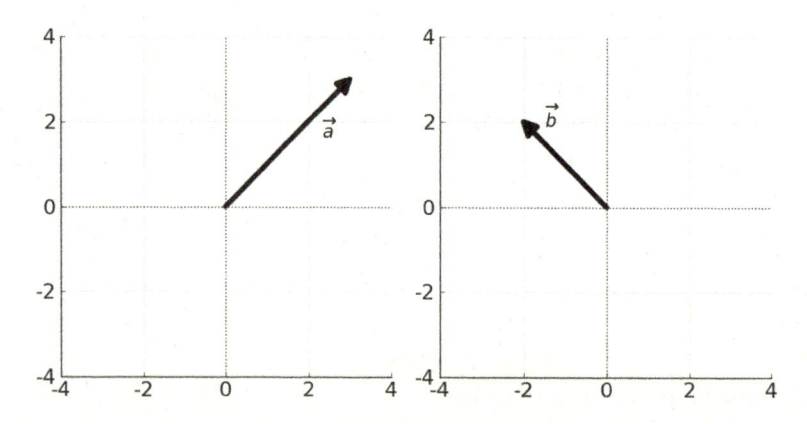

Figure 2.6: Another two vectors whose dot product is 0.

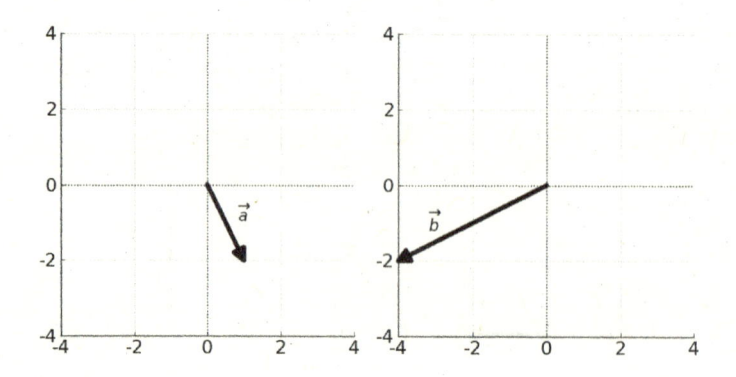

Figure 2.7: Yet another two vectors whose dot product is 0.

Three pairs of vectors, all of which have zero dot products. Now what's common to all three examples? Answer: *the vectors are perpendicular to each other.* This is easier to see when we plot each pair on the same graph, as in Figure 2.8.

Whenever you have two vectors at exactly right angles to each other, their dot product will be at a minimum; namely, zero. Our linear algebra term for this, annoyingly, is not "perpendicular" (a word you already know) but **orthogonal**. When two vectors are orthogonal, they're "as unaligned as possible."

Think of it this way. Pick any of the three pairs of vectors in Figure 2.8, and pretend that your goal is to go in the $\vec{b}$ direction. You

2.5. THE VECTOR OPERATIONS IN ACTION

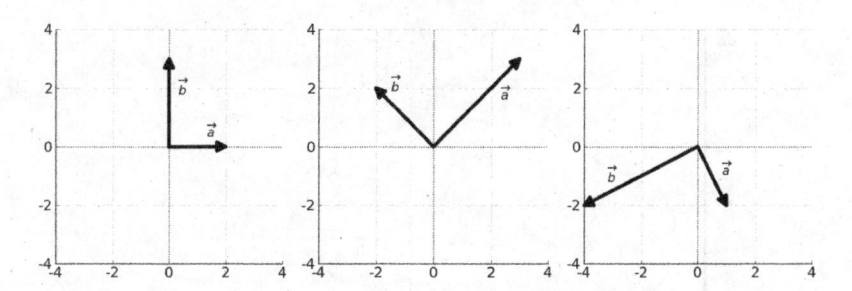

Figure 2.8: The three pairs of vectors plotted together. The fact that they are orthogonal to each other is what makes their dot products zero.

want to get "as b-ward as possible." But suppose your only option was to go in the direction of $\vec{a}$. Would you make any meaningful progress towards your goal? The answer is no: $\vec{a}$ is exactly the direction that doesn't let you move *anywhere* you want to go. On the left-most figure, for example, if your goal was to get from the origin due north to the point $(0, 15)$, you can't make any progress whatsoever if you're allowed only to travel along the x-axis. And that's true for all three of those pairs.

To get a non-zero dot product, the two vectors at least have to point *somewhat* in the same direction. Take the two in Figure 2.9, where $\vec{a}$ = [3   − 3] and $\vec{b}$ = [2   − 4]. These vectors are clearly *not* orthogonal, and hence their dot product is non-zero: $3 \cdot 2 + -3 \cdot -4 = 18$.

In general, the more the arrows point in the same direction, the higher the dot product, holding everything else equal. The more they diverge to right angles, the more the dot product drops to zero. I'll have more to say about this in Section 2.6 when we look at an alternate way to compute the dot product geometrically.

2.5 The vector operations in action

This book is chock full of examples of using vectors in the real world. Let me give one now which illustrates the eminent usefulness

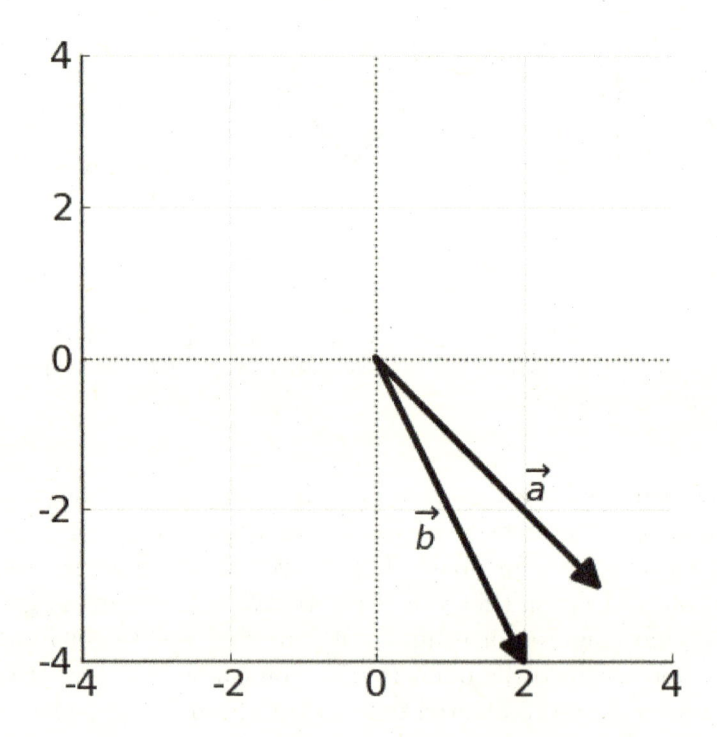

Figure 2.9: Two *non*-orthogonal vectors, whose dot product is 18.

of these three vector operations.

Let's say we've been tasked with baking goodies for a bake sale. There are three recipes we're planning on making in bulk: chocolate chippers (my personal fave), brownies, and fudge. Upon consulting our recipe book, we write down an ingredient list for each:

$$\overrightarrow{\text{chippers}} = [\underset{\text{butter}}{2} \quad \underset{\text{sugar}}{1} \quad \underset{\text{chips}}{1} \quad \underset{\text{flour}}{1} \quad \underset{\text{eggs}}{3}]$$

$$\overrightarrow{\text{brownies}} = [\underset{\text{butter}}{1} \quad \underset{\text{sugar}}{1} \quad \underset{\text{chips}}{4} \quad \underset{\text{flour}}{2} \quad \underset{\text{eggs}}{2}]$$

$$\overrightarrow{\text{fudge}} = [\underset{\text{butter}}{2} \quad \underset{\text{sugar}}{2} \quad \underset{\text{chips}}{4} \quad \underset{\text{flour}}{0} \quad \underset{\text{eggs}}{0}].$$

2.5. THE VECTOR OPERATIONS IN ACTION

This shows, for each of our five ingredients, how many "units" of each one is required for one recipe's worth.[3] Chocolate chip cookies evidently require two sticks of butter, one cup of sugar, one package of Ghirardelli chocolate chips, *etc.*

Additionally, we define these two vectors:

$$\vec{\text{wegmans}} = [\underset{\text{butter}}{1.59} \quad \underset{\text{sugar}}{2.79} \quad \underset{\text{chips}}{3.49} \quad \underset{\text{flour}}{1.67} \quad \underset{\text{eggs}}{.4}]$$

$$\vec{\text{satfat}} = [\underset{\text{butter}}{56} \quad \underset{\text{sugar}}{0} \quad \underset{\text{chips}}{24} \quad \underset{\text{flour}}{1} \quad \underset{\text{eggs}}{1.6}]$$

The first shows how much each of these ingredients is currently selling for at Wegmans. For the health-conscious, the second shows how many grams of saturated fat is present in each unit of the various ingredients. (*shudder*)

Now, let's consider some common questions we might need to answer:

1. "If we want to bake five batches of chocolate chippers for our bake sale, what's on our shopping list?"

    The answer is a simple vector operation:

    $$\vec{\text{shoppinglist}} = 5\,\vec{\text{chippers}}$$
    $$= [\underset{\text{butter}}{10} \quad \underset{\text{sugar}}{5} \quad \underset{\text{chips}}{5} \quad \underset{\text{flour}}{5} \quad \underset{\text{eggs}}{15}]$$

    Scalar-vector multiplication gives us exactly what we want: multiply the number of recipes by each ingredient's per-recipe quantity.

---

[3] Warning: do *not* attempt to use these ingredient lists to actually make real goodies! I have left many things out for simplicity. These would taste ratchet if you made them. Consult a real recipe book.

2. "We've decided on six recipes of brownies and fudge, plus a dozen batches of chocolate chippers. What's on our shopping list?"

   Putting vector addition into the mix (see what I did there?) gives us our elegant answer:

   $$\overrightarrow{\text{shoppinglist}} = 6\,\overrightarrow{\text{brownies}} + 6\,\overrightarrow{\text{fudge}} + 12\,\overrightarrow{\text{chippers}}$$
   $$= \begin{bmatrix} \underset{\text{butter}}{42} & \underset{\text{sugar}}{30} & \underset{\text{chips}}{60} & \underset{\text{flour}}{24} & \underset{\text{eggs}}{48} \end{bmatrix}$$

3. "My recipe tells me there are 16 brownies in a batch. How much saturated fat is in each brownie?"

   Here's where the dot product comes in handy. We have a vector ($\overrightarrow{\text{brownies}}$) that gives us the amount of each ingredient, and another ($\overrightarrow{\text{satfat}}$) that gives us per-unit fat content. The dot product is just what we need: multiply each ingredient amount by its fat content, and add up the results. It's a snap! All we then need to do is find the per-serving total by taking only a sixteenth of a batch, which is scalar-vector multiplication again. Putting it all together:

   $$fatPerBrownie = \frac{1}{16}(\overrightarrow{\text{brownies}} \cdot \overrightarrow{\text{satfat}})$$
   $$= \frac{1}{16}(1 \cdot 56 + 1 \cdot 0 + 4 \cdot 24 + 2 \cdot 1 + 2 \cdot 1.6)$$
   $$= 9.825 \text{ grams.}$$

   Ouch. Better sneak just one of those.

4. Finally, "how much is this all going to cost me at Wegmans?"

   We already computed the grand shopping list in question 2, above. To get the cost of this list, we again simply use the dot product:

$$totalCost = \overrightarrow{\textbf{shoppinglist}} \cdot \overrightarrow{\textbf{wegmans}}$$
$$= 42 \cdot 1.59 + 30 \cdot 2.79 + 60 \cdot 3.49 + 24 \cdot 1.67 + 48 \cdot .4$$
$$= \$419.16.$$

Wowza: I sure hope we sell all these!

Hopefully this gives you a feel for why the three operations – and especially the dot product – are eminently useful. They turn out to be exactly what we want to do with vectors much of the time, which is why they were invented. Get to know them intimately.

2.6 More about magnitude

Flip for a moment back to Figure 2.3 on p. 18. You'll recall that we defined the "magnitude" of the $\overrightarrow{\textbf{v}}$ vector as r: the crow-flies distance from its tail to its tip, as computed by the Pythagorean Theorem. In that case, we computed $r = \sqrt{v_0^2 + v_1^2} = 22.8$ for $\overrightarrow{\textbf{v}}$'s magnitude.

Now like all of mathematics, we can define things however we want. It turns out that this crow-flies distance thing – also called the **Euclidean distance** after Euclid, the ancient Greek geometer – is only one possible way to define the "length" or "magnitude" of a vector. This section includes several others which prove useful in various settings.

Oh, and before we get started, here's yet another piece of verbiage. The preferred mathematical term for the sort of generalized magnitude measurement presented below is the "**norm**" of a vector. We'll define several different norms, each of which offers a different take on measuring a vector's "size" or "bigness." No matter how we define it, *the norm of a vector is always a scalar*. We use double-pipe signs to represent it, like this: $\|\overrightarrow{\textbf{v}}\|$.

The Euclidean ("ℓ^2") norm

The most common norm is the **Euclidean norm**, which is just what we covered on p. 18. The Pythagorean Theorem is your friend.

The Euclidean norm is used for many, many things, one of which is a second, equally legitimate way to compute and to think about the dot product between two vectors. First, recall the cosine operation from trigonometry. The cosine of a 0° angle is 1, the cosine of a 90° angle is zero, and in between those two extremes the cosine varies smoothly from 1 down to 0.

Now suppose we have a couple of two-dimensional vectors $\vec{a}$ and $\vec{b}$. We'll use the same ones from the example on p. 32, shown here in Figure 2.10. To refresh your memory, the vector $\vec{a}$ is [3 −3] and $\vec{b}$ is [2 −4].

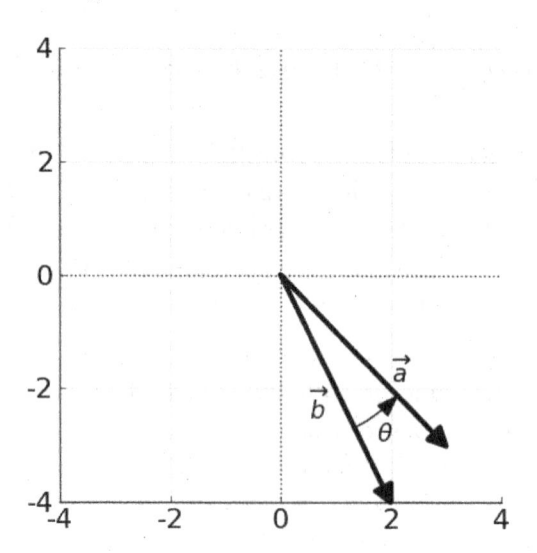

Figure 2.10: An alternate way to compute the dot product of two vectors, using the angle between them in the calculation.

We've learned that one way to compute the dot product between $\vec{a}$ and $\vec{b}$ is to multiply their corresponding entries:

$$\vec{a} \cdot \vec{b} = 3 \cdot 2 + (-3) \cdot (-4) = 18.$$

2.6. MORE ABOUT MAGNITUDE

Here's another way. We can *multiply the two norms together, and then multiply by the cosine of the angle between them.* You can really see why it's called the dot "product" when you think of it this way. Multiplying vectors is just multiplying their lengths...but there's a catch. We also multiply by the cosine of their angle, so that the more they diverge from each other, the lower the dot product.

In this example, we compute the angle between them (called θ in the figure):

$$\text{angle of } \vec{a} = \tan^{-1} \frac{-3}{3} = -45°$$

$$\text{angle of } \vec{b} = \tan^{-1} \frac{-4}{2} = -63.43°$$

$$\theta = \text{angle between } \vec{a} \text{ and } \vec{b} = -45° - (-63.43°) = 18.43°$$

Now we can compute the dot product our new way:

$$\vec{a} \cdot \vec{b} = \|\vec{a}\| \cdot \|\vec{b}\| \cdot \cos\theta =$$
$$\sqrt{3^2 + (-3)^2} \cdot \sqrt{2^2 + (-4)^2} \cdot \cos 18.43° =$$
$$4.243 \cdot 4.472 \cdot .948 = 18.$$

Yay! Same answer. I've found this a super useful way to visualize the dot product, even though it's often more convenient to calculate it the original way. A long vector times a long vector will give a large answer...provided those long vectors are kinda sort pointing in the same direction. If they're not – and most especially, if they're at right angles to each other, a la the Figure 2.8 examples (p. 31) – then the dot product can be miniscule even if the vectors themselves are long.

Okay, enough about the dot product. Back to the Euclidean norm itself. So far we've been assuming two dimensions. But importantly, the Euclidean norm applies equally well in *any* number of dimensions. Suppose we had a five-dimensional vector, like this one:

$$\vec{\mathbf{f}} = [\ 3\ \ -4\ \ 5\ \ 17\ \ 0\ ].$$

The Pythagorean Theorem – which in high school you may have only learned in a two-dimensional setting – still works just fine:

$$\|\vec{\mathbf{f}}\| = \sqrt{3^2 + (-4)^2 + 5^2 + 17^2 + 0^2} = 18.412.$$

Note: you still *square* the entries and take the *square* root of the sum. (You don't take the fifth power of the entries and the fifth root of the sum, like I expected when I first learned this.)

The result is (*deep breath*): "the length of the straight line from the origin to the point $(3, -4, 5, 17, 0)$ in five-dimensional space." You can't visualize it, so don't try. Just believe. No matter how many entries a vector has, you can compute its crow-flies length this way.

Now for weird but ultimately consistent reasons, this Euclidean norm is also called the "ℓ^2 norm"[4] of the vector. And we will sometimes write the 2 in as a subscript to the double-pipe, like this:

$$\|\vec{\mathbf{f}}\|_2 = 18.412.$$

I know it seems strange, but just go with it for now. And remember this, too: if we *don't* have any subscript after the $\|\cdot\|$ signs, *the default is 2*. In other words, unless explicitly stated, the "normal" meaning of *norm* is the ℓ^2 norm, a.k.a. Euclidean distance, computed by the Pythagorean Theorem.

---

[4] Pronounced "ell two," not "ell squared."

2.6. MORE ABOUT MAGNITUDE

The Manhattan ("ℓ^1") norm

Imagine yourself in downtown Manhattan, New York City. You're a software developer on an upper floor of the sleek new building at the corner of 33rd Street and 8th Avenue. It's just about time for lunch, and you and your fellow developers are discussing where to go – the Thai place on 25th St. and 10th Ave.? The new Hungarian restaurant that opened up on 44th St. and 6th Ave.? Or will it be just the greasy subway shop four blocks uptown today?

One of the factors in your decision is the distance: you can't take forever for lunch because you have a team meeting at 1:30pm. So you need to work out how long it will take to walk (or take a taxicab) to each of these places.

Now one (stupid) approach would be to use find the latitude and longitude of both your office and each of the restaurants, and compute the Euclidean distance. I say "stupid" because this is really only useful if you have a helicopter. (We can dream.) In my world, you can't fly over buildings; you have to walk around them. There's no point in computing the crow-flies distance if you're not a crow.

So how do we determine the distance? Simple: it's just the number of blocks you have to walk. Consider the Thai place. To get from 35th Street to 24th, we have to walk five blocks. To get from 8th Avenue to 10th, we have to walk two. Therefore, the walking distance between these two restaurants is "ten blocks." Note that it doesn't matter whether we walk the blocks west first and then south, or south first and then west, or zig-zag back and forth between streets and avenues: as long as we travel one of the shortest routes through the buildings (which means never going east or north), it'll be ten blocks.

For reasons which should now be obvious, this way to measure distance is called the **Manhattan norm** (or **taxicab norm**). You can measure the Manhattan distance between two points by simply *adding the absolute value of the pairwise differences between elements*. That's easier to do than to say. For our office-to-Thai-restaurant journey:

$$\text{dist}_{\text{Manhattan}} = |33 - 25| + |8 - 10| = 8 + 2 = 10 \text{ blocks}$$

The Euclidean distance, of course, is somewhat less:

$$\text{dist}_{\text{Euclidean}} = \sqrt{(33-25)^2 + (8-10)^2} = 8.246 \text{ blocks}$$

which is why helicopters can be useful.

When speaking of the norm of a vector, we always start at the origin and travel out from there. The Manhattan norm of a vector $\vec{v}$, which is written $\|\vec{v}\|_1$, is thus:

$$\|\vec{v}\|_1 = |v_0| + |v_1| + \cdots + |v_{n-1}|,$$

where n is the vector's number of dimensions. For example, let's compute the Manhattan norm of the 5-d vector $\vec{f}$ we previously used (with value [3 −4 5 17 0], you'll recall):

$$\|\vec{f}\|_1 = |3| + |-4| + |5| + |17| + |0| = 29.$$

Quite a bit higher than the Euclidean norm of 18.412, as expected.

By the way, just as the Euclidean norm was called the ℓ^2 norm, the Manhattan norm is called the ℓ^1 ("ell one") norm. You might take a moment to mull over why, and then see if you're right when I unveil the explanation in the next section.

This "$\ell^\#$" business

Okay. Here's how the Euclidean, Manhattan, and all the other norms we haven't yet discussed are related.

First, I'm going to write the formula for the Manhattan norm in a slightly different way. You'll probably wonder why I would complicate the expression, but suspend your disbelief for a moment. Instead of this:

2.6. MORE ABOUT MAGNITUDE

$$\|\vec{v}\|_1 = |v_0| + |v_1| + \cdots + |v_{n-1}|,$$

I'm going to write it this way:

$$\|\vec{v}\|_1 = \sqrt[1]{|v_0|^1 + |v_1|^1 + \cdots + |v_{n-1}|^1}.$$

Wut? Yeah. First, convince yourself that I haven't actually changed anything. Remember that any number "to the first power" is just the number itself. And notice that I'm not taking the *square* root here, but "the *first* root." If you didn't know this, "the first root" of a number is also just the number itself.

Bottom line is that these two formulas for the Manhattan norm are identical.

All right, but why do this? Here's why. Check out these two expressions, back to back:

$$\|\vec{v}\|_1 = \sqrt[1]{|v_0|^1 + |v_1|^1 + \cdots + |v_{n-1}|^1} \quad \text{(Manhattan norm)}$$
$$\|\vec{v}\|_2 = \sqrt[2]{|v_0|^2 + |v_1|^2 + \cdots + |v_{n-1}|^2} \quad \text{(Euclidean norm)}$$

Aha. See where I'm going with this? I've slipped in absolute value signs in the Euclidean norm elements – but that's okay, since if you square a negative number you get a positive result anyway. And I put a "2" above the root sign, to be explicit that it's the *square* root. Now the formulas are identical except for "1" vs. "2."

And now I'm going to tell you that we can use *any* number, not just 1 or 2. The others don't have special names, but they're legit nonetheless:

$$\|\vec{v}\|_1 = \sqrt[1]{|v_0|^1 + |v_1|^1 + \cdots + |v_{n-1}|^1} \quad \text{(Manhattan norm)}$$
$$\|\vec{v}\|_2 = \sqrt[2]{|v_0|^2 + |v_1|^2 + \cdots + |v_{n-1}|^2} \quad \text{(Euclidean norm)}$$
$$\|\vec{v}\|_3 = \sqrt[3]{|v_0|^3 + |v_1|^3 + \cdots + |v_{n-1}|^3} \quad (\ell^3 \text{ norm})$$
$$\|\vec{v}\|_4 = \sqrt[4]{|v_0|^4 + |v_1|^4 + \cdots + |v_{n-1}|^4} \quad (\ell^4 \text{ norm})$$
$$\|\vec{v}\|_5 = \sqrt[5]{|v_0|^5 + |v_1|^5 + \cdots + |v_{n-1}|^5} \quad (\ell^5 \text{ norm})$$
$$\vdots$$
$$\|\vec{v}\|_\infty = \sqrt[\infty]{|v_0|^\infty + |v_1|^\infty + \cdots + |v_{n-1}|^\infty} \quad (\ell^\infty \text{ norm})$$

That's right, we can even have an "infinity norm." So what do all these options do?

ℓ^3 and higher norms

Let's go back to our friend $\vec{f}$ whose value is [3 −4 5 17 0]. We've already computed the first two norms; let's keep going and see what happens:

$$\|\vec{f}\|_1 = \sqrt[1]{|3|^1 + |-4|^1 + |5|^1 + |17|^1 + |0|^1} = 29$$
$$\|\vec{f}\|_2 = \sqrt[2]{|3|^2 + |-4|^2 + |5|^2 + |17|^2 + |0|^2} = 18.412$$
$$\|\vec{f}\|_3 = \sqrt[3]{|3|^3 + |-4|^3 + |5|^3 + |17|^3 + |0|^3} = 17.246$$
$$\|\vec{f}\|_4 = \sqrt[4]{|3|^4 + |-4|^4 + |5|^4 + |17|^4 + |0|^4} = 17.049$$
$$\|\vec{f}\|_5 = \sqrt[5]{|3|^5 + |-4|^5 + |5|^5 + |17|^5 + |0|^5} = 17.010$$
$$\vdots$$
$$\|\vec{f}\|_\infty = \sqrt[\infty]{|3|^\infty + |-4|^\infty + |5|^\infty + |17|^\infty + |0|^\infty} = 17.$$

It's interesting: the numbers get smaller and smaller as we increase the # in "$\ell^\#$", and they finally converge on *the highest individual*

2.7. NORMALIZING

element of the vector. Cool! $\vec{f}$'s highest entry was 17, and lo and behold that's what the ℓ^∞ norm gives us.

The method to the madness is this: the higher the norm we take of a vector, the more that only the single largest element matters. The lower the norm we take, the more that all the elements equally matter. Think about the Manhattan norm: we simply added up the (absolute value of the) elements. Every element had a chance to shine. Higher and higher norms squeeze the life out of everything except the single highest value.

The ℓ^0 norm

Lastly, and mostly for fun, I'll throw a "ℓ^0" norm in. What does the "zero norm" do? It's defined to be *the number of non-zero elements* in the vector. So for our friend $\vec{f}$, we say that $\|\vec{f}\|_0 = 4$. This is at the other extreme from the infinity norm: now not only do all the elements count, but they count *equally*. I don't care if you're 17 or 3; as long as you're not zero you count towards my ℓ^0 norm.

2.7 Normalizing

Finally, let me mention the concept of **"normalizing"** a vector. To normalize a vector means to whack it down to size: make its length be exactly 1. We do this when we only care about a vector's *direction*, not its magnitude, and when the magnitude might actually get in the way.

First I'll tell you how to do this, and then give you an idea of why we'd want to. The how part is easy: you just divide the vector by its norm. (We can choose whichever norm is appropriate, often Euclidean.) Just as "subtracting two vectors" meant "multiply the second vector by −1 and add them," so "dividing a vector by a scalar" means "multiply the vector by 1-over-the-scalar."

For example, if we normalize our vector $\vec{b} = [\ 2\ \ -4\ ]$ from the last section, we get:

$$\frac{\vec{b}}{\|\vec{b}\|} = \frac{[\ 2\ \ -4\ ]}{\|[\ 2\ \ -4\ ]\|} = \frac{[\ 2\ \ -4\ ]}{\sqrt{2^2 + (-4)^2}} = \frac{[\ 2\ \ -4\ ]}{4.472} = [\ .447\ \ -.894\ ].$$

This is a vector that's in the same direction as $\vec{b}$, but of magnitude 1. We can verify this:

$$\text{angle} = \tan^{-1}\frac{-.894}{.447} = -63.43°,$$
$$\text{magnitude} = \sqrt{.447^2 + (-.894)^2} = 1.$$

Okay, now why would we want to normalize a vector? Isn't throwing away the magnitude tantamount to losing important information? Well, it depends. Let's return to our matchmaker dating site (p. 27). You'll recall that the odious Mr. Right was trying to game the system by answering 10 to all the survey questions. "Action movies? I love 'em! Hiking! Love it! Candlelight dinners? Love 'em!..." He figured he could be every woman's dream match because he'd have the maximum dot product with all of them.

But if we *normalize* each person's vector before taking the dot product, we put everybody on the same playing field. Effectively, each person has the same amount of points to "spend" on the various survey questions, and giving a high answer to one question means you're essentially going to have to give a low answer to others.

Consider Filbert, whose answers were:

$$\overrightarrow{\text{filbert}} = [\ \ \underset{\text{action}}{6}\ \ \ \underset{\text{hiking}}{2}\ \ \ \underset{\text{candlelight}}{8}\ \ \ \underset{\text{mystery}}{4}\ \ ]$$

His norm was $\sqrt{6^2 + 2^2 + 8^2 + 4^2} = 10.95$, so when we normalize him, we get:

$$\frac{\overrightarrow{\text{filbert}}}{\|\overrightarrow{\text{filbert}}\|} = [\ \ \underset{\text{action}}{.548}\ \ \ \underset{\text{hiking}}{.183}\ \ \ \underset{\text{candlelight}}{.730}\ \ \ \underset{\text{mystery}}{.365}\ \ ]$$

2.7. NORMALIZING

Biff's norm was $\sqrt{10^2 + 10^2 + 1^2 + 1^2} = 14.21$, so when we normalize him, we get:

$$\frac{\overrightarrow{\text{biff}}}{\|\overrightarrow{\text{biff}}\|} = [\quad .704 \quad .704 \quad .070 \quad .070 \quad]$$
$$\qquad\qquad\text{action}\quad\text{hiking}\quad\text{candlelight}\quad\text{mystery}$$

As for Mr. Right, he has the largest norm: $\sqrt{10^2 + 10^2 + 10^2 + 10^2} = 20$. So no matter how much he tries to fool the ladies with his huge answers, his normalized version is simply:

$$\frac{\overrightarrow{\text{mrright}}}{\|\overrightarrow{\text{mrright}}\|} = [\quad .5 \quad .5 \quad .5 \quad .5 \quad]$$
$$\qquad\qquad\text{action}\quad\text{hiking}\quad\text{candlelight}\quad\text{mystery}$$

See how that works? Your survey responses now become relative to your *other* survey responses. Answering 10 to everything is the same as answering 5 to everything, or even 0 to everything: you're effectively saying "I like all these activities equally." The only way to *truly* say "I really do love candlelight dinners" is to rank candlelight dinners higher than other activities which you admit you like less.

Using normalized versions of the vectors, let's see how each of our eligible bachelors pairs up with Jezebel:

$\overrightarrow{\text{jezebel}} \cdot \overrightarrow{\text{biff}} = .434 \cdot .704 + .173 \cdot .704 + .867 \cdot .070 + .173 \cdot .070 = .5$

$\overrightarrow{\text{jezebel}} \cdot \overrightarrow{\text{filbert}} = .434 \cdot .548 + .173 \cdot .183 + .867 \cdot .730 + .173 \cdot .365 = \mathbf{.966}$

$\overrightarrow{\text{jezebel}} \cdot \overrightarrow{\text{wendell}} = .434 \cdot .092 + .173 \cdot .275 + .867 \cdot .275 + .173 \cdot .917 = .485$

$\overrightarrow{\text{jezebel}} \cdot \overrightarrow{\text{mrright}} = .434 \cdot .500 + .173 \cdot .500 + .867 \cdot .500 + .173 \cdot .500 = .824$

Filbert wins, and Mr. Right is defeated: normalization revealed that Filbert is truly more compatible with Jezebel than he is.

Let's bring this chapter to a close, and wish Filbert and Jezebel a very romantic evening together. :)

🐍 *Appendix: Python*

In this Python appendix, we'll focus mostly on how to create vectors in Python, and how to perform operations on them. For this, we'll use the `ndarray` type from the NumPy library. Creating an `ndarray` (or just "array" for short)[5] has the effect of introducing a named variable whose value is a whole sequence of numbers, not just a single number as with a scalar variable. In Python, each element of an array has a consecutive index number, and as I mentioned on p. 16, these indices start at 0 instead of at 1.

Creating vectors (arrays)

In our first example, we use the `array()` NumPy function to create a brief history of local temperatures[6]:

```
temps = array([42,48,47,51,32])
```

(This line of code, and all others, must come *after* the standard "`from numpy import *`" preamble mentioned on p. 9, of course.)

Notice very carefully that the above line of code has a pair of "boxies" (square brackets) inside the pair of parentheses. It won't work without both pairs, in the correct nesting order. Anyway, after running that code we now have a new array that goes by the name `temps`. We can use the `print()` function to see all its values:

```
print(temps)
```

---

[5] An "array" is basically another name for a list of items. Python also has a simpler type – called a **list** – that could be used as a primitive, makeshift sort of vector. NumPy arrays are the better choice for data-centric applications, though, and have many convenient features over plain-Jane lists. By the way, the first two letters of `ndarray` stand for "n-dimensional."

[6] I'm writing this chapter in the wintertime, by the way, which may explain my frosty Fredericksburg.

2.7. NORMALIZING

> [42 48 47 51 32]

It will also be useful sometimes to create a vector of all zeros. (This is helpful when we have an array of different cumulative counts.) The `zeros()` function can be used here:

```
nada = zeros(6)
print(nada)
```

> [0. 0. 0. 0. 0. 0.]

(The trailing decimal points, by the way, indicate that these entries are stored as floating-point numbers ("decimal numbers") instead of integers. This won't be super important for us.)

It's also common to create a vector with a sequence of consecutive entries. For this, we have the `arange()` function[7] which can be given one, two, or three numbers inside the parens:

```
a = arange(7)
b = arange(5,12)
c = arange(5,50,5)
print(a)
print(b)
print(c)
```

> [0 1 2 3 4 5 6]
> [5 6 7 8 9 10 11]
> [5 10 15 20 25 30 35 40 45]

---

[7] Be careful – this is *not* the English word *arrange* which has two r's in it! Instead, it's an amalgamation of the phrase "array range."

As you can see, the first version yields a vector of the appropriate length whose entries start at 0; the second version goes from a specific starting point up to (but not including) a specific end point; and the third version goes from a starting point to (but again, not including) an ending point by a particular step size. The fact that 12 is *not* included in the vector produced by `arange(5,12)` is another minor but weird thing you have to get used to. (Maybe you should make a list of these.)

There will be cases where we want to get vectors full of *random* numbers. NumPy gives us many, many ways to do this, most of which are outside the scope of this book. I'll just mention one, which is to get a vector of random numbers between 0 and 1:

```
r = random.rand(4)
print(r)
```

```
[0.64039213 0.2164199  0.48690418 0.72351423]
```

The "4" specifies how long the vector should be.

Finally, a very common way to create a vector is to load its contents from a data file. Suppose there were a file on your computer called `somedata.txt` which had a long list of numbers, one number per line. You could import the whole thing into a NumPy array called `my_data` like this:

```
my_data = loadtxt("somedata.txt")
```

The file must be in "plain-text" format (*i.e.*, not a Word document or a PDF file or any other such formatted thing). Often, but not always, such files have a ".txt" extension to indicate that.

2.7. NORMALIZING

Working with vectors (arrays)

To retrieve individual elements from a vector, we can specify numbered indices inside a pair of boxies after the array name:

```
print(temps)
print(temps[0])
print(temps[4])
```

```
[42 48 47 51 32]
42
32
```

Heads up! In a five-element array, since element #0 is the first one, element #4 is the last one.

We can ask an array how long it is by appending `.size` to its name:

```
print(temps.size)
```

```
5
```

We can also get a **slice** of a vector by specifying a range of indices. It works like this:

```
print(temps[1:4])
```

```
[48 47 51]
```

The "1:4" inside the boxies means "I'd like all elements numbered 1 (inclusive) through 4 (exclusive)." This is a total of *three* elements: the ones at index numbers 1, 2, and 3. (Again, 4 itself is not included, and yes that's annoying.)

To round a vector's elements to the nearest integer, or to simply drop the part after the decimal point, we can use the functions round_()[8] or trunc(), respectively:

```
weights = array([ 145.6, 212.9, 156.4 ])
print(weights)
print(round_(weights))
print(trunc(weights))
```

```
[145.6 212.9 156.4]
[146. 213. 156.]
[145. 212. 156.]
```

We can also add up the elements in a vector, find the smallest and largest, and find the *index of* the smallest and of the largest:

```
print(weights.sum())
print(weights.min())
print(weights.max())
print(weights.argmin())
print(weights.argmax())
```

```
514.9
145.6
212.9
0
1
```

The value printed by ".argmin()" is the index of the smallest value in the vector, which in this case is element #0 (whose value is 145.6). The value printed by ".argmax()" is 1, since element #1 (whose value is 212.9) is the highest.

---

[8] Careful: don't forget the trailing underscore!

2.7. NORMALIZING

And finally, our actual linear algebra operations. To perform scalar-vector multiplication, just use the splat ("*") symbol:

```
weights_kg = (1/2.2) * weights
print(weights_kg)
```

[66.18181818 96.77272727 71.09090909]

And to perform vector addition, just use the plus ("+") symbol:

```
holiday_gains = array([8.5, 10, 11])
print(weights + holiday_gains)
```

[154.1 222.9 167.4]

(Oof. Too much milk chocolate fudge.)

You could've guessed how to do those two operations without me even telling you. The only slightly weird-looking one is the dot product. It requires typing ".dot()" (which I always pronounce "dot-dot"):

```
abc = array([5,3,0,2])
def = array([0,1,9,6])
print(abc.dot(def))
```

15

And lastly, norms. To compute a vector's Euclidean norm, we use the `linalg.norm()` function with the vector in the parens:

```
print(linalg.norm(abc))
```

6.164414002968976

If you're feeling paranoid, we can compute it by hand using the Pythagorean theorem to confirm this is the correct answer:

```
print(sqrt(abc[0]**2 + abc[1]**2 + abc[2]**2 + abc[3]**2))
```

6.164414002968976

If you want any norm other than the Euclidean, you can specify the "order" of the norm as a second number in the parens:

```
print(linalg.norm(abc,0))
print(linalg.norm(abc,1))
print(linalg.norm(abc,2))
print(linalg.norm(abc,3))
print(linalg.norm(abc,4))
print(linalg.norm(abc,Inf))
```

3.0
10.0
6.164414002968976
5.428835233189813
5.183633637236413
5.0

This prints for us the ℓ^0, ℓ^1, ℓ^2, ℓ^3, ℓ^4, and ℓ^∞ norms of our `abc` vector. In particular, the ℓ^0 is the number of non-zero entries, the ℓ^1 is the sum of the entries, the ℓ^∞ is the maximum entry, and of course the ℓ^2 norm is the same as the Euclidean norm.

Chapter 3

Linear independence

One of the deepest and most central concepts in linear algebra – in fact, if I were to make a top ten ranking, this one might just make #1 – is that of **linear independence**. It's not about mechanical computations, but conceptual truths. Learn this chapter well.

3.1 The Domino Game

I've thought long and hard about the best way to teach the material in this chapter, and I've come up with a game. I call it "the Domino Game." Here are the rules:

---

1. You are given one or more **yellow**[1] "starter dominoes."
2. The object of the game is to build the white "goal domino" from these starter dominoes.
3. You can "use" any number of each starter domino (even a fraction, even negative), and add them together (left sides add together, and right sides add together).
4. You *cannot* use only one side of a domino.
5. You *cannot* turn a domino around so the left side and right sides flip.

Example. Suppose your starter dominoes are:

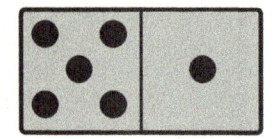

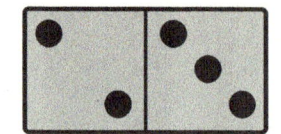

and your goal domino is:

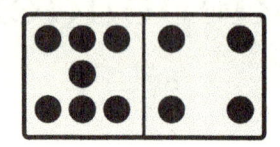

A solution would be "**one** and **one**." This means that you'll take *one* copy of the first starter domino, and *one* copy of the second, and add them together.

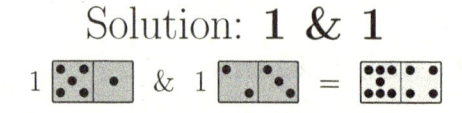

Solution: **1** & **1**

1 [5-1] & 1 [2-3] = [7-4]

Stare carefully at that until you master how it works; the rest of this chapter will be a complete waste of time if this operation is not fully grasped. Adding domino 5–1 to 2–3 means adding the left sides together, and separately adding the right sides together, to produce a new domino 7–4 (since 5 + 2 = 7 and 1 + 3 = 4).

Actually do this

All right, let's test your skillz. I want you to *actually* work out the answers to the following Domino Game puzzles on your own. There are six of them, so it might take you a while (perhaps as long as 6 minutes). But it's vital to cement your understanding of how this works...*and* to set up the crucial punchline later on in this chapter.

---
[1] Light gray, actually, since I made this book black&white to keep costs down.

3.1. THE DOMINO GAME

Answers to each puzzle are given at the end of the chapter. Maybe your answers will not be the same as mine...or maybe they will? That itself is actually a very important question we'll consider in a few minutes.

Enough preamble. Go!

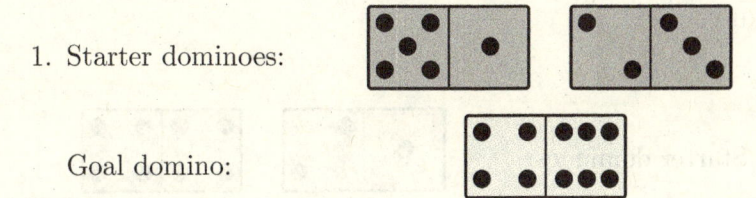

1. Starter dominoes: [5|1] [1|2]

   Goal domino: [3|6]

   (Hint: it's okay to take *zero* of one of the dominoes; *i.e.*, to completely ignore it.)

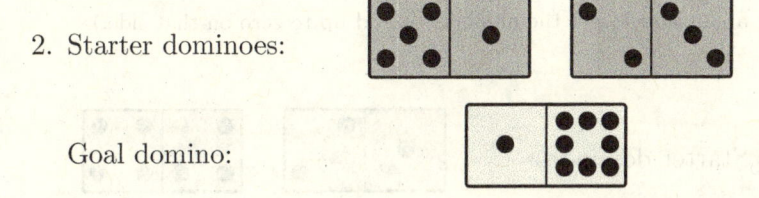

2. Starter dominoes: [4|1] [1|2]

   Goal domino: [1|6]

   (Hint: you may, if you wish, take "a *negative* number" of one of the dominoes. In other words, you can multiply the entire domino by a negative number and then add it to your multiples of the other one.)

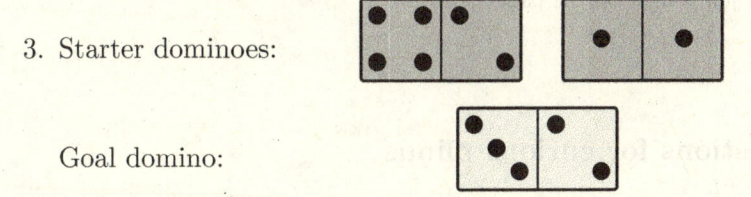

3. Starter dominoes: [3|2] [1|1]

   Goal domino: [2|3]

   (Hint: you can even take a *fraction* of a domino, provided you take the same fraction of both left and right sides. This means that just as you can multiply an entire domino by a positive or negative number, or zero, you can also multiply it by non-integers.)

4. Starter dominoes: [1|2] [3|3 3|3]

   Goal domino: [5|1]

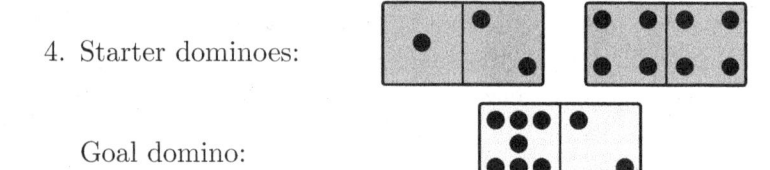

   (Hint: sometimes you have to go pretty far afield to get a solution, meaning a large number of one domino and a large *negative* number of the other.)

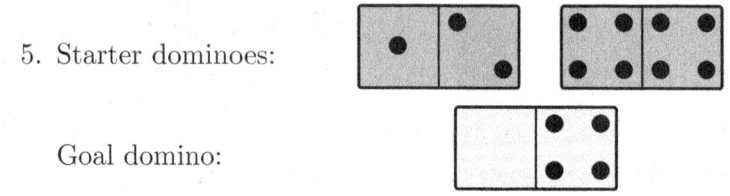

5. Starter dominoes: [1|2] [3|3 3|3]

   Goal domino: [0|4]

   (Hint: the goal domino can have a zero on it, just like the starter dominoes did. But it's really no different; you just have to think creatively about how to get the numbers to add up to zero on that side.)

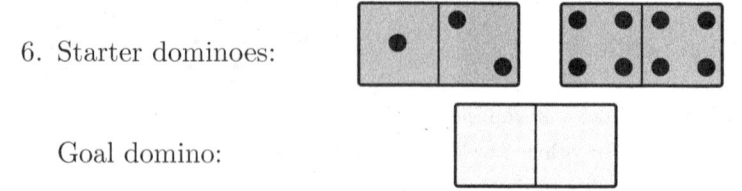

6. Starter dominoes: [1|2] [3|3 3|3]

   Goal domino: [0|0]

   (Hint: and yeah, the goal domino might even be *completely* zero. That's really not any different either, and in fact the solution will probably just jump right off the page at you.)

Questions for curious minds

I presume you have tried, and hopefully succeeded at most of these puzzles by trial and error. Even if you didn't, I hope you've looked at and understood the solutions I gave at the end of the chapter (p. 81).

3.2. THE DOMINO GAME, REDUX

It's well worth taking a moment after all that fiddling around to consider some interesting questions:

1. Were your solutions that same as mine in each case? If so, do you think that was just coincidence? If not, how many different solutions do you think are possible?

2. Is it always possible to solve a puzzle like this, no matter what the *goal* domino is? Or are only a small number of goal dominoes actually possible to produce?

3. Is it always possible to solve a puzzle like this, no matter what the *starter* dominoes are? Or is it only in a few cleverly crafted scenarios where the numbers happen to work out just right?

These matters turn out to be at the heart of the subject of linear algebra. We'll shed light on all of them as we move forward.

3.2 The Domino Game, Redux

I'm now going to give you one more domino puzzle, which is going to seem at first just like the others. But it turns out that hidden inside is a mystery, a paradox, a conundrum that will shake our foundations in chapters to come. Here it is:

Starter dominoes:

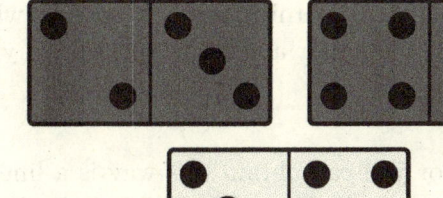

Goal domino:

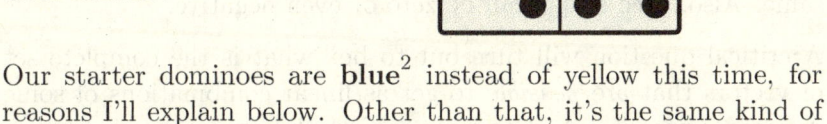

Our starter dominoes are **blue**[2] instead of yellow this time, for reasons I'll explain below. Other than that, it's the same kind of

---
[2]Dark gray, actually, since I made this book black&white to keep costs down.

problem. Go ahead – try it!

I'll mail you $5 if you can figure it out and send me a solution.

Actually, I'll make it $5,000.

Don't get too frustrated before you realize the simple truth: it's not possible.

The key point: *why* blue dominoes don't work

You don't have to be too clever to recognize that this whole Domino Game thing is really math in disguise. And if you haven't seen the connection yet, let me just point out the following so you can do a face palm:

- Dominoes are just two-dimensional vectors.
- "Taking some number of the left (or right) domino" is just scalar-vector multiplication.
- Adding together your copies-of-the-left-domino and your copies-of-the-right-domino is just vector addition.

The central theme of the game is figuring out "which vectors you can make from which other vectors." The result of "making" a new domino is called a linear combination:

You get a **linear combination** of vectors when you multiply each of them by a scalar and add them up (to yield another vector).

Any vector you can obtain this way is a linear combination of the vectors you used. The scalars definitely don't have to all be the same. Also, each scalar can be zero or even negative.

A critical question will turn out to be: what is the complete set of vectors that are *possible* to get as linear combinations of some "starter vectors?" And to answer that, I'm going to give you a whole new perspective on dominoes.

3.2. THE DOMINO GAME, REDUX

Dominoes are vectors

Several of our puzzles involved the yellow starter dominoes 1–2 and 4–4. As I indicated, dominoes are really vectors in disguise. So I have plotted these two "dominoes" in Figure 3.1.

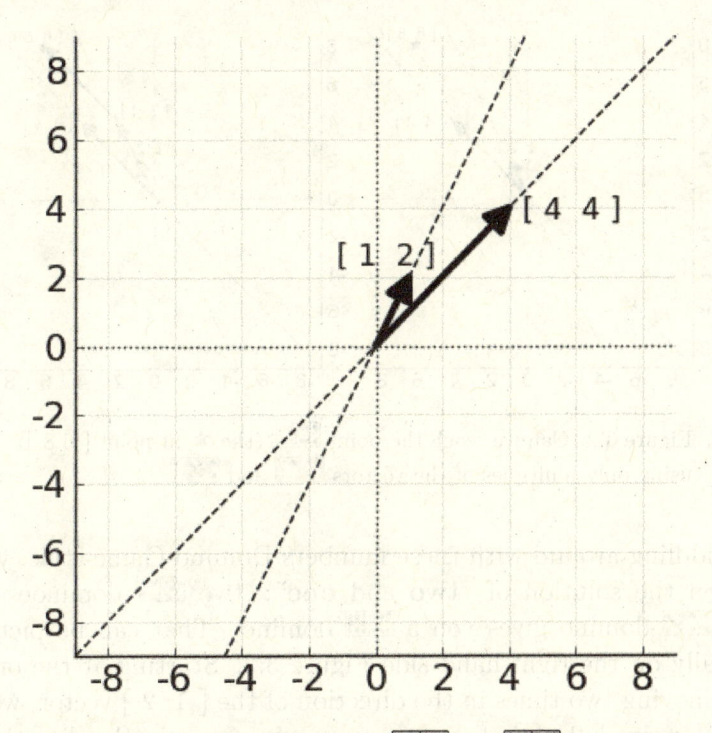

Figure 3.1: Plotting the dominoes ⚁ and ⚃ as vectors.

Also on the diagram are two dashed lines, each going off to infinity in both directions. Consider first the steepest of the two lines. It's pointing in exactly the same direction as the [1 2] vector. It represents *all the points you can get to by multiplying that vector by a scalar.* Take a moment and digest that thought completely. You'll see that some of the points that dashed line goes through are $(2, 4)$, $(4, 8)$, $(0, 0)$, $(-\frac{1}{2}, -1)$, and $(-4, -8)$. Those points are the tips of the vectors you would get if you multiplied [1 2] by 2, 4, 0, $-\frac{1}{2}$, and -4, respectively. Similar comments apply to the dashed line that extends the [4 4] vector.

Now consider the process of trying to reach a goal domino like ⚅⚃, also known as [6 8]. What we're effectively asking is: is there any linear combination of [1 2] and [4 4] that will reach the point [6 8]? The setting for this problem is on the left-hand side of Figure 3.2.

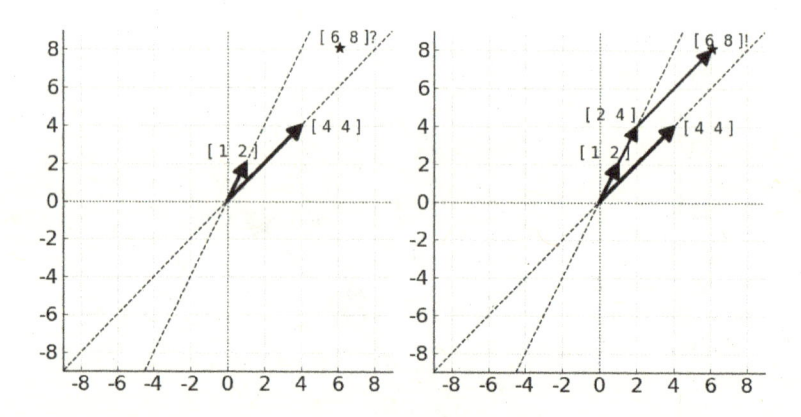

Figure 3.2: Can we reach the point ⚅⚃ (the ★ at point [6 8]) using only multiples of the vectors ⚁ and ⚃? *Yes!*

By fiddling around with these numbers Domino-Game-style, you'll hit on the solution of "**two** and **one**": two ⚁ dominoes plus one ⚃ domino gives you a ⚅⚃ domino. That can be pictured visually on the right-hand side Figure 3.2. Starting at the origin, and moving two times in the direction of the [1 2] vector, we get to the point [2 4]. From there, moving once in the direction of the [4 4] vector lands us exactly on the point [6 8]. Voilà!

That was fun – let's try some more. What about the point [3 2]. Can we reach *it* by using only multiples of [1 2] and [4 4]?

At first glance, it doesn't seem so; after all, the point (3,2) is outside the "windshield wiper" angle between the two dashed lines. But it turns out we can, if we go against the grain. Moving "−1 times in the [1 2] direction" takes us to the point [−1 − 2]. From there, we do *almost* a complete 180°. Heading back northeast once in the [4 4] direction lands us on [3 2] as desired. Bingo! (See Figure 3.3.)

3.2. THE DOMINO GAME, REDUX 61

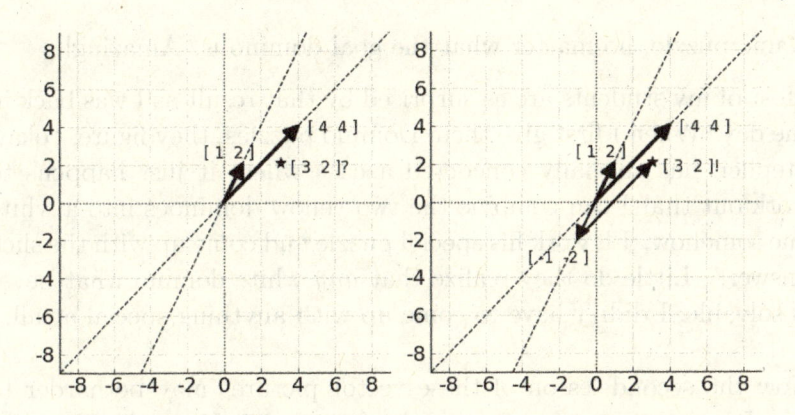

Figure 3.3: Can we reach the point [3 2] using only [1 2] and [4 4]? *Yes!*

And how about [0 4]? This time it's the ⚃ domino that we use "backwards." Going four times in the [1 2] direction followed by −1 in the [4 4] direction gives us the solution "4 & −1," as depicted in Figure 3.4.

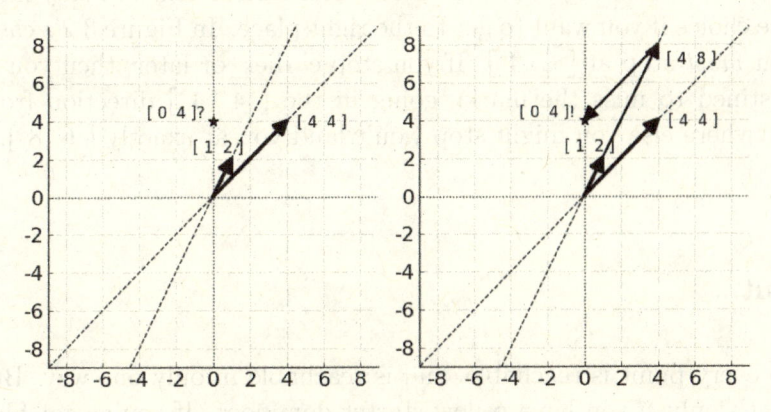

Figure 3.4: Can we reach the point [0 4] using only [1 2] and [4 4]? *Yes!*

At this point, you'll probably guess what I'm going to say next. Yes indeed, *any* point in the entire x, y plane can be reached through some combination of the [1 2] and [4 4] vectors. And that gives us the answer to one of our questions from p. 57 (question #2): surprisingly, *yes* we can always find a solution to the Domino

Game puzzle, no matter what the goal domino is. Amazing!

Most of my students are as surprised by that result as I was back in the day. When I first give them Domino puzzles, they figure, "okay, Stephen has specially concocted a case where it just happens to work out that I can combine the two yellow dominoes into a white one somehow. I'll work his special puzzle and come up with the slick answer." Little do they realize that *any* white domino whatsoever is solvable; I didn't have to come up with anything special at all.

Now the second lesson of these vector pictures may be harder to see. It's the answer to question #1 from p. 57. Not only can every Domino problem be solved, but *it can be solved in only one way*.

If you did it right, your answers to the six puzzles on pp. 55-56 were exactly the same as mine on p. 81. Perhaps that struck you as a coincidence at first: "gee, it's sure funny that I always keep hitting on the exact same solution that Stephen did!" But if you stare at Figure 3.2 and friends, you might see the reason. Starting from the origin, and striking out in the first vector's direction, you only have one choice if you want to get to the right place. In Figure 3.2's case, you *must* stop at [2 4]. If you stop earlier, or later, then you're destined to miss the mark: going in the [4 4] direction from anywhere else you might stop won't land you at exactly [6 8].

But...

So every point is reachable, and is reachable in only one way. But that's only *if* you have yellow starter dominoes. If you've got blue ones, it's a totally different story.

Figure 3.5 shows the hopeless situation. The telltale sign of misery is that *there's only one dashed line*. The ▨ and ▨ vectors point in *exactly* the same direction, so no matter how hard we try, there's no getting off that one line. In the middle of a promising two-dimensional landscape, we're stuck in a one-dimensional subworld.

3.3. LINEAR INDEPENDENCE IN TWO DIMENSIONS

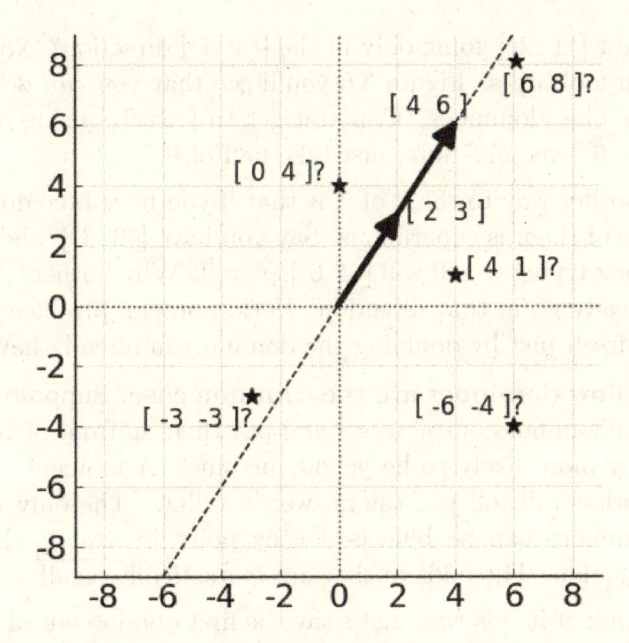

Figure 3.5: Can we reach the points [6 8], [0 4], [4 1], [−6 − 4], [−3 − 3]...or virtually anything else using only [2 3] and [4 6]? **No.**

3.3 Linear independence in two dimensions

The yellow ⚀ and ⚄ vectors are called **linearly independent**. By contrast, the blue ⚁ and ⚃ vectors are **linearly dependent**. Figure 3.6 (p. 65) sums up some extremely important facts about these two cases in one handy table. Let me explain each item in turn.

- **Yellow dominoes are linearly independent.** This means they point in different directions, so that each one gives you a "fresh" degree of freedom to travel in.

- **You can't get one yellow domino from the other.** A corollary of the "different directions" thing is that if you tried to get to the tip of the first yellow domino using only the second, you couldn't do it. Look back at Figure 3.1 (p. 59) if you don't believe me. From the origin, can you get to the point [1 2] going only in the [4 4] direction? No. But if you look up at Figure 3.5 you'll see that you *can* do it with our blue dominoes. Can you get to [2 3] using only the [4 6] vector? Sure, just take half of it.

Another way to think of it is that if you have blue dominoes, one of them is superfluous. Say you have [2 3], and I come along trying to sell you [4 6] as well. Why bother? You can already go in that direction! Heck, you can produce [4 6] yourself just by doubling the domino you already have.

- **Yellow dominoes are the common case.** Suppose I picked two dominoes out of a bag and put them in front of you. Are they more likely to be yellow, or blue? A moment's consideration will tell you the answer is yellow. The only way the dominoes can be blue is if they point in *exactly* the same direction. The odds of that are fantastically small.

  Think of it this way. Let's say the first domino out of the bag is [1 3]. And let's say the left half of the second domino is 4, so that the second domino is [4 ?]. Think about what would have to happen for the pair of dominoes to be blue. That question mark would have to be exactly 12. *Only* 12. Absolutely any other number for the question mark would give you yellow dominoes.

- **With yellow dominoes, you can get *any* white domino.** This is perhaps the most important point. The yellow dominoes have enough coverage that any point in the entire plane is reachable using them. The sorry blue dominoes, on the other hand, are inbred; you can't get anywhere on the plane except the points along their shared, lonely line.

- **With yellow dominoes, each solution is unique.** This may or may not have been obvious to you from the diagrams, but I promise it's so. You can reach each point in only one way. By contrast, everything the blue dominoes can reach – which admittedly, ain't much – can be reached in multiple ways (including the origin; see the next point).

- **Yellow dominoes can't get to the origin, except "trivially."** One last point is that with yellow dominoes, the only way to get to the origin is to take zero of the first domino and zero of the second. (This is called a **trivial solution**.) That's because once you set out in the first domino's direction, using the second one has to take you in a *different* direction, and hence not back to where you came. With blue dominoes, you can do this in many different ways: take six [2 3]'s minus three [4 6]'s, or −1 [2 3]'s and half a [4 6], *etc.* I guess that's some small recompense for having to stay on that one line: blue dominoes truly *own* that line and can tread it to their heart's content. This seemingly obscure fact will actually play a surprising role later on.

By the way, a student once asked me, "what if you get one yellow domino and one blue? What happens then?" Perhaps you'll see the answer immediately as one of my other students did. The answer is *that can't happen*. No domino is, by itself, intrinsically yellow or blue: it's only yellow or blue *with respect to another one*. It's the *pair* of dominoes that are yellow if they point in different directions, or blue if they point in the same direction.

Yellow dominoes	Blue dominos
linearly **independent**	linearly **dependent**
can't get any yellow from others	can get each blue from others
"common"	"rare"
can make *any* white domino	can make only a few
each goal reachable in one way	each goal reachable *many* ways
can only get ▢▢ "trivially"	can get ▢▢ in many ways

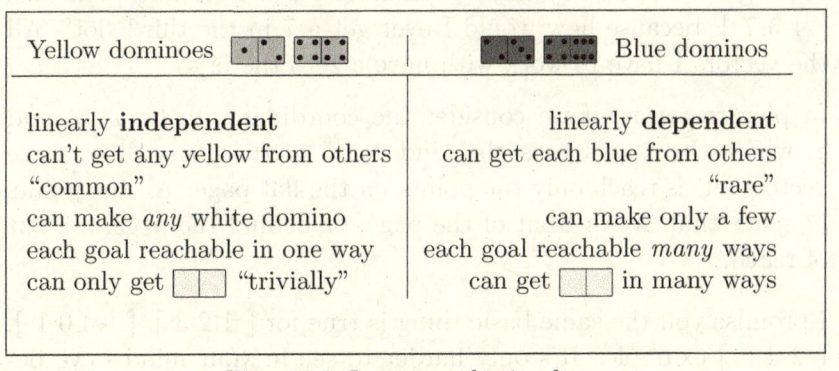

Figure 3.6: Important domino facts.

3.4 Linear independence in more dimensions

Now I wish things could stay that easy but they just can't. When we move to three dimensions (and beyond) things become more subtle, even besides being harder to visualize.

First let's look at an easy case. Suppose you have the three "triominoes" [1 2 3], [−4 0 1], and [2 4 6]. You can probably eyeball those and see that they are *not* linearly independent, because the first and third dominoes are multiples of each other. (Multiply [1 2 3] by 2 and you get [2 4 6].) And if you can get one vector from one of the others, that's the death knell for our yellow hopes and dreams: These vectors are unavoidably blue.

In three dimensions, blue triominoes mean that we can't get to every point in three-dimensional **space** just by using those vectors. That's hard to visualize, but if you can picture the following, you'll get the idea. Recall that in 2-d, blue vectors sat on the same dashed line. You couldn't get to the rest of the plane. In 3-d, blue vectors all sit on the same *plane*. You can get anywhere on that two-dimensional surface, but not anywhere else in the vastness of three-dimensional space.

Perhaps this is easier to see if I change the example. Suppose my three triominoes are [4 2 0], [2 3 0], and [6 5 0]. Now you can add multiples of these three vectors together all day, but you'll never get a third entry other than zero. I can't get to a point like [4 3 7], because how would I ever get a 7 in the third slot? All the vectors I have to work with have a zero there!

In picture terms, if we consider the coordinates to be x, y, and z, where the z axis goes "in" and "out" of the page, those three vectors let us reach only the points *on* the flat page. All the points in space that are in front of the page, or behind the page, are out of reach.

I promise you the same basic thing is true for [1 2 3], [−4 0 1], [2 4 6] example. It's only harder to see in your mind's eye because in this case, the plane we're trapped on isn't flat. It's angled through space, slicing slant-wise through the origin. But it's still true that the vast majority of 3-d points can't be reached. The problem here, just like with blue dominoes, is that one of the vectors in the list (the third one) doesn't give us any power we didn't already have with one of the others (the first one).

Now so far, this seems just the same as the two-dimensional case,

3.4. LINEAR INDEPENDENCE IN MORE DIMENSIONS 67

except that we have three entries per vector to work with. But unfortunately, even if none of the three vectors is a multiple of any of the other, that's *not* enough to guarantee linear independence. Three vectors which are "pairwise independent" from each other – meaning $\vec{v_1}$ is not a multiple of $\vec{v_2}$, nor $\vec{v_2}$ of $\vec{v_3}$, nor $\vec{v_3}$ of $\vec{v_1}$ – can still be a linearly dependent set.

How? *If one is a linear combination of the other two.* Consider these three vectors:

$$\begin{aligned} \vec{v_1} &= [\quad 2 \quad 0 \quad -3 \quad] \\ \vec{v_2} &= [\quad -1 \quad 4 \quad 4 \quad] \\ \vec{v_3} &= [\quad 3 \quad 4 \quad -2 \quad] \end{aligned}$$

Those look pretty linearly independent to me. But they're not. If you take twice the first vector plus the second vector, you get the third vector:

$$2\vec{v_1} + 1\vec{v_2} = [\ 4\ \ 0\ \ -6\ ] + [\ -1\ \ 4\ \ 4\ ] = [\ 3\ \ 4\ \ -2\ ] = \vec{v_3}$$

As before, then, the third vector *didn't give us any additional power.* If we wanted to move in the [3 4 − 2] direction, we could do so using only vectors $\vec{v_1}$ and $\vec{v_2}$ in the right quantities. The offer of that $\vec{v_3}$ vector leaves us with an awkward pause and saying as politely as possible "no, thanks."

Now finally, we're ready for our supreme definition of linear independence, no matter how many dimensions. Here goes:

> A set of vectors is **linearly independent** only if none of them can be made from a linear combination of the others.

If you're given a set of vectors, and you can find a superfluous one in the bunch, remove it so you whittle the set down to size. When you get to the point where none of the remaining vectors can be deleted without losing the ability to reach some points, then you know you have a linearly independent set.

3.5 Foundational definitions

We close this heady chapter by defining a few more crucial terms that we'll make use of again and again.

> A **"vector space"** is a world of n dimensions in which n-dimensional vectors live. (like the x-y plane, or the 3-d space.)

I hinted at this term back on p. 19, and mentioned that it's sometimes used in a very abstract way. The above definition, believe it or not, is a pretty brass-tacks definition, since we're defining it in terms of dimensions and coordinates. Just think of a "vector space" as "the place where vectors (of a particular length) live" and you won't be too far off.

> The set of *all* linear combinations of a set of vectors is called the **span** of that set.

This is precisely the question of "where can I *get* using these starter dominoes?" that we asked in the Domino Game. I can combine starter vectors with each other in numerous ways to get other vectors. If I kept doing that and doing that infinitely, what is my *entire* set of possible vacation spots? Answer: the **span**.

To be concrete:

- The span of { ▫, ▫ } is **the whole x-y plane**.
- The span of { ▫, ▫ }, on the other hand, is merely **the line through the origin with slope $\frac{3}{2}$** ("rise over run").
- The span of { [2 3 1], [0 − 9 0], [0 1 1] } is **the whole three-dimensional x-y-z space**, since that set is linearly

3.5. FOUNDATIONAL DEFINITIONS

independent. (You can believe me or not, but it is. We'll figure out how to verify that later on.)

- The span of { [2 0 −3], [−1 4 4], [3 4 −2] } is *not* the whole x-y-z space, since as we learned above, that set is not linearly independent. Its span is merely **a 2-d plane slicing through the origin** of three-dimensional space.

> A **basis** for a vector space is a *linearly independent* set of vectors that *spans* the space.

Note that two-part definition. Your vectors have to (1) be independent of one another, and (2) span the entire space. Only then do they constitute a basis.

Important fact: if you have a basis, then every vector in the entire vector space can be expressed as a linear combination of the basis vectors in exactly one way.

For example, we saw that { [1 2], [4 4] } was a basis for the x-y plane. Therefore, every point on the x-y plane can be formed by a unique linear combination of those vectors:

$$[\ 6\ 8\ ] = 2\,[\ 1\ 2\ ] + 1\,[\ 4\ 4\ ]$$
$$[\ 0\ 4\ ] = 4\,[\ 1\ 2\ ] - 1\,[\ 4\ 4\ ]$$
$$[\ 4\ -4\ ] = -8\,[\ 1\ 2\ ] + 3\,[\ 4\ 4\ ]$$
$$etc.$$

We'll look at this in a new and deep way later on, but you can begin to grasp it now: using a basis kind of gives us *a new coordinate system* in which to express a vector. For example, as shown above, the vector [4 −4] can be expressed as **−8** of the [1 2] vector plus **3** of the [4 4] vector. That means that its coordinates are kinda sorta "(−8, 3)" in this basis rather than "(4, −4)" in the original basis. Dude, that's mind-blowing.

> The **"standard basis"** is a basis whose vectors have norm 1 and which point in each axis direction.

In other words:

- In two dimensions, the standard basis is the vectors [1 0] and [0 1].
- In three dimensions, it's the vectors [1 0 0], [0 1 0], and [0 0 1].
- In four dimensions, it's the vectors [1 0 0 0], [0 1 0 0], [0 0 1 0], and [0 0 0 1].
- *Etc.*

Note that in the standard basis, we have:

$$[\,6\ \ 8\,] = 6[\,1\ \ 0\,] + 8[\,0\ \ 1\,]$$
$$[\,0\ \ 4\,] = 0[\,1\ \ 0\,] + 4[\,0\ \ 1\,]$$
$$[\,4\ \ -4\,] = 4[\,1\ \ 0\,] - 4[\,0\ \ 1\,]$$

etc.

Thus in some ways, the standard basis is sort of the "natural" coordinate system. (Hang on to your hats in Chapter 8, though, when we consider a different "natural" one.)

Fact: all possible bases for a vector space have the *same* number of vectors in them. Why? Well, you can't span the space with any fewer. And you can't be linearly independent if you have any more. So no matter what basis you tell me you have for the x-y plane, I know it'd better have exactly two vectors in it or you're a liar. If you tell me you have a basis for x-y-z space, it'd better have three vectors in it: no more, and no fewer.

Last one, which you might already be able to guess:

> The **dimension** of a vector space is the number of elements in a basis for it.

3.6. CHANGING BASES

We've talked about the dimension of a *vector* before, but not of a vector space. The dimension of a vector space is how many vectors are required to get everywhere in it. And that in turn is simply the dimension of the vectors that live in it. It's no accident that for *three*-dimensional space, a basis has *three* vectors with *three* elements each.

3.6 Changing bases

If each basis is merely a new coordinate system in which to express vectors, we ought to be able to change between bases at will. And in fact we can. Let's see how.

Changing *to* the standard basis

Ron has a two-dimensional vector called $\vec{r}$. I'll tell you that its coordinates are 3 and −1, BUT before you try to visualize it, there's a catch: these coordinates are *not* expressed in the standard basis, but in the *"domino basis"* we've used several times in this chapter: ⚀⚁ / ⚂⚃.

This is the first time I've used the phrase "expressed as coordinates in a certain basis," because up until now, we've always been implicitly assuming the standard basis. If I said a vector had components "7" and "4," it has gone without saying that I meant "7 units in the [1 0] direction, and 4 units in the [0 1] direction." Viewed in this way, a vector with coordinates 7 and 4 is really a linear combination of the two (standard) basis vectors:

$$7 \cdot \begin{bmatrix} 1 \\ 0 \end{bmatrix} + 4 \cdot \begin{bmatrix} 0 \\ 1 \end{bmatrix} = \begin{bmatrix} 7 \\ 4 \end{bmatrix}.$$

Sometimes we need to be explicit about which basis is being used to express a vector's components. To do that, we'll put a subscript on our vector notation, labeled with the basis it uses. We'll use the symbol "B_s" to mean the standard basis; B_s thus equals

{[1 0],[0 1]}. So we would write down this example vector as follows:

$$\begin{bmatrix} 7 \\ 4 \end{bmatrix}_{B_s}.$$

Now Ron, on the other hand, insists on using the domino basis ▨ / ▨. We'll call it "B_d" (d for "dominoes.") Thus B_d = {[1 2],[4 4]}, and we write Ron's vector like this:

$$\vec{r} = \begin{bmatrix} 3 \\ -1 \end{bmatrix}_{B_d}.$$

Our question is one of translation: what are Ron's coordinates in the *standard* basis?

If you think about it, that's a pretty easy question to answer. When Ron says his coordinates are "3" and "−1," he merely means "I've got three ▨'s and negative one ▨'s." Computing his standard-basis coordinates is just a matter of taking that linear combination:

$$\vec{r} = 3 \cdot \begin{bmatrix} 1 \\ 2 \end{bmatrix} + (-1) \cdot \begin{bmatrix} 4 \\ 4 \end{bmatrix} = \begin{bmatrix} -1 \\ 2 \end{bmatrix}_{B_s}.$$

This is called a **change of basis** operation. It's important to understand that Ron's vector *itself* did not change: only the coordinate system in which we expressed it. In other words, these two vector representations are exactly equal:

$$\begin{bmatrix} 3 \\ -1 \end{bmatrix}_{B_d} = \begin{bmatrix} -1 \\ 2 \end{bmatrix}_{B_s}.$$

You can see in Figure 3.7 that whether we say "three $\begin{bmatrix} 1 \\ 2 \end{bmatrix}$'s and negative one $\begin{bmatrix} 4 \\ 4 \end{bmatrix}$," or "negative one $\begin{bmatrix} 1 \\ 0 \end{bmatrix}$'s and two $\begin{bmatrix} 0 \\ 1 \end{bmatrix}$'s," we get the same vector $\vec{r}$.

3.6. CHANGING BASES

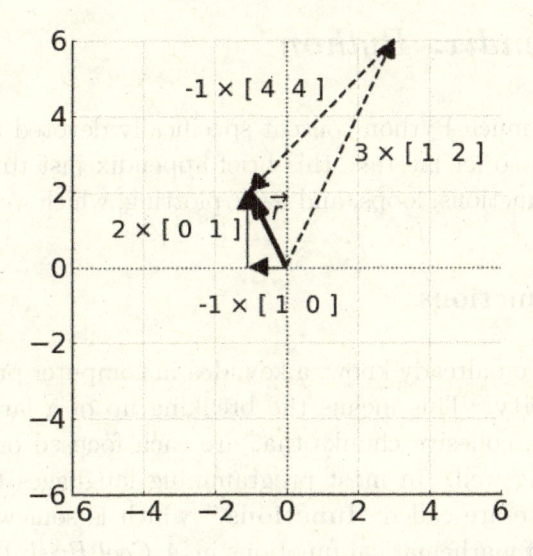

Figure 3.7: In either the domino basis (dashed lines) or the standard basis (thin solid lines), Ron's vector (thick solid line) is the same.

Changing *from* the standard basis

By the way, what if we want to go the other way? Suppose Hermione has a vector $\vec{h}$ which, expressed as coordinates in the *standard* basis, is [5 2]. Again, this means that her vector is a linear combination of the two standard basis vectors:

$$\vec{h} = 5 \cdot \begin{bmatrix} 1 \\ 0 \end{bmatrix} + 2 \cdot \begin{bmatrix} 0 \\ 1 \end{bmatrix} = \begin{bmatrix} 5 \\ 2 \end{bmatrix}_{B_s}.$$

But what are her coordinates in the domino basis?

I'm going to need to put you off on this all the way to p. 165, since it will involve a few concepts we haven't covered yet. I promise we'll return to Hermione, though!

🐍 *Appendix: Python*

There's not much Python content specifically devoted to linear independence, so let me take this brief appendix just to outline the syntax for functions, loops, and basic plotting, which we'll use later.

Python functions

As most of you already know, a key idea in computer programming is **modularity**. This means the breaking up of a large program into smaller, cohesive chunks that are each focused on doing one specific thing well. In most programming languages (Python included) these are called "**functions**," which is somewhat related to our use of mathematical functions in *A Cool Brisk Walk* in that they map inputs to outputs.

Here's how they work in Python. To create a function, you use this syntax:

```
def functionName(argument1, argument2, ...):
    ... statements ...
    return output
```

The word "`def`" is literal: it means you're **def**ining a function. The words "`functionName`, `argument1`, and `statements`" are *not* literal: they are placeholders for the name of your function, the names of the inputs it accepts, and the code that comprises the function. "Argument" is the nutty word that programmers use for "an input given to a function"; each one has a name, and these are separated by commas inside a pair of parens, followed by a colon.

Important: all the Python code that comprises the **body** of the function must be *indented one tab to the right*. Python is almost the only language that delineates its structure through indentation, and this can cause students hangups if they're not on their guard. The indented code actually in the function can be any Python code

3.6. CHANGING BASES

at all. At one (or more[3]) places in the code, a **"return statement"** will indicate a value that is given as the function's output.

Here's a very short example of a function we might write:

```
def average(my_vector):
    return my_vector.sum() / my_vector.size
```

We learned in the last appendix how to sum up the values in an array, and also how to obtain the number of elements it contains. This function combines these two operations and takes the arithmetic mean, or average, of the results.

To actually make use of this function, we **"call"** it by typing its name, parens, and an input value, then either printing the output or capturing it in another variable. Here goes:

```
weights = np.array([ 145.6, 212.9, 156.4 ])

avg_weight = average(weights)
print("The avg weight is {} pounds.".format(avg_weight))
```

> The avg weight is 171.63333333333333 pounds.

Notice carefully that although the `average()` function named its argument "`my_vector`," when we called the function we specified a different name ("`weights`"). This is a happy healthy thing, and you should get used to it. All you have to remember is that whatever is given as an input to the function, *the function will itself temporarily name it with its own name* for use in calculation.

In the case of two or more arguments, the order in which they are listed is what keeps everything in sync between the function and the

---

[3]You might wonder why a function would have more than one **return** statement, since a **return** stops the function and gives an output. We'll see an example of multiple **returns** on p. 109.

code that calls it. Here's an example which uses both scalar-vector multiplication and vector addition:

```
def next_years_salary(salaries, increases, cost_of_living_raise):
    new_salaries = salaries + increases
    return new_salaries + (cost_of_living_raise * new_salaries)

eng = np.array([86000, 91000, 86000])
eng_bumps = np.array([2000, 3000, 4000])
eng = next_years_salary(eng, eng_bumps, .02)
print("Next year's engineering salaries are: {}.".format(eng))
```

> Next year's engineering salaries are: [89760. 95880. 91800.].

In this case, the function itself named its arguments **salaries**, **increases**, and **cost_of_living_raise**. When we called it, however, we gave it different names for the first two arguments, and didn't even *have* a name for the third one! (We just specified the literal value .02 as the third input.)

Python loops

Another programming technique we'll use is that of a **loop**, specifically a **for loop**. These work very much the same as for loops do in any other language. They are used when the programmer wants a certain block of code to be repeated multiple times, possibly with minor changes each time. Importantly, for loops are used when the programmer knows at the outset how many times the loop needs to execute. (When she doesn't know this, she should use a **while loop** instead, which we won't cover in this book.)

One bit of lingo: each time the block of statements is executed is called an **iteration**. You'll may hear people say that a chunk of code "**iterates**" or "works **iteratively**"; by this they simply mean it contains a loop.

In Python, the pattern we'll use is as follows:

3.6. CHANGING BASES

```
for i in arange(n):
    ...statements...
```

Again, the indentation is key: the only way Python knows when the to-be-repeated code block ends, and the code after the loop resumes, is that the former is tabbed over whereas the latter is flush-left.

The `i` that appears after `for` is called the **loop variable**: it is the only thing about the block of statements that may vary between iterations. And this is only because the statements themselves often have a reference to `i`, as we'll see in a moment.

Finally, you'll recognize "`arange`" in the first line as our new friend from p. 47. (Remember: only one 'r'!) That line of code says: "run the following block of statements multiple times. In the first iteration, set the `i` variable to the value 0. The second time, set it to 1. Continue all the way up to n-1."

As an example, let's write our own function to compute a vector's Euclidean norm (even though NumPy gives us this out-of-the-box):

```
def euclidean_norm(x):
    total = 0
    for i in arange(x.size):
        total = total + x[i]**2
    return sqrt(total)
```

Notice how the loop variable (`i`) is being used as an index to the `x` array, so that a different element is selected each time for squaring and adding to the running total. In the call to `arange()`, we used `x.size`, so that we would run the loop exactly once for each element. Let's take it for a spin:

```
abc = array([5,3,0,2])
print(euclidean_norm(abc))
```

> 6.164414002968976

This does match our result from p. 52 exactly.

Python plotting

Finally, let's just learn a few simple plotting commands so we can reproduce the kinds of figures that are in this book. Python has a plethora of different plotting libraries, all of which have different features and pros and cons. Just to keep things super simple, we'll use the `pylab` library which requires a minimum of fuss.

First, you import it with your other imported things by typing "`import pylab`" at the top of your program.

Then, to plot a single point, you can use the `pylab.plot()` function. It takes three arguments: an x and a y coordinate, and then a character indicating the "shape" of the plotted point, for which we'll use `'o'` to get a circle. (There are boatloads of other options.)

It's also useful to be able to set the overall ranges of your plot (in both x and y directions) so you can zoom in or out as desired. For this, we call `pylab.xlim(`*min*`,`*max*`)` to set the x-axis range, and similarly for the y-axis range.

Finally, in your Python environment you may need `pylab.show()` to get it to actually render the plot in a window.

Let's put this all together. We'll first write a function `linearCombo` that will compute a linear combination of two dominos.

3.6. CHANGING BASES

```
def linearCombo(n1,n2):
    domino1 = array([1,2])
    domino2 = array([4,4])
    return n1 * domino1 + n2 * domino2
```

This uses our yellow dominos from this chapter. Now we'll call this function by generating a hundred random linear combinations of these dominos, and plotting each. Here's the code:

```
for i in range(100):
    n1 = (random.rand(1) * 4) - 2
    n2 = (random.rand(1) * 4) - 2
    randomCombo = linearCombo(n1,n2)
    pylab.plot(randomCombo[0],randomCombo[1],'o')
pylab.xlim(-10,10)
pylab.ylim(-10,10)
pylab.show()
```

If you stare at the "n1" line inside the loop, you'll realize that it's generating a random number between -2 and 2. (`random.rand(1)`, you'll recall, gives us a random number between 0 and 1. By multiplying that number by 4 and subtracting 2, we've spread its possible values over the desired range. We do the same for n2. So the function is basically plotting "a random linear combination of the yellow dominos" a hundred times.

The result is on the left side of Figure 3.8. You'll see the bulk of the dots fall on a southwest-ish-to-northeast-ish line. That's because both of our dominoes (⚅ and ⚅) do point in that general direction. But if we got really lucky (?) with our random number draws, we could conceivably get *any* point on the plane, even a really northwest or a really southeast one.

With the blue dominoes, as you've hopefully learned this chapter, that's not possible. If you change the first two lines of the `linearCombo()` function to this:

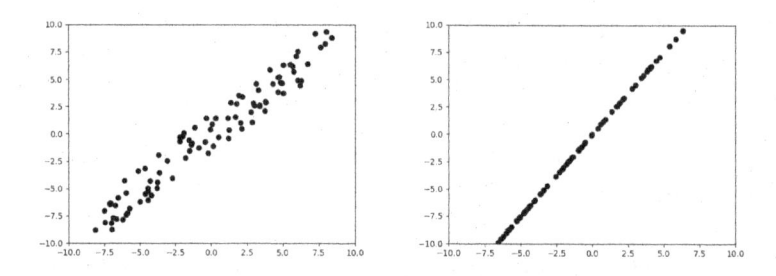

Figure 3.8: A hundred random linear combinations of the yellow dominos (left) and the blue dominos (right).

```
      ...
domino1 = array([2,3])
domino2 = array([4,6])
      ...
```

and re-run the code, you get the right side of Figure 3.8, in which every single point, no matter the random numbers, is exactly on the ▨ line (which is precisely the same line as the ▨ line, of course), giving a very warped view of our supposedly two-dimensional universe. Alas, that's life with blue dominoes.

3.6. CHANGING BASES

Answers to Domino Game puzzles from pp. 55-56

1. Solution: **0 & 2**

   0 [🁣] & 2 [🁣] = [🁣]

2. Solution: **−1 & 3**

   −1 [🁣] & 3 [🁣] = [🁣]

3. Solution: $\frac{1}{2}$ & **1**

   $\frac{1}{2}$ [🁣] & 1 [🁣] = [🁣]

4. Solution: **-5 & 3**

   −5 [🁣] & 3 [🁣] = [🁣]

5. Solution: **4 & −1**

   4 [🁣] & −1 [🁣] = [🁣]

6. Solution: **0 & 0**

   0 [🁣] & 0 [🁣] = [🁣]

Chapter 4

Matrices

It's now time for the granddaddy of all linear algebra entities: the **matrix**. When we've finished this part of our climb, you'll actually be able to see the summit we'll eventually reach.

By the way, the plural of *matrix* is **matrices** (pronounced MAY-trih-sees), kind of like the plural of *index* is *indices*. But don't forget the singular is still *"matrix!"* Don't let me (or anyone else) catch you uttering the non-word "matrice" – you'll sound like a dweeb and drive me up a wall.

4.1 Row and column vectors

Up to now, a vector has simply been a vector. I haven't made a big deal about how you write it on the page. We've been free to write a vector $\vec{x}$ with the three elements 6, 2, and 9 in either of these ways:

$$\vec{x} = [\ 6 \ \ 2 \ \ 9\ ] \qquad ...or... \qquad \vec{x} = \begin{bmatrix} 6 \\ 2 \\ 9 \end{bmatrix}$$

Or heck, you could even write it diagonally if you want. This flexibility is because all that really matters is the *function* view of a vector that we discussed in section 2.3. All that ultimately matters is that you associate the correct index number with the correct element. However I might draw $\vec{x}$ on paper, if I asked you for the value of "element #0," you'd say 6, and if I asked for "element #2," you'd say 9. The way it looks has been immaterial up until now.

That will still be true sometimes. But beginning with this chapter, it's going to sometimes turn out to matter whether or not we think of a vector as a **row vector** (the left-hand-side version of $\vec{x}$, above) or a **column vector** (the right-hand-side). Memorize these terms: they matter, and you'll have to have them on the tip of your neural cortex. A row goes horizontally, side-to-side; and a column goes vertically, up-to-down.

I'll try to always be very careful to emphasize the row vs. column nature of a vector in those cases where it turns out to matter.

By the way, one surprising thing (at least, it was to me) is that the "default" is for an unspecified vector to be treated as a *column* vector, not a row. Column vectors take up more room on the page, and aren't as natural when you're writing on paper, which I guess is why it surprised me. At any rate, whenever a vector is under discussion, try to visualize it as an up-and-down column of entries, unless the accompanying text explicitly says otherwise.

4.2 The matrix

At last, the matrix. This will seem underwhelming at first, but *boy* does it pack a wallop.

A matrix is simply a two-dimensional rectangular grid of entries, kind of like a spreadsheet. We'll use capital letters to designate them, with no special arrow-like or other adornment. Here's our first example:

$$A = \begin{bmatrix} 5 & -7 & 3 & 9 \\ 18 & 4 & 1 & 1 \\ 3 & -3 & \pi & 4 \end{bmatrix}$$

4.2. THE MATRIX

Matrices are always rectangular, but not always square. The A matrix is called a "3 × 4" (three-by-four) matrix, since it has three **row**s and four **column**s. We say that 3×4 are the matrix's **dimensions**. Again, it's important to master all this terminology. When giving the dimensions of a matrix, you always list the number of rows first, and then the number of columns.

To specify an individual element, we need *two* indices instead of just one as we did for a vector. We'll use Python-style numbering (starting with 0) and write the row and column as a two-part comma-separated subscript:

$$A_{0,0} = 5$$
$$A_{1,0} = 18$$
$$A_{0,3} = 9$$
$$A_{2,2} = \pi$$

Just practice first moving down to the correct row, then moving over to the correct column, and you'll be fine.

Labels

As with vectors, we won't always use index numbers to designate rows and columns: sometimes we'll use labels. Check out this matrix W (for "weather"):

$$\begin{array}{c} \text{D.C.} \\ \text{Fredericksburg} \\ \text{Richmond} \end{array} \begin{bmatrix} 81 & 86 & 78 & 74 & 77 \\ 83 & 86 & 79 & 79 & 82 \\ 82 & 86 & 84 & 87 & 87 \end{bmatrix}$$
$$\text{Mon} \quad \text{Tue} \quad \text{Wed} \quad \text{Thu} \quad \text{Fri}$$

Here we're using city names for the row labels, and days of the week as the column labels. It's still easy peasy to interpret – how hot did it get in the nation's capital on Tuesday? 86°, of course. Using the same subscript notation as above, we could say:

$$W_{\text{D.C.,Mon}} = 81$$
$$W_{\text{Fredericksburg,Wed}} = 79$$
$$W_{\text{Fredericksburg,Thu}} = 79$$
$$W_{\text{Richmond,Thu}} = 87$$
$$\vdots$$

and so forth. D.C. and Fred had a bit of a cool-down midweek, thank God, while Richmond was all the while cooking in the upper 80's.

4.3 A matrix is also a function

Remember back in section 2.3 (p. 20) when I explained that a vector, viewed in a sufficiently weird way, was actually a function? The same thing is true for matrices, just by adding one more input to the function.

Put another way, let's consider the row labels (or numbers, if we want to be boring) as the set C (for "cities"). And let's consider the column labels as the set D (for "days-of-the-week"). Then, you can see that a matrix is precisely maps a pair of a city and a day to a high temperature. (The high temperatures are in the set $\mathbb{R}$, which are the real numbers.) In symbols, W is defined as this function:

$$W : C \times D \to \mathbb{R}$$

Recall that function syntax. W is the name of the function. The part before the arrow is the **domain** of the function: the set which its inputs are drawn from. Since it's the Cartesian product of two sets (cities and days) this domain is really all the ordered pairs of cities-and-days, like (D.C., Thurs) and (Richmond, Monday). The function takes any ordered pair like that and gives you a number telling you how hot that city was on that day. It's a snap when seen this way.

4.4 Matrix operations

Just as section 2.4 listed the permissible actions we could perform on vectors (and scalars), so this section lists the operations we can perform on matrices (and vectors, and scalars). There's one other big one which I'll save for entire separate chapter, but there are still four useful ones we'll cover here.

Operation #1: scalar-matrix multiplication

This one's a piece of cake. Recall that multiplying a scalar by a vector amounted to multiplying the scalar by each of its elements, producing a vector of the same dimension. Same here: we get a matrix of the same dimension by multiplying individually:

$$4 \cdot \begin{bmatrix} 3 & 2 & 9 \\ 1 & -1 & 0 \end{bmatrix} = \begin{bmatrix} 12 & 8 & 36 \\ 4 & -4 & 0 \end{bmatrix}.$$

Sometimes we'll put a dot between the two, as above, though we'll often omit that and just write the scalar and matrix side-by-side. Either way, it means scalar-matrix multiplication.

Operation #2: matrix addition

Also a piece of cake, and just what you'd expect:

$$\begin{bmatrix} 4 & 1 \\ 1 & -2 \\ 3 & 18 \end{bmatrix} \begin{bmatrix} 1 & 2 \\ 5 & 2 \\ -10 & -10 \end{bmatrix} + \begin{bmatrix} 5 & 3 \\ 6 & 0 \\ -7 & 8 \end{bmatrix}.$$

The only hard part is not going cross-eyed as you zigzag your eyeballs across the page to match up entries.

As with vector addition, you simply can't add two matrices at all if they don't have the same dimensions. Also just like vectors, we can *subtract* one matrix from another just by adding the first matrix to "−1 times the second matrix."

Operation #3: transpose

Now here's kind of a strange one that's more structural than arithmetical. It's called the **transpose** operator. Unlike the previous ones, this is a **unary operator** which means it acts on only one operand (input) instead of two. (When we did scalar-matrix multiplication, we needed two things to act on: a scalar and a matrix. With matrix addition, we needed two matrices. But here, we only need one "thing" that we do the transpose to.)

The symbol for this is a superscript "T" written just after the matrix. Its purpose is to *interchange the rows and the columns*. The rows of the original matrix become the columns (in the same order) of the transposed matrix, and vice versa. So,

$$\text{If } A = \begin{bmatrix} 4 & 1 \\ 1 & -2 \\ 3 & 18 \end{bmatrix}, \text{ then } A^\mathsf{T} = \begin{bmatrix} 4 & 1 & 3 \\ 1 & -2 & 18 \end{bmatrix}.$$

As you can see, if we start with an $m \times n$ matrix, transposing it gives us an $n \times m$ matrix. Fat-and-wide becomes tall-and-skinny, and vice versa. And in symbols,

$$A_{i,j} = A^\mathsf{T}_{j,i}$$

for all the rows i and columns j of the A matrix. Note how the i and j swapped places in the subscript. The element at row 7, column 19 of A is the same as the one at row 19, column 7 of A^T.

You can probably also tell that if we transpose a column vector, we get a row vector, and vice versa. As I mentioned, there are times that we'll treat a vector as just a sequence of elements, and won't care about its "shape." Other times, though (including the next operation) we'll really be treating it as a sort of degenerate matrix with only one row or one column. At those times, it makes sense to say things like:

$$\text{If } \vec{x} = \begin{bmatrix} 9 \\ 2 \\ 4 \end{bmatrix}, \text{ then } \vec{x}^\mathsf{T} = \begin{bmatrix} 9 & 2 & 4 \end{bmatrix}.$$

4.4. MATRIX OPERATIONS

When speaking, by the way, you pronounce $\vec{x}^\mathsf{T}$ as "x-transpose" and A^T as "A-transpose."

Operation #4: matrix-vector multiplication

Okay, heads-up. Here's the toughie.

What do you think it would mean to multiply a *matrix* by a *vector*? You might think of several plausible ways to define such an operation, but I doubt you'll think of the one that's actually in use. It's weird for a number of reasons, one of which is that the thing you get back often isn't the same dimensions as *either* of the operands!

Let me just do one and see if you can reverse engineer how I got the answer. Here goes:

$$\begin{bmatrix} 2 & 2 & 7 \\ 1 & 4 & 0 \end{bmatrix} \cdot \begin{bmatrix} 1 \\ -1 \\ 4 \end{bmatrix} = \begin{bmatrix} 28 \\ -3 \end{bmatrix}.$$

Can you figure out why in the world that would be the answer?

Surprise number one is the *type* of thing we got back. We multiplied a 2 × 3 matrix by a three-dimensional column vector and this produced...a *two*-dimensional column vector. Ooookay. Surprise number two are the contents of that vector. 28 and −3, what the...?

Things will get considerably clearer if you remember the *dot product* operator from section 2.4 (p. 24). What we did here was *separately compute <u>each</u> row of the matrix dot-product-ed with the vector*. A dot product, you'll recall, gives us a single scalar as an answer. So, since [2 2 7]·[1 −1 4] is 28, and [1 4 0]·[1 −1 4] is −3, our result is a vector containing those two results.

This can really trip you up later if you don't master it now, so take a minute and master the above calculation. Make sure you understand how the *rows* of the matrix are each dot-product-ed with the *column* vector to produce an answer. And since there are two such dot products, there are two such answers, and the result is a column vector with two entries.

The rules for when matrix-vector multiplication are possible are:

1. The vector must be a column vector, or at least treated as such for purposes of performing the operation.
2. The number of *columns* (not rows) in the matrix must be the same as the dimension of (the number of entries in) the vector. If these do not match, the game is over.

If these two check out, then the operation is permissible, and the result is a column vector whose dimension (number of entries) is the same as the number of *rows* (not columns) in the matrix.

For example:

- A wide 5 × 17 matrix times a 17-dimensional column vector is legal, and gives a 5-dimensional vector result.
- A tall 17 × 5 matrix times a 5-dimensional column vector is legal, and gives an 17-dimensional vector result.
- A wide 5 × 17 matrix times a 5-dimensional column vector is illegal.
- A wide 5 × 17 matrix times any *row* vector is illegal.

Sometimes it helps to stretch your neck out a bit before attempting matrix-vector multiplication. That's because you have to visualize a (potentially long) row of numbers being paired up, one-by-one, with a (potentially tall) column of numbers. It's not too hard once you get used to it, but it can be surprisingly difficult at first to move across the page with your left eyeball at the same time you're moving *down* the page with your right eyeball. Like all things, practice.

Two ways to think about matrix-vector multiplication

Now there are two different ways to think about the matrix-vector product. Each one is useful in certain situations, so it's very important to master *both* interpretations. Here they are:

4.4. MATRIX OPERATIONS

Two different ways to think about $A \cdot \vec{x}$:
1. All of the dot products between the *rows* of A with $\vec{x}$.
2. A linear combination of A's *columns*. ($\vec{x}$'s elements are the coefficients of the linear combination.)

The first interpretation is what we've learned operationally so far. To compute $A \cdot \vec{x}$, we take each of A's rows, in turn, and dot-product them with the vector, producing a new vector of answers.

When does it make sense to think of it this way? Think back to Jezebel and friends (p. 27). Let's say we have Jezebel's (normalized) survey answers in a vector $\vec{j}$:

$$\vec{j} = \begin{bmatrix} .434 & .173 & .867 & .173 \end{bmatrix}.$$
$$\phantom{\vec{j} = [}\text{action hiking candle mystery}$$

Now suppose we have all the eligible Men's (normalized) survey answers in a matrix M, like so:

$$\begin{matrix}\text{biff}\\\text{filbert}\\\text{wendell}\end{matrix}\begin{bmatrix} .704 & .704 & .070 & .070 \\ .548 & .183 & .730 & .365 \\ .092 & .275 & .275 & .917 \end{bmatrix}$$
$$\text{action hiking candle mystery}$$

A very reasonable way to store these entries, I think you'll agree. Each row represent one man's (normalized) survey responses, where each column is one of the questions.

Now we can compute Jezebel's compatibility with every guy under the sun in one fell swoop! All we need to do is transpose her vector into a column vector, and perform matrix-vector multiplication:

$$M \cdot \vec{j}^\top = \begin{bmatrix} .704 & .704 & .070 & .070 \\ .548 & .183 & .730 & .365 \\ .092 & .275 & .275 & .917 \end{bmatrix} \cdot \begin{bmatrix} .434 \\ .173 \\ .867 \\ .173 \end{bmatrix} = \begin{bmatrix} .500 \\ .966 \\ .484 \end{bmatrix}.$$

Boom! The elements of our answer represent Jezebel's compatibility with Biff, Filbert, and Wendell, respectively. That's because the *first* element of our answer was the dot product of the *first* row of M (Biff's row) with $\vec{j}$. Ditto for the other two.

As you can see, this is really nothing more than automating and repeating our individual dot product calculations, since that's what the matrix-vector product *is*, according to interpretation 1. Instead of just multiplying Jezebel's vector times Biff's, we can multiply it times a thousand different guys all at once, to get a thousand different compatibilities. In the end, we see that Filbert and Jezebel are paired together as expected, which means all is right with the world.

The other way to think about the matrix-vector product is as a linear combination of the matrix's *columns*. The bake sale example from p. 32 is a case where it makes sense to think about it this way. Let's make a "Recipes matrix" R in which each column is one recipe, and each row corresponds to an ingredient. The entries tell us the quantity of that ingredient required for one batch of each of the recipes:

$$\begin{array}{r} \text{butter} \\ \text{sugar} \\ \text{chips} \\ \text{flour} \\ \text{eggs} \\ \text{marshmallow} \\ \text{rice krispies} \end{array} \begin{bmatrix} 2 & 1 & 2 & 2 \\ 1 & 1 & 2 & 0 \\ 1 & 4 & 4 & 0 \\ 1 & 2 & 0 & 0 \\ 3 & 2 & 0 & 0 \\ 0 & 0 & 0 & 5 \\ 0 & 0 & 0 & 2 \end{bmatrix}$$

$$\text{chippers} \quad \text{brownies} \quad \text{fudge} \quad \text{rice krispies}$$

When we do our bake sale planning, we decide we want to bake the following number of batches for our first day of the sale:

$$\vec{b} = [\quad 5 \quad\quad 5 \quad\quad 2 \quad\quad 6 \quad].$$
$$\text{chippers} \quad \text{brownies} \quad \text{fudge} \quad \text{rice krispies}$$

4.4. MATRIX OPERATIONS

How do we compute our complete shopping list? Simple: transpose $\vec{b}$ and do matrix-vector multiplication:

$$R \cdot \vec{b}^{\mathsf{T}} = \begin{bmatrix} 2 & 1 & 2 & 2 \\ 1 & 1 & 2 & 0 \\ 1 & 4 & 4 & 0 \\ 1 & 2 & 0 & 0 \\ 3 & 2 & 0 & 0 \\ 0 & 0 & 0 & 5 \\ 0 & 0 & 0 & 2 \end{bmatrix} \cdot \begin{bmatrix} 5 \\ 5 \\ 2 \\ 6 \end{bmatrix} = \begin{bmatrix} 31 \\ 14 \\ 33 \\ 15 \\ 25 \\ 30 \\ 12 \end{bmatrix}.$$

We'll clean out Publix by purchasing 31 sticks of butter, 14 cups of sugar, 33 bags of chocolate chips, and so on.

Now why do I say that the *second* interpretation from p. 91 is the right one here? Because we're treating the columns as meaningful entities. The left-most column is "how much stuff to buy for *each* chocolate chip cookie batch." The second column is "how much stuff to buy for each brownie batch." And so forth. So what we're really doing in this calculation is saying "we want 5 chipper recipes, so 5 times the first column; and also 5 brownie recipes, so 5 times the second column; 2 batches of fudge, so twice the third column; plus 6 times the last column for our 6 trays of Rice Krispie treats." Mathematically, we're doing this:

$$5\begin{bmatrix} 2 \\ 1 \\ 1 \\ 1 \\ 3 \\ 0 \\ 0 \end{bmatrix} + 5\begin{bmatrix} 1 \\ 1 \\ 4 \\ 2 \\ 2 \\ 0 \\ 0 \end{bmatrix} + 2\begin{bmatrix} 2 \\ 2 \\ 4 \\ 0 \\ 0 \\ 0 \\ 0 \end{bmatrix} + 6\begin{bmatrix} 2 \\ 0 \\ 0 \\ 0 \\ 0 \\ 5 \\ 2 \end{bmatrix} = \begin{bmatrix} 31 \\ 14 \\ 33 \\ 15 \\ 25 \\ 30 \\ 12 \end{bmatrix},$$

which is exactly a linear combination of the recipes. The coefficient of each vector – the scalar in each scalar-vector multiplication – is the corresponding element of our $\vec{b}$ vector, telling us how much of each recipe to make.

A couple additional thoughts before we leave this section. First, I don't know about you, but I think it's actually quite remarkable that these two different definitions of matrix-vector multiplication turn out to give the same answer. In #1, we're taking the dot product of each of the matrix's rows with the entire vector. In #2, we're working with the columns of the matrix, not the rows, and we're not doing any dot products at all; we're treating the vector as a sequence of coefficients and doing scalar-vector multiplication with them. These seem like totally different – perhaps even opposite, or competing – operations, yet they always work out to the same result.

Finally, I'll just say that if you think it's annoying to take the transpose of the vector and write it up-and-down, I feel your pain. It does seem much more sensible (and less prone to error) to just leave the row vector as a row vector, because then it lines up visually with the *rows* of the matrix that we're taking its dot product with anyway. It's hard enough to keep all the numbers straight without having to constantly shift between horizontal and vertical vision *as* you're calculating! Anyway, I guess I've just learned to accept this over the years, since it's universal to define the operation this way. My advice is to grumble to yourself a while and then try to do the same.

4.5 Change-of-basis matrices (*to* standard)

Remember back to last chapter (specifically, p. 71) when we discussed how a vector can be expressed as coordinates in *any* basis, not merely in the standard basis. We had our Ron vector $\vec{r}$ that could be expressed in either the standard basis B_s or equivalently in the "domino basis" B_d:

$$\vec{r} = \begin{bmatrix} 3 \\ -1 \end{bmatrix}_{B_d} = \begin{bmatrix} -1 \\ 2 \end{bmatrix}_{B_s}.$$

(Our domino basis, you'll recall, had the dominoes and in it, so $B_d = \{[\ 1\ \ 2\ ], [\ 4\ \ 4\ ]\}$.)

We can translate between the two bases using matrix-vector multiplication. To go from domino to standard, we merely put the dominoes into the columns of a matrix:

$$\text{COB}_{B_d \to B_s} = \begin{bmatrix} 1 & 4 \\ 2 & 4 \end{bmatrix}$$

because

$$\vec{r}_{B_s} = \begin{bmatrix} 1 & 4 \\ 2 & 4 \end{bmatrix} \cdot \vec{r}_{B_d} = \begin{bmatrix} 1 & 4 \\ 2 & 4 \end{bmatrix} \cdot \begin{bmatrix} 3 \\ -1 \end{bmatrix}_{B_d} = \begin{bmatrix} -1 \\ 2 \end{bmatrix}_{B_s}.$$

This $\text{COB}_{B_d \to B_s}$ matrix is called the **change-of-basis matrix** from the domino basis to the standard basis.

What if we want to go in the other direction? Remember, Hermione had a vector $\vec{h}$ which, when expressed in the standard basis, was $\begin{bmatrix} 5 \\ 2 \end{bmatrix}$. What are her coordinates in the domino basis?

Hate to still leave you hanging on Hermione, but for that, we'll need a new concept called the **matrix inverse**, which we won't get to until p. 157. Stay tuned.

4.6 "Special" matrices

Finally, there are some terms for "special" matrices that satisfy certain properties, which will come up for us in important contexts. We'll start with the least restrictive definition and repeatedly add further constraints to it for successively more restrictive ones.

Easiest of all, a **square** matrix is simply one that has the same number of rows and columns. Any 4×4 matrix is square, and no 6×7 matrix is square. Simple. And yes, in case you're wondering, we can have a 1×1 matrix, which is considered square.

In order for a matrix to be **symmetric**, it has to be square.[1] Further, in a symmetric matrix *the rows and the columns are interchangeable*. For example:

$$\begin{bmatrix} 9 & 7 & 2 & 8 \\ 7 & -3 & 0 & -1 \\ 2 & 0 & 5 & 4 \\ 8 & -1 & 4 & 16 \end{bmatrix}$$

In this matrix, row #0 is [9 7 2 8], and column #0 is *also* [9 7 2 8]. Similarly, row #1 and column #1 are the same, as are row #2 and column #2, and row #3 and column #3.

Mathematically, a matrix M is symmetric only if:

$$\forall i, j \ M_{i,j} = M_{j,i}.$$

In other words, you must be able to swap the row and column numbers and get the same value. The entry at row 5 column 8 must be the same as the one at row 8 column 5, *etc.* If that's not true every time, it's not a symmetric matrix.

It might help you understand the meaning of "symmetric" if you mentally visualize a line from the upper-left entry to the lower-right entry of the matrix:

$$\begin{bmatrix} 9 & 7 & 2 & 8 \\ 7 & -3 & 0 & -1 \\ 2 & 0 & 5 & 4 \\ 8 & -1 & 4 & 16 \end{bmatrix}$$

These entries, by the way, where the row number equals the column number, are called the **main diagonal** (or just the **diagonal**) of the matrix. If a matrix is symmetric, you could imagine that line being a mirror: and it perfectly reflects one side to the other. The two 7's are on matching, opposite sides of that line, as are the two

---

[1] There are more advanced versions of some of the definitions in this section that don't require square-ness, but they won't come up for us.

4.6. "SPECIAL" MATRICES

2's, the two 0's, the two 8's, the two −1's, and the two 4's. Note that the entries *on* the main diagonal can be anything at all – they don't affect the symmetric-ness (or not) of the matrix.

This property may seem obscure, but it will come up surprisingly often.

By the way, you might have expected a "symmetric matrix" to be one that was a mirror image of itself left-to-right-wise, or top-to-bottom-wise. Nope. That doesn't turn out to be a useful concept. The definition above, however – reflection along the main diagonal – turns out to be immensely useful.

Okay, next one. A matrix is said to be **upper-triangular** if *all entries below the main diagonal are zero*. Example:

$$\begin{bmatrix} 9 & 7 & 2 & 8 \\ 0 & -3 & 0 & -1 \\ 0 & 0 & 5 & 4 \\ 0 & 0 & 0 & 16 \end{bmatrix}$$

This matrix is upper-triangular because I've zeroed-out everything below the 9, −3, 5, 16 entries of the main diagonal. Note that it's perfectly fine to also have a 0 above – or even on – the diagonal. The existence of such a zero doesn't disqualify you from upper-triangular-ness. The only requirement is that all entries *below* the diagonal must be zero.

You can probably tell why the word "triangular" is used: the possibly-nonzero entries are all arranged in a right triangle in the upper-right half of the matrix. Occasionally it will also be useful to talk about a **lower-triangular** matrix, which has zeroes in every entry *above* the diagonal. And again, you have to be square for your upper- or lower- triangular-ness to even be under consideration.

Also common is the notion of a **diagonal matrix**. Be careful: a "a diagonal matrix" is different from "the diagonal *of* a matrix!" A diagonal matrix is one where all entries *not* on the diagonal must be zero. Example:

$$\begin{bmatrix} 9 & 0 & 0 & 0 \\ 0 & -3 & 0 & 0 \\ 0 & 0 & 5 & 0 \\ 0 & 0 & 0 & 16 \end{bmatrix}$$

Food for thought: a diagonal matrix is both upper-triangular *and* lower-triangular.

Like I said, we're getting more and more restrictive as we go. If you're planning on being a 6 × 6 diagonal matrix, there's a whole lot of your life already set in stone. The only choices you have are what to put on your diagonal.

But we can get more restrictive still! Believe it or not, a very common and interesting type of matrix will be a so-called **identity matrix**. Get this: an identity matrix is a diagonal matrix *with only 1's on the diagonal*. Talk about confining. Once you've decided on your size, you have literally no choices. The one and only 4 × 4 identity matrix is this one:

$$\begin{bmatrix} 1 & 0 & 0 & 0 \\ 0 & 1 & 0 & 0 \\ 0 & 0 & 1 & 0 \\ 0 & 0 & 0 & 1 \end{bmatrix}$$

For every natural number n, there's one and only one identity matrix of that size. Sometimes we call that matrix I_n for short; in other words, the matrix above is sometimes called I_4.

In the next chapter (p. 157, to be exact), you'll learn the excellent reason that this kind of matrix is called an "identity" matrix. For now, test yourself with these questions:

1. Are all square matrices symmetric?
2. Are all symmetric matrices square?
3. Are all symmetric matrices upper-triangular?
4. Are all upper-triangular matrices symmetric?
5. Are all diagonal matrices upper-triangular?

4.6. "SPECIAL" MATRICES

6. Are all upper-triangular matrices diagonal?
7. Are all diagonal matrices symmetric?
8. Are all diagonal matrices identity matrices?
9. Are all identity matrices upper-triangular?
10. Are all identity matrices diagonal?

The answers are at the end of the chapter (p. 112).

Rounding out our list, I'll mention two more types of "special" matrices that are a bit different from the previous ones. The first is called a **block diagonal matrix**. A matrix is block diagonal if it can be partitioned into rectangular chunks (called "blocks") such that each chunk on the diagonal is square, and all entries in the non-diagonal chunks must be all zeros.

Whoa, that's hard to visualize. Let's look at some examples:

$$\begin{bmatrix} 3 & 2 & 0 & 0 \\ 4 & 4 & 0 & 0 \\ 0 & 0 & 9 & 7 \\ 0 & 0 & 2 & 6 \end{bmatrix}$$

This is a block diagonal matrix. Why? Because if we break it up this way:

$$\left[\begin{array}{cc|cc} 3 & 2 & 0 & 0 \\ 4 & 4 & 0 & 0 \\ \hline 0 & 0 & 9 & 7 \\ 0 & 0 & 2 & 6 \end{array}\right]$$

we can see that it satisfies the conditions. The two blocks on the diagonal (which are the 3-2-4-4 block and the 9-7-2-6 block) are square (2 × 2), and all the entries in the off-diagonal blocks are zeroes.

Sometimes it can take a little fiddling around to find the right partition. Try this one:

$$\begin{bmatrix} 1 & 4 & 3 & 0 \\ 6 & 8 & 2 & 0 \\ 5 & 1 & 5 & 0 \\ 0 & 0 & 0 & 7 \end{bmatrix}$$

Does that one look block diagonal to you? It is:

$$\left[\begin{array}{ccc|c} 1 & 4 & 3 & 0 \\ 6 & 8 & 2 & 0 \\ 5 & 1 & 5 & 0 \\ \hline 0 & 0 & 0 & 7 \end{array} \right]$$

Notice that the blocks that are *not* on the diagonal don't have to be square. All that matters are the diagonal blocks, and here we have a 3 × 3 and a 1 × 1, so we're good.

Here's one more for the road:

$$\begin{bmatrix} 4 & 0 & 0 & 0 & 0 & 0 & 0 \\ 0 & 9 & 0 & 3 & 3 & 0 & 0 \\ 0 & 0 & 0 & 0 & 0 & 0 & 0 \\ 0 & 0 & 2 & 0 & 0 & 0 & 0 \\ 0 & 7 & 0 & 0 & 5 & 0 & 0 \\ 0 & 0 & 0 & 0 & 0 & 6 & 3 \\ 0 & 0 & 0 & 0 & 0 & 1 & 0 \end{bmatrix}$$

Is this one, too, block diagonal? All the extra (and unnecessary) zeroes might fool you, but if you partition it this way:

$$\left[\begin{array}{c|cccc|cc} 4 & 0 & 0 & 0 & 0 & 0 & 0 \\ \hline 0 & 9 & 0 & 3 & 3 & 0 & 0 \\ 0 & 0 & 0 & 0 & 0 & 0 & 0 \\ 0 & 0 & 2 & 0 & 0 & 0 & 0 \\ 0 & 7 & 0 & 0 & 5 & 0 & 0 \\ \hline 0 & 0 & 0 & 0 & 0 & 6 & 3 \\ 0 & 0 & 0 & 0 & 0 & 1 & 0 \end{array} \right]$$

you can see that it is.

4.6. "SPECIAL" MATRICES

Finally finally, let me introduce the concept of an "**orthogonal matrix**." A matrix must meet two criteria in order to deserve the title "orthogonal":

1. Each of its *columns* must be orthogonal to each of the other columns. (Recall from p. 30 that two vectors are orthogonal if their dot product is zero.)
2. The (Euclidean) norm of each of its columns must be equal to 1. (Recall that to compute the Euclidean norm of a vector, you just take the square-root-of-the-sum-of-its-elements-squared, a.k.a. the Pythagorean Theorem. See p. 36.)

Okay, that seemed kind of random. But it actually has important implications, which will come up later in the book. For now, let me just show some examples of each:

$$A = \begin{bmatrix} 2 & 1 \\ -2 & 1 \end{bmatrix}, \quad B = \begin{bmatrix} \frac{\sqrt{2}}{2} & 1 \\ \frac{\sqrt{2}}{2} & 0 \end{bmatrix}, \quad C = \begin{bmatrix} \frac{2}{5} & \frac{3}{5} \\ \frac{3}{5} & -\frac{2}{5} \end{bmatrix}, \quad D = \begin{bmatrix} 1 & 0 \\ 0 & 1 \end{bmatrix}.$$

Question: which of these matrices are orthogonal? Answers:

- A is *not*. It passes the first criterion, since $\begin{bmatrix} 2 \\ -1 \end{bmatrix} \cdot \begin{bmatrix} 1 \\ 1 \end{bmatrix}$ does equal zero (check my math!) but the two columns don't have Euclidean length 1. (The norm of the left column for instance, is $\sqrt{2^2 + (-2)^2} = 2.828\ldots$) Next!

- B is *not*. It passes the second criterion (the Euclidean norms of both columns are 0 – double-check that) but not the first, since the dot product of the two columns is $\frac{\sqrt{2}}{2} = .707\ldots$ (Double-check that, too.) Next!

- Matrix C, on the other hand, *is* orthogonal. The dot product of its two columns is zero:

$$\frac{2}{5} \cdot \frac{3}{5} + \frac{3}{5} \cdot \left(-\frac{2}{5}\right) = \frac{6}{25} - \frac{6}{25} = 0,$$

and each column has norm 1:

$$\left(\sqrt{\frac{2}{5}}\right)^2 + \left(\sqrt{\frac{3}{5}}\right)^2 = 1, \text{ and}$$

$$\left(\sqrt{\frac{3}{5}}\right)^2 + \left(-\sqrt{\frac{2}{5}}\right)^2 = 1.$$

Yay!

- And lastly, realize that the identity matrix D is also orthogonal! Both criteria are satisfied by inspection. This is true of any identity matrix, you'll realize as soon as you consider it.

I haven't yet told you why orthogonal matrices are important, but we'll return to this in future chapters.

By the way, if I were King of the World, I wouldn't have called these "orthogonal matrices." I would have called them "**orthonormal matrices.**" That's because two vectors which are both perpendicular to each other (with zero dot product, and therefore orthogonal) *and* which also each have Euclidean norm 1 (and thus are "normalized" in length) are called **orthonormal vectors**.

When I'm King, I'll redefine these terms so that "orthogonal matrix" means any matrix that satisfies criterion #1, above (but not necessarily #2), and reserve the new term "orthonormal matrix" for any matrix that satisfies *both* criteria. Until then, we'll have to keep using the misleading term "orthogonal matrix." (Keep a watch on your news feed for that Stephen-becomes-King-of-the-World thing – I'm still working on it.)

🐍 *Appendix: Python*

With NumPy, a matrix is very similar to a vector. That's because they're both `ndarrays`. They only vary in the number of **dimensions**, but we have to be careful here because NumPy uses the term "dimension" in a different way than we've been doing (say, on p. 85). In our lingo, a matrix with three rows and four columns has dimensions 3 × 4. But NumPy would say that this matrix – and *all* matrices – has dimension **2**. Why 2? Because it has a left-to-right dimension (rows) and an up-and-down dimension (columns).

For us, this won't be too complicated, because we won't be dealing with objects of higher dimension (which are called **tensors**, by the way) than 2. So all this really means for us is that a one-dimensional `ndarray` is a vector, and a two-dimensional `ndarray` is a matrix. And when we want to zero in on a particular element of a matrix, we need *two* index numbers: one for the row and one for the column.

Creating matrices (2-d arrays)

Creating a NumPy matrix is a snap – you just need to be prepared to type a lot of boxies. Here's a 3 × 2 matrix:

```
mat = array([[6,9],[4,5],[1,4]])
```

Notice the boxies-within-boxies: the very outermost pair is for the entire array, where each inner pair specifies one row. In this way, you see that a matrix is an array-of-arrays; or, if you prefer, a list of rows. We can print them the same way we did vectors:

```
print(mat)
```

```
[[6 9]
 [4 5]
 [7 4]]
```

The `zeros()` function works for matrices, but with a slightly different syntax: we specify the dimensions we'd like after the word `shape` and a comma:

```
nada = zeros(shape=(4,7))
print(nada)
```

```
[[0. 0. 0. 0. 0. 0. 0.]
 [0. 0. 0. 0. 0. 0. 0.]
 [0. 0. 0. 0. 0. 0. 0.]
 [0. 0. 0. 0. 0. 0. 0.]]
```

And we can do the random number thing, too, by passing the `random.rand()` function dimension numbers:

```
crazy = random.rand(3,5)
print(crazy)
```

```
[[0.09121684 0.3084825  0.2529024  0.78089448 0.46138631]
 [0.30003058 0.9275848  0.72649169 0.10995998 0.97565467]
 [0.32876047 0.25447349 0.78955441 0.07921066 0.20986057]]
```

(As before, each number is between 0 and 1.)

Lastly, we can read a matrix from a file just like we did with a vector. Most commonly, such files will use a comma as a **delimiter** to separate entries on a line, so we'll specify that in our function call:

```
my_matrix = loadtxt("somematrixdata.txt", delimiter=",")
```

By the way, often files like these will have a `.csv` extension instead of `.txt`; this stands for **comma-separated values**, for obvious reasons.

4.6. "SPECIAL" MATRICES

Working with matrices (arrays)

indexshape@.shape

To learn the dimensions of a matrix, use .shape which gives a vector of the dimensions:

```
print(mat)
print(mat.shape)
print("The matrix has {} rows.".format(mat.shape[0]))
print("The matrix has {} columns.".format(mat.shape[1]))
```

```
[[6 9]
 [4 5]
 [1 4]]
(3, 2)
The matrix has 3 rows.
The matrix has 2 columns.
```

We can give a matrix *two* index numbers (comma-separated) to retrieve or change individual elements:

```
print(mat[0,1])
print(mat[2,0])
mat[1,1] = 19
print(mat)
```

```
2
7
[[ 3  2]
 [ 4 19]
 [ 7  4]]
```

Note that both rows and columns are indexed starting at 0.

We can get an entire row, or an entire column, by using a colon (":") in place of one of the indices:

```
print(mat[2,:])
print(mat[:,1])
```

```
[1 4]
[ 9 19  4]
```

Somewhat weirdly, getting exactly one column (as we did in the second operation just now) gives us back the correct (column) vector, but instead of printing it out as a column, NumPy prints it as a row. Trying to save screen space? Not sure.

Our slicing technique works the same as before (p. 49), on the rows and/or the columns. Let's create a slightly bigger matrix to show it off:

```
bigger = array([[-9,-8,-7],[2,4,-6],[0,0,0],[1,9,6]])
print(bigger)
```

```
[[-9 -8 -7]
 [ 2  4 -6]
 [ 0  0  0]
 [ 1  9  6]]
```

```
print(bigger[1,0:2])
```

```
[2 4]
```

```
print(bigger[0:3,1:3])
```

```
[[-8 -7]
 [ 4 -6]
 [ 0  0]]
```

4.6. "SPECIAL" MATRICES

```
print(bigger[0:3,2])
```

```
[-7 -6  0]
```

(Yeah, displays as row vector, it's weird I agree.)

Finally, some linear algebra operations. We can take the transpose of a matrix by appending .transpose():

```
print(bigger.transpose())
```

```
[[-9  2  0  1]
 [-8  4  0  9]
 [-7 -6  0  6]]
```

And matrix-vector multiplication also uses the .dot() syntax:

```
x = array([4,5,6])
print(bigger.dot(x))
```

```
[-118   -8    0   85]
```

Python branching

Finally, one more Python programming thing. Every programming language has ways to **branch**, which means to control the flow of the program so that the lines aren't executed in strict sequential order, depending on the situation. Python uses the "if statement" for this, and again relies on indentation to know where the relevant block of code ends. They are often used in conjunction with for loops. Example:

```
weights = np.array([ 145.6, 212.9, 126.4 ])

for i in arange(weights.size):
    if weights[i] < 150:
        print("You weigh {} lbs and might consider eating more."
            .format(weights[i]))
    print("Thanks for weighing in!")
```

```
You weigh 145.6 lbs and might consider eating more.
Thanks for weighing in!
Thanks for weighing in!
You weigh 126.4 lbs and might consider eating more.
Thanks for weighing in!
```

Each time the loop is executed, i has a different value, and hence the next element of the `weights` vector is considered. Only if that particular element satisfies the condition (less than 150) does the indented code under the `if` get executed. Note that the "`Thanks!`" message gets printed out *regardless* of the weight. Only lines indented to the right of the `if` are what the `if` statement controls.

The "`weights[i] < 150`" part is called the `if` statement's **condition**, and there is some wacky syntax you have to master to write them correctly. Here it is:

Operator	Meaning
>	greater than
<	less than
>=	greater than or equal to
<=	less than or equal to
!=	*not* equal to
==	equal to
and	and
or	or
not	not

The last three of those are used when creating a **compound condition** comprised of more than one test. For example:

4.6. "SPECIAL" MATRICES

```
if (sex[i] == "male" and weights[i] < 160  or
    sex[i] == "female" and weights[i] < 140):
    ...
```

Here, the body of the `if` statement will only be executed for males under 160 lbs and for females under 140 lbs.

Boolean variables in Python

The raw material that `if` statements work with is of the **Boolean** type, not numbers, strings, or anything else. A Boolean variable, named after 19th-century logician George Boole, holds either the value `True` or `False`. (And these are capitalized in Python.)

It's common for a function to return a Boolean when its purpose is to check whether some condition holds. Let's write a function called `is_square()` to determine whether a matrix is square. Here goes:

indexshape@.shape

```
def is_square(m):
    if m.shape[0] == m.shape[1]:
        return True
    else:
        return False
```

Here we've added another feature to our `if` statement, namely an **else branch**. I'm sure you can guess what it means, even if you've never seen an `if`/`else` construction before: the code indented under `else` gets executed *only* if the condition in the `if` statement is `False`. So an `if`/`else` is simply an either/or.

You'll remember I mentioned in the last chapter that some functions have more than one `return` statement in them. Now you can see why that would be useful. A function finishes immediately as soon as it encounters a `return`, and does not execute any code below it. However, because of `if` statements, the path through a function might zigzag over and past some `return` statements before reaching others.

Anyway, you can see how this function works: it simply compares the number of rows in the matrix with the number of columns, and returns `True` if these are the same. That, after all, is the definition of squareness.

Here's another example:

```
def is_diagonal(m):
    if m.shape[0] != m.shape[1]:
        return False
    for i in arange(m.shape[0]):
        for j in arange(m.shape[1]):
            if i != j and m[i,j] != 0:
                return False
    return True
```

That one packs a wallop. Can you figure out how it works?

First, we check to see if the matrix is square, since the way we've defined diagonal matrices in this book, they must be square. If that check fails, we immediately return our answer – `False` – and unpause our Netflix video. If it *is* square, however, we have more work to do.

The further work involves a **nested for loop**, since we need to examine all elements of the matrix m: every row and every column. I have the `i` loop variable going through the rows, and for *each* row, the `j` loop goes through all the columns. (It's important that you see how each iteration of the outer (`i`) loop results in *multiple* iterations of the inner (`j`) loop.)

Now for every element, I check two things. First, does its row number equal its column number? If these are equal, then that means

4.6. "SPECIAL" MATRICES

the element I'm examining is on the diagonal. Nothing special is required in this case; a diagonal matrix is free to have anything it wants on its diagonal. However, if `i` does *not* equal `j`, then I'm examining an off-diagonal entry. If the matrix in question is truly diagonal, all of those off-diagonal entries had better be 0. As soon as I find an off-diagonal, non-zero entry, I immediately raise my red flag and return from the function, again with a negative answer.

Only after I've gone through *every* entry, and confirmed that *all* of the off-diagonal entries are zero, can I declare victory and return `True`. Many students mess up on this part: they often put an `else` branch on that `if`. This is fine syntactically, but wrong logically: just because I find a single entry that satisfies my criteria does not mean the entire matrix is therefore diagonal! No, I can only dare to return `True` at the very, very end, after checking everything out.

Let's see whether our functions work. First, we'll create three matrices of varying contents, and print them out:

```
m1 = array([[2,3,4],[5,6,7]])
m2 = array([[5,0,1],[0,3,0],[0,0,9]])
m3 = array([[16,0,0],[0,27,0],[0,0,5]])
print(m1)
print(m2)
print(m3)
```

```
[[2 3 4]
 [5 6 7]]

[[5 0 1]
 [0 3 0]
 [0 0 9]]

[[16  0  0]
 [ 0 27  0]
 [ 0  0  5]]
```

Then, let's call both functions on each of them, and see which ones return `True`:

```
if is_square(m1):
    print("m1 is square!")
if is_diagonal(m1):
    print("m1 is diagonal!")
if is_diagonal(m2):
    print("m2 is diagonal!")
if is_square(m2):
    print("m2 is square!")
if is_square(m3):
    print("m3 is square!")
if is_diagonal(m3):
    print("m3 is diagonal!")
```

```
m2 is square!
m3 is square!
m3 is diagonal!
```

We hereby declare victory.

Do you think you could write an `is_upper_triangular()` function in this vein? `is_identity()`? `is_symmetric()`? How about `is_orthogonal()` or `is_block_diagonal()`? Clearly, some of these are way harder than others to write the code for, but all are indeed possible with Python.

Answers to "special" matrix quiz from p. 98

1. No.
2. Yes.
3. No.
4. No.
5. Yes.
6. No.
7. Yes.
8. No.
9. Yes.
10. Yes.

Chapter 5

Linear transformations

A **linear transformation** is actually just another spin on matrix-vector multiplication. It's also yet another way to view a matrix as a *function*. Back on p. 86, I made the point that instead of drawing numbers in a grid, you could view a matrix itself as a function, where the input is an ordered pair (row and column numbers) and the output is the element at that entry. In this chapter, we explore a deeper and richer interpretation of a matrix as a *different* sort of function.

5.1 Transforming one vector into another

Recall how matrix-vector multiplication works. We'll write it notationally as $A \cdot \vec{x} = \vec{y}$, where $\vec{y}$ is the result of the multiplication. Now we could think about the operation like this:

- A is a "function" of sorts, which works on vectors to produce other vectors.
- $\vec{x}$ is the input vector we give to that function.
- $\vec{y}$ is the function's output (result).

We're thinking of A as a long-lasting, reusable thing, whereas $\vec{x}$ and $\vec{y}$ stand for the temporary inputs & outputs that we give to A and compute on the fly. My mental image is of A as a machine, $\vec{x}$ as the raw materials we might feed to the machine, and $\vec{y}$ as the machine's completed work.

One natural question is: "what is the domain, and the range, of this A function?" That depends on A's dimensions. Suppose it's a 3 × 2 matrix:

$$\begin{bmatrix} 2 & 3 \\ 1 & -4 \\ 0 & 5 \end{bmatrix} \cdot ? = ?$$

We know from the rules of matrix-vector multiplication (p. 90) that the first question mark has to be a **2**-dimensional column vector, else the operation is impossible. And we know that the output will be a **3**-dimensional column vector. This means that the domain of the A "function" is 2-d vectors and the codomain is 3-d vectors. Most commonly, this is written as follows:

$$A : \mathbb{R}^2 \to \mathbb{R}^3.$$

Remember from *A Cool, Brisk Walk* that the $\mathbb{R}$ sign means "the set of real numbers." When we say "$\mathbb{R}^2$" we're saying "the set of vectors with two real-numbered entries." And $\mathbb{R}^3$ is the set of *three*-dimensional real vectors, *etc.*

Put all together, the purpose of our A matrix is to map each two-dimensional vector to a particular three-dimensional vector. For instance, it maps the 2-d vector [2 1] to:

$$\begin{bmatrix} 2 & 3 \\ 1 & -4 \\ 0 & 5 \end{bmatrix} \cdot \begin{bmatrix} 2 \\ 1 \end{bmatrix} = \begin{bmatrix} 7 \\ -2 \\ 5 \end{bmatrix}.$$

The particular vector it chooses seems kind of random so far, and indeed this first example is just pulled from the air. Normally there will be some "meaning" to the transformation.

By the way, a linear transformation is sometimes called a **linear map** because it performs this "mapping" operation, like a function does. The two terms (linear transformation and linear map) are exact synonyms.

5.1. TRANSFORMING ONE VECTOR INTO ANOTHER

Meaningful examples

Before we go any further, let's at least show that this is useful. I'm going to create a machine (matrix) B (for "Body," sort of) that transforms certain 4-dimensional vectors into 2-dimensional ones. Here it is:

$$B = \begin{bmatrix} 12 & 1 & 0 & 0 \\ 0 & 0 & 2.2 & 0 \end{bmatrix}.$$

The kind of input this matrix/function is intended to act on a vector such as $\overrightarrow{\textbf{stephen}}$, which is structured like this:

$$\begin{array}{r} \text{height: whole feet} \to \\ \text{height: extra inches} \to \\ \text{weight: kilograms} \to \\ \text{shoe size} \to \end{array} \begin{bmatrix} 6 \\ 2 \\ 95.5 \\ 13 \end{bmatrix}$$

This rather revealing vector contains some of my vital bodily stats. I'm 6'2" tall, and hence don't fit on airplanes; I weigh too much at 95.5 kg; and I wear an impossible-to-fit 13 shoe (13AAA, actually; blame my mom's side of the family).

Now what happens when we feed this to the B machine?

$$B \cdot \overrightarrow{\textbf{stephen}} = \begin{bmatrix} 12 & 1 & 0 & 0 \\ 0 & 0 & 2.2 & 0 \end{bmatrix} \cdot \begin{bmatrix} 6 \\ 2 \\ 95.5 \\ 13 \end{bmatrix} = \begin{bmatrix} 74 \\ 210 \end{bmatrix} \begin{array}{l} \leftarrow \text{height in inches} \\ \leftarrow \text{weight in pounds} \end{array}$$

This matrix-vector multiplication produces a 2-element vector, since

$$B : \mathbb{R}^4 \to \mathbb{R}^2.$$

The first element is my height in total inches, and the second element is my weight in pounds. B will produce a 2-dimensional vector like this for every person whose 4-dimensional vector it's multiplied by. Interestingly, the shoe size of the input vector plays no role in the value of the output vector, because there are zero elements at both $B_{0,3}$ and $B_{1,3}$. And that's okay.

By the way, you might think about expanding this example to calculate something more complex like a BMI (body-mass index). After all, BMI is a straightforward function of a person's weight and height[1], as you might know:

$$\text{BMI} = 703 \times \frac{\text{weights (lbs)}}{\text{height (in)}^2}.$$

However, it turns out this is *impossible* to do with a linear transformation. The reason is it's not linear! The only operations that can be included in a linear transformation are dot products, because that's what matrix-vector multiplication *is*. So for each element of our output vector, we can (1) take the elements of the input vector, (2) multiply each of them by any constant we like, and (3) add up the results. The BMI formula, by contrast, requires us to *divide* one of our inputs by another, and in fact requires us to *square* that second input before dividing. These are both decidedly non-linear operations that cannot be expressed with a matrix.

This may seem limiting, and in a way it is, but keep in mind two things. First, there are lots and lots and lots of common operations that *are* linear, and all of those come under our power in this book on linear algebra. Second, when we do have linear operations, we can take advantage of all kinds of computational simplifications and analytical tricks, so concentrating on the linear case is most definitely worth our time.

Here's a second example. Suppose I have the following odd-looking matrix S (for "stocks," sort of):

---

[1](Mine's about 27, which puts me in the "obese" range I'm sorry to say.)

5.2. LINEAR OPERATORS

$$S = \begin{bmatrix} 0 & 1 & 0 \\ 0 & .69 & 0 \\ 0 & 111.1 & 0 \\ 0 & .88 & 0 \\ 0 & 6.48 & 0 \\ 0 & 17.37 & 0 \end{bmatrix}$$

What does it do? Well, it's designed for us to feed it vectors representing Wall Street stocks, like so:

$$\overrightarrow{\text{mcdonalds}} = \begin{bmatrix} 1965 \\ 183.52 \\ 2606707 \end{bmatrix} \begin{array}{l} \leftarrow \text{year founded} \\ \leftarrow \text{current share price} \\ \leftarrow \text{trading volume} \end{array}$$

The result of multiplying S by this vector is to give us a convenient list of the McDonald's current stock price in various currencies:

$$S \cdot \overrightarrow{\text{mcdonalds}} = \begin{bmatrix} 183.52 \\ 126.93 \\ 20389.10 \\ 161.50 \\ 1189.21 \\ 3187.74 \end{bmatrix} \begin{array}{l} \leftarrow \$ \text{ (U.S. dollars)} \\ \leftarrow £ \text{ (British pounds sterling)} \\ \leftarrow ¥ \text{ (Japanese Yen)} \\ \leftarrow € \text{ (Euros)} \\ \leftarrow ¥ \text{ (Chinese Yuan)} \\ \leftarrow P \text{ (Mexican Pesos)} \end{array}$$

Again, the S matrix is simply ignoring the information we don't care about, and that's okay. It's still a function:

$$S : \mathbb{R}^3 \to \mathbb{R}^6.$$

5.2 Linear operators

So every matrix gives us a linear transformation, no matter its shape. But if the matrix is *square*, we use a special name for the linear transformation it carries out: a **linear operator**.

A matrix being square, of course, would imply that the input vectors and the output vectors (or the domain and codomain, if you prefer) are the *same dimension*: the function will map vectors in $\mathbb{R}^3$ to other vectors in $\mathbb{R}^3$, for instance, or from $\mathbb{R}^{81}$ to $\mathbb{R}^{81}$.

Let's restrict our attention for the moment to just two dimensions, and see what effect certain 2 × 2 linear operator matrices have on the vectors they act upon.

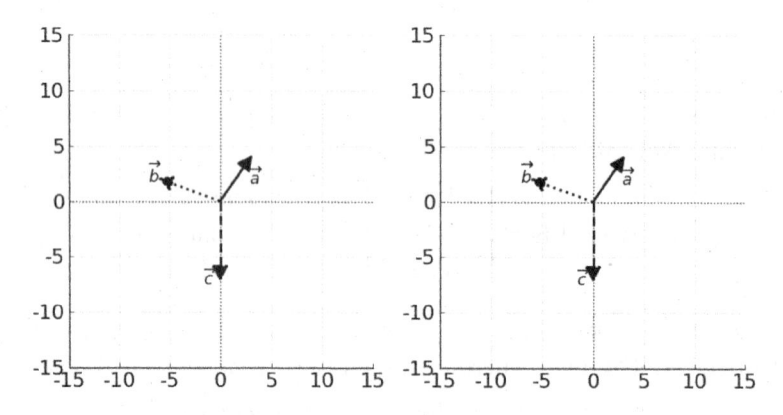

Figure 5.1: Three vectors, and their transformations under the super boring linear operator $\begin{bmatrix} 1 & 0 \\ 0 & 1 \end{bmatrix}$.

We'll have three guinea pig vectors, which are: $\vec{a}$ = [3 4] (solid), $\vec{b}$ = [−6 2] (dotted), and $\vec{c}$ = [0 − 7] (dashed). They're plotted in the left half of Figure 5.1. First, we'll try the identity matrix, which you'll remember in two dimensions is simply:

$$I_2 = \begin{bmatrix} 1 & 0 \\ 0 & 1 \end{bmatrix}$$

Let's multiply our three guinea pigs by this matrix to transform them:

$$I_2 \cdot \vec{a} = \begin{bmatrix} 1 & 0 \\ 0 & 1 \end{bmatrix} \cdot \begin{bmatrix} 3 \\ 4 \end{bmatrix} = \begin{bmatrix} 3 \\ 4 \end{bmatrix}.$$

$$I_2 \cdot \vec{b} = \begin{bmatrix} 1 & 0 \\ 0 & 1 \end{bmatrix} \cdot \begin{bmatrix} -6 \\ 2 \end{bmatrix} = \begin{bmatrix} -6 \\ 2 \end{bmatrix}.$$

5.2. LINEAR OPERATORS

$$I_2 \cdot \vec{c} = \begin{bmatrix} 1 & 0 \\ 0 & 1 \end{bmatrix} \cdot \begin{bmatrix} 0 \\ -7 \end{bmatrix} = \begin{bmatrix} 0 \\ -7 \end{bmatrix}.$$

The effect, you'll agree, is underwhelming. Double-check my math, and convince yourself that *the function of the identity matrix is to convert a vector into itself.* This is why it's called the "identity" matrix, in fact. The "identity element" of addition is 0, which means if you add anything to zero, you get your number back as an answer. The identity element of multiplication is 1, of course. And the identity *matrix* (in two dimensions) is the matrix $\begin{bmatrix} 1 & 0 \\ 0 & 1 \end{bmatrix}$.

The right half of Figure 5.1 illustrates this boring fact: under the identity matrix's linear operator, all three vectors look exactly the same after the transformation.

K, let's shake things up a bit then. Let's try this operator:

$$S_{v=2} = \begin{bmatrix} 1 & 0 \\ 0 & 2 \end{bmatrix}.$$

I'll reveal why I chose $S_{v=2}$ as the name of this matrix in a moment. Notice that it is the same as I_2 except for the 2 in the bottom-right corner. What does it do when it maps vectors? Let's give it a shot:

$$S_{v=2} \cdot \vec{a} = \begin{bmatrix} 1 & 0 \\ 0 & 2 \end{bmatrix} \cdot \begin{bmatrix} 3 \\ 4 \end{bmatrix} = \begin{bmatrix} 3 \\ 8 \end{bmatrix},$$

$$S_{v=2} \cdot \vec{b} = \begin{bmatrix} 1 & 0 \\ 0 & 2 \end{bmatrix} \cdot \begin{bmatrix} -6 \\ 2 \end{bmatrix} = \begin{bmatrix} -6 \\ 4 \end{bmatrix},$$

$$S_{v=2} \cdot \vec{c} = \begin{bmatrix} 1 & 0 \\ 0 & 2 \end{bmatrix} \cdot \begin{bmatrix} 0 \\ -7 \end{bmatrix} = \begin{bmatrix} 0 \\ -14 \end{bmatrix}.$$

Can you see what it did in Figure 5.2? It *stretched all the points vertically by a factor of 2.* In other words, every vector is now pointing at a point twice as far from the *x*-axis. This is why I chose the name $S_{v=2}$ – it stands for "**S**tretch vertically by a factor of **2**."

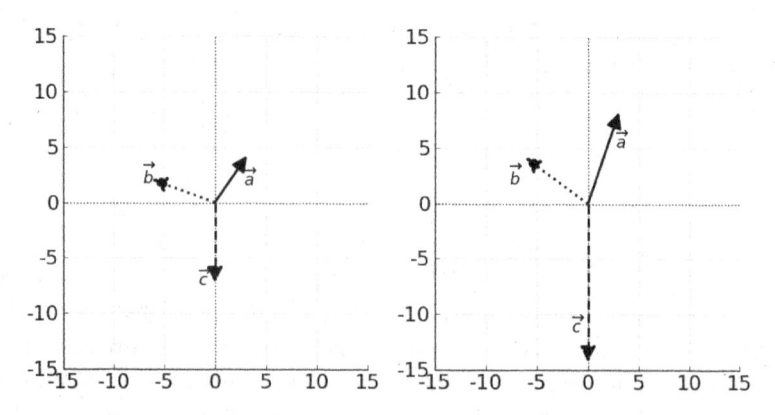

Figure 5.2: Three vectors, and their transformations under the slightly more interesting linear operator $\begin{bmatrix} 1 & 0 \\ 0 & 2 \end{bmatrix}$.

Playing on the same theme, we can try:

$$S_{v=\frac{1}{2}, h=2\frac{1}{2}} = \begin{bmatrix} 2\frac{1}{2} & 0 \\ 0 & \frac{1}{2} \end{bmatrix}.$$

Let's see what this does to our vectors:

$$S_{v=\frac{1}{2}, h=2\frac{1}{2}} \cdot \vec{a} = \begin{bmatrix} 2\frac{1}{2} & 0 \\ 0 & \frac{1}{2} \end{bmatrix} \cdot \begin{bmatrix} 3 \\ 4 \end{bmatrix} = \begin{bmatrix} 7\frac{1}{2} \\ 2 \end{bmatrix},$$

$$S_{v=\frac{1}{2}, h=2\frac{1}{2}} \cdot \vec{b} = \begin{bmatrix} 2\frac{1}{2} & 0 \\ 0 & \frac{1}{2} \end{bmatrix} \cdot \begin{bmatrix} -6 \\ 2 \end{bmatrix} = \begin{bmatrix} -15 \\ 1 \end{bmatrix}.$$

$$S_{v=\frac{1}{2}, h=2\frac{1}{2}} \cdot \vec{c} = \begin{bmatrix} 2\frac{1}{2} & 0 \\ 0 & \frac{1}{2} \end{bmatrix} \cdot \begin{bmatrix} 0 \\ -7 \end{bmatrix} = \begin{bmatrix} 0 \\ -3.5 \end{bmatrix}.$$

Figure 5.3 (p. 121) shows the results. Our vectors have been both stretched and squished: stretched wide away horizontally from the y-axis, and squished towards the x-axis. It's like a hippo sat down on the x-axis – and his evil twin hippo below him sat "up" on the x-axis, so that their butts nearly met in the middle. All the

5.2. LINEAR OPERATORS

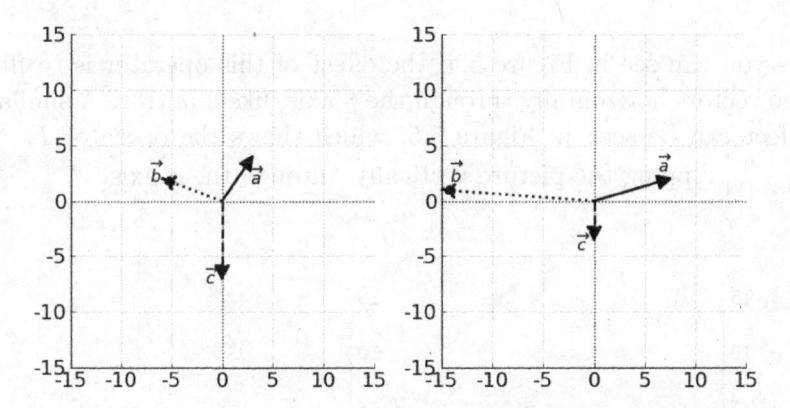

Figure 5.3: The transformations under the linear operator $\begin{bmatrix} 2\frac{1}{2} & 0 \\ 0 & \frac{1}{2} \end{bmatrix}$, which is a bit like being simultaneously sat on by two mirror-image hippos.

blades of grass on both sides of the axis were smooshed under the composite load. (Btw, if this visual image isn't doing it for you, by all means disregard it.)

Okay, now some other things than squishing and stretching. Let's investigate this smooth operator:

$$F_h = \begin{bmatrix} -1 & 0 \\ 0 & 1 \end{bmatrix}.$$

Almost the same as the identity matrix, except for that minus sign. What does it do?

$$F_h \cdot \vec{a} = \begin{bmatrix} -1 & 0 \\ 0 & 1 \end{bmatrix} \cdot \begin{bmatrix} 3 \\ 4 \end{bmatrix} = \begin{bmatrix} -3 \\ 4 \end{bmatrix},$$

$$F_h \cdot \vec{b} = \begin{bmatrix} -1 & 0 \\ 0 & 1 \end{bmatrix} \cdot \begin{bmatrix} -6 \\ 2 \end{bmatrix} = \begin{bmatrix} 6 \\ 2 \end{bmatrix}.$$

$$F_h \cdot \vec{c} = \begin{bmatrix} -1 & 0 \\ 0 & 1 \end{bmatrix} \cdot \begin{bmatrix} 0 \\ -7 \end{bmatrix} = \begin{bmatrix} 0 \\ -7 \end{bmatrix}.$$

As you can see in Figure 5.4, the effect of this operator is to flip the vectors horizontally through the y axis, like a mirror. A similar effect can be seen in Figure 5.5, which shows the operator $F_v = \begin{bmatrix} 1 & 0 \\ 0 & -1 \end{bmatrix}$ flipping the picture vertically, through the x axis.

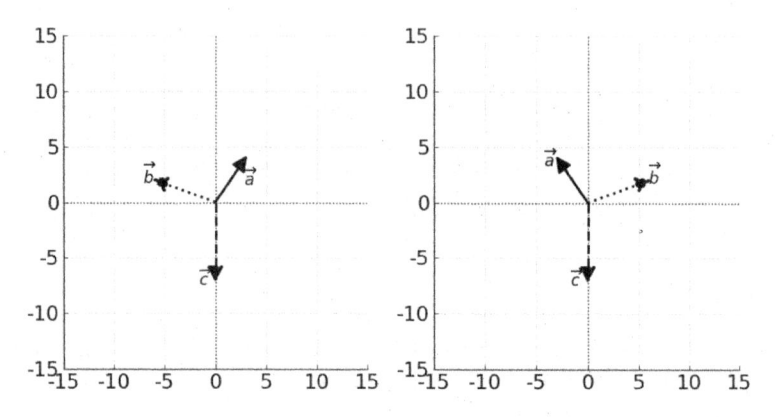

Figure 5.4: The action of the linear operator $\begin{bmatrix} -1 & 0 \\ 0 & 1 \end{bmatrix}$, which flips everything mirror-image-wise across the y-axis. To the $\vec{c}$ vector, this had no effect.

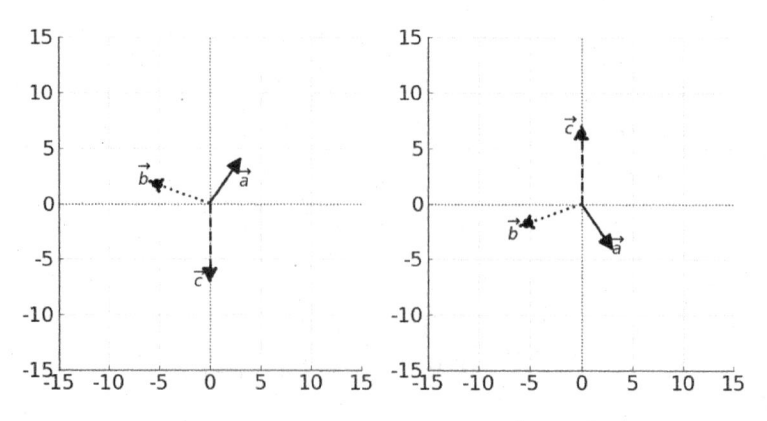

Figure 5.5: The action of the linear operator $\begin{bmatrix} 1 & 0 \\ 0 & -1 \end{bmatrix}$, which flips everything mirror-image-wise across the x-axis.

5.2. LINEAR OPERATORS

Okay, now my favorite ones. Check out this bad boy:

$$R_{+90°} = \begin{bmatrix} 0 & -1 \\ 1 & 0 \end{bmatrix}.$$

Can you guess why I named it the way I did? Check out its operation, and the resulting graph:

$$R_{+90°} \cdot \vec{a} = \begin{bmatrix} 0 & -1 \\ 1 & 0 \end{bmatrix} \cdot \begin{bmatrix} 3 \\ 4 \end{bmatrix} = \begin{bmatrix} -4 \\ 3 \end{bmatrix},$$

$$R_{+90°} \cdot \vec{b} = \begin{bmatrix} 0 & -1 \\ 1 & 0 \end{bmatrix} \cdot \begin{bmatrix} -6 \\ 2 \end{bmatrix} = \begin{bmatrix} -2 \\ -6 \end{bmatrix}.$$

$$R_{+90°} \cdot \vec{c} = \begin{bmatrix} 0 & -1 \\ 1 & 0 \end{bmatrix} \cdot \begin{bmatrix} 0 \\ -7 \end{bmatrix} = \begin{bmatrix} 7 \\ 0 \end{bmatrix}.$$

It *rotates* the vectors 90° counter-clockwise. Neato!

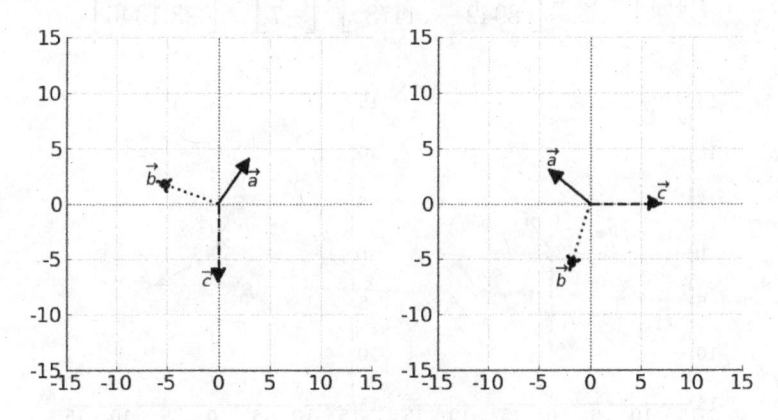

Figure 5.6: The linear operator $\begin{bmatrix} 0 & -1 \\ 1 & 0 \end{bmatrix}$, which rotates them 90° counter-clockwise.

As a matter of fact, we can create a linear operator to rotate vectors *any* angle we want. Suppose we want to rotate them 63.4°

counter-clockwise (just to pick an angle at random). The formula for computing the rotation matrix is:

$$R_\theta = \begin{bmatrix} \cos\theta & -\sin\theta \\ \sin\theta & \cos\theta \end{bmatrix},$$

where θ is the angle we wish to rotate. We plug in $\theta = 63.4°$ to get:

$$R_{+63.4°} = \begin{bmatrix} .4478 & -.8942 \\ .8942 & .4478 \end{bmatrix}.$$

Applying this linear operator to our three vectors, we get these results and the picture in Figure 5.7.

$$R_{+63.4°} \cdot \vec{a} = \begin{bmatrix} .4478 & -.8942 \\ .8942 & .4478 \end{bmatrix} \cdot \begin{bmatrix} 3 \\ 4 \end{bmatrix} = \begin{bmatrix} -2.2334 \\ 4.4738 \end{bmatrix},$$

$$R_{+63.4°} \cdot \vec{b} = \begin{bmatrix} .4478 & -.8942 \\ .8942 & .4478 \end{bmatrix} \cdot \begin{bmatrix} -6 \\ 2 \end{bmatrix} = \begin{bmatrix} -4.4752 \\ -4.4696 \end{bmatrix}.$$

$$R_{+63.4°} \cdot \vec{c} = \begin{bmatrix} .4478 & -.8942 \\ .8942 & .4478 \end{bmatrix} \cdot \begin{bmatrix} 0 \\ -7 \end{bmatrix} = \begin{bmatrix} 6.2594 \\ -3.1346 \end{bmatrix}.$$

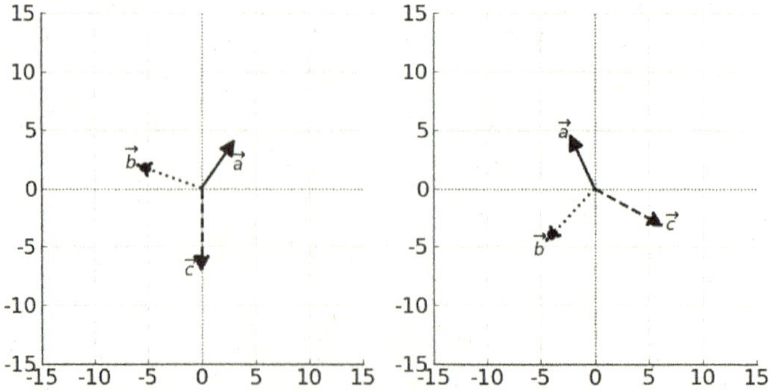

Figure 5.7: The vectors under rotation by 63.4° CCW.

I think you get the idea. Linear operators are simple matrices that can perform a variety of transformative effects on vectors. They're

5.3. THE KERNEL

especially helpful (and easy to visualize) in graphics settings. Every time your Mario Kart character turns slightly, and sees a different angle of the race track, all of the scenery and opposing racers have to be drawn in exactly the right places. This can involve shrinkage, stretching, skewing, rotation, and a variety of other effects, all of which boil down to linear algebra operations. The same could be said for CGI movie effects.

Many people are surprised to learn that underneath the breathtaking scenery and fist-clenching action sequences of movies and games is a bunch of math. Watching Lt. Kara Thrace's viper arc towards the Cylon Resurrection ship seems like the least "mathy" thing in the world: it's all art and images and motion. But the reason it looks cool (and "correct" to the viewer, who has seen many objects move around in the world before) is that the linear algebra operations that govern movement and perspective are calculated properly. Truly, there's nothing cool without math.

5.3 The kernel

One curious-sounding mathematical term is "**kernel**," which is a property of linear operators (and therefore, square matrices). Another word for a matrix's kernel is its **nullspace**, which means the same thing.

The kernel of a linear operator is simply this: *the set of input vectors that it maps to the zero vector.* (A **zero vector** is just a vector with all zeroes in it.) Recall that a linear operator acts on vectors of a particular dimension to produce other vectors of the same dimension. What's under consideration here is: "what can we feed in to this operator and get all zeroes?" That may not seem like a very interesting question, but it turns out to be.

Let's start with an example. On p. 121 we had this linear operator:

$$F_h = \begin{bmatrix} -1 & 0 \\ 0 & 1 \end{bmatrix},$$

whose function, when we worked it out, was to flip vectors horizontally through the y-axis. The vector [2 3] was transformed to [−2 3]; the vector [−4 − 1] was mapped to [4 − 1]; and the like. Each input was mapped to its mirror image.

Now consider the kernel question. What is the complete set of vectors which, when subjected to the operation of F_h, would turn into [0 0]? I think you'll see in a moment's thought that there is only one such vector; namely, [0 0] itself. Only if you're already *on* the origin is your mirror image in the y-axis also going to be the origin. Hence, the kernel of F_h is only the zero vector. Notationally, we write:

$$\ker F_h = \left\{ \begin{bmatrix} 0 \\ 0 \end{bmatrix} \right\}.$$

The word "ker" stands for kernel, of course, and since we defined an operator's kernel as the *set* of vectors that get mapped to the zero vector, we put our one and only kernel vector in curly braces to designate that.

Now do you remember way back on p. 64 when we spoke of the "trivial solution" of a pair of dominoes? You might want to flip back to that page and refresh your memory. The subject under discussion was how to get to the *origin* via a linear transformation of a set of dominoes. In Domino Game fashion, you could add any multiple of the first domino to any multiple of the second, and in this case the goal was to get the domino ▢▢. The conclusion we came to was that if the dominoes were *yellow* (*i.e.*, if they were linearly independent of one another) there was no way to get to the origin except by, duh, taking zero of the first domino and zero of the second.

You should immediately see the tie-in with the kernel concept. Since every matrix-vector multiplication is a linear combination of the matrix's columns (interpretation #2 on p. 91), asking which vectors get mapped to the zero vector is the same as asking which linear combinations take you to the origin. And the fact of the matter is that if your matrix has linearly independent columns (yellow

5.3. THE KERNEL

dominoes) then there is only one such linear combination: zero of the first, and zero of the second.

What about our rotation matrix?

$$R_{+90°} = \begin{bmatrix} 0 & -1 \\ 1 & 0 \end{bmatrix}.$$

Again, visualizing it geometrically tells you the answer. Every point is rotated 90° counter-clockwise about the origin. So the only way to *land* in the middle of the whirlpool is to *start* in the middle of the whirlpool. Again, we have just the zero vector: ker $R_{+90°} = \{\begin{bmatrix} 0 \\ 0 \end{bmatrix}\}$.

What about our squishing/stretching matrices, like this one:

$$S_{v=\frac{1}{2}, h=2\frac{1}{2}} = \begin{bmatrix} 2\frac{1}{2} & 0 \\ 0 & \frac{1}{2} \end{bmatrix}?$$

Same thing. Every point will be (1) moved halfway closer to the x-axis than it was, and (2) moved two-and-a-half times further from the y-axis than it was. So the only way to land on the origin is to start on the origin, and once again we have ker $S_{v=\frac{1}{2}, h=2\frac{1}{2}} = \{\begin{bmatrix} 0 \\ 0 \end{bmatrix}\}$.

You're probably starting to wonder whether this is always the case. Does *any* linear operator have a bigger kernel?

But the answer, as you may remember from p. 64, is **yes**: if our columns are *blue dominoes*. Linearly *de*pendent vectors makes it so that there are many ways to get to the origin.

Let's try a linear operator with blue domino columns, like this one:

$$B = \begin{bmatrix} \frac{1}{2} & 1 \\ -1 & -2 \end{bmatrix}.$$

First, convince yourself that the columns are indeed linearly dependent. If you took the left column, [$\frac{1}{2}$ -1], and you multiplied that column by 2, you would get [1 -2], which is the right column. So yes, they are.

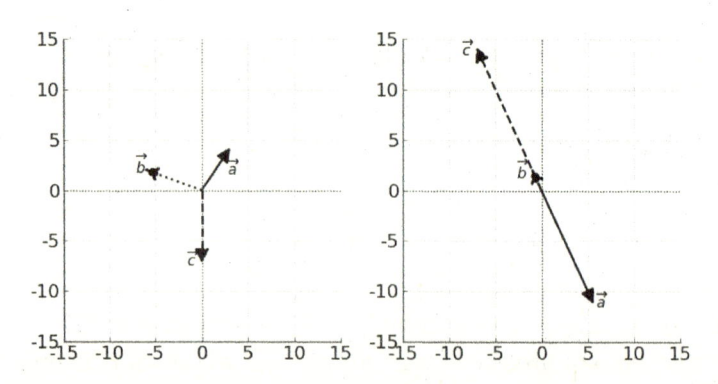

Figure 5.8: The vectors transformed by an operator B whose columns are linearly dependent.

The effect, shown in Figure 5.8, is rather jarring. This narrow-minded matrix slapped all three vectors down in exactly the same direction! This is because just as blue dominoes can only move you on a certain line of the two-dimensional plane, so *they can only map input vectors to that line.*

Now the "good news" (if you call it that) for blue dominoes is that there is indeed more than one way to get to the origin by using them – more than just the "trivial solution." And this in turn means that the *kernel* is larger than just the zero vector. Just check out all these vectors that get mapped to the origin:

$$\text{the vector } \begin{bmatrix} -2 \\ 1 \end{bmatrix}: \quad \begin{bmatrix} \frac{1}{2} & 1 \\ -1 & -2 \end{bmatrix} \cdot \begin{bmatrix} -2 \\ 1 \end{bmatrix} = \begin{bmatrix} 0 \\ 0 \end{bmatrix} \checkmark$$

$$\text{the vector } \begin{bmatrix} -4 \\ 2 \end{bmatrix}: \quad \begin{bmatrix} \frac{1}{2} & 1 \\ -1 & -2 \end{bmatrix} \cdot \begin{bmatrix} -4 \\ 2 \end{bmatrix} = \begin{bmatrix} 0 \\ 0 \end{bmatrix} \checkmark$$

$$\text{the vector } \begin{bmatrix} 6 \\ -3 \end{bmatrix}: \quad \begin{bmatrix} \frac{1}{2} & 1 \\ -1 & -2 \end{bmatrix} \cdot \begin{bmatrix} 6 \\ -3 \end{bmatrix} = \begin{bmatrix} 0 \\ 0 \end{bmatrix} \checkmark$$

$$\text{the vector } \begin{bmatrix} 67 \\ -33\frac{1}{2} \end{bmatrix}: \quad \begin{bmatrix} \frac{1}{2} & 1 \\ -1 & -2 \end{bmatrix} \cdot \begin{bmatrix} 67 \\ -33\frac{1}{2} \end{bmatrix} = \begin{bmatrix} 0 \\ 0 \end{bmatrix} \checkmark$$

$$\text{the vector } \begin{bmatrix} -\frac{1}{9} \\ \frac{1}{18} \end{bmatrix}: \quad \begin{bmatrix} \frac{1}{2} & 1 \\ -1 & -2 \end{bmatrix} \cdot \begin{bmatrix} -\frac{1}{9} \\ \frac{1}{18} \end{bmatrix} = \begin{bmatrix} 0 \\ 0 \end{bmatrix} \checkmark$$

5.3. THE KERNEL

So at this point, we've discovered that the kernel of B has *at least* these vectors in it:

$$\ker B = \left\{ \begin{bmatrix} -2 \\ 1 \end{bmatrix}, \begin{bmatrix} -4 \\ 2 \end{bmatrix}, \begin{bmatrix} 6 \\ -3 \end{bmatrix}, \begin{bmatrix} 67 \\ -33\frac{1}{2} \end{bmatrix}, \begin{bmatrix} -\frac{1}{9} \\ \frac{1}{18} \end{bmatrix}, \cdots \right\}$$

Now the shrewd reader will notice something interesting about all those vectors in the kernel. Can you spot the pattern?

It's actually pretty simple. Whatever number you choose for the first element of the vector, the second element has to be negative-half-of that. The first example, [−2 1], has −2 in the first element, and negative-half-of-that (which is 1) as its second element. Similarly, 2 is negative-half-of −4, −3 is negative-half-of 6, and so forth.

Now a subtle but important fact here is that our "choice process" for finding vectors in ker B has *one degree of freedom* to it. We're free to choose whatever we like for one of the vector's elements. But then, if we want the vector to be in the kernel of B, we have no flexibility in what we choose for the other. Our only choice is to divide it by 2 and change its sign. Any other choice for that second element won't result in a vector that maps to $\begin{bmatrix} 0 \\ 0 \end{bmatrix}$.

We could express this in symbols by saying that you get one variable – call it x – for your free choice, at which point you can declare this vector to be in B's kernel:

$$\begin{bmatrix} x \\ -\frac{x}{2} \end{bmatrix}.$$

If you're a visual person, you can let x freely range from $-\infty$ to ∞, and plot this vector for all possible values of x plugged in. Your plot would look like Figure 5.9: a one-dimensional straight line.

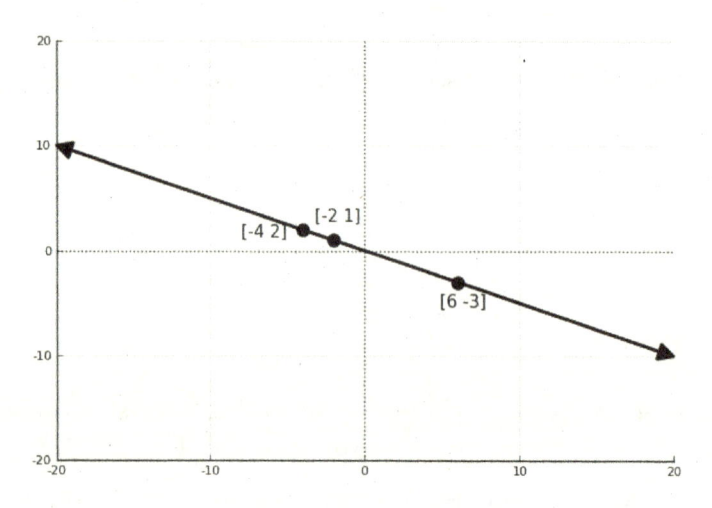

Figure 5.9: The kernel (nullspace) of B, plotted visually. Any vector whose tip lies on that straight line will be in $\ker B$, which means we have a one-dimensional kernel.

5.4 Nullity

Okay, so with B, we had one degree of freedom in constructing a vector in the kernel. Now with our other linear operators from this chapter – like F_h, $R_{63.4°}$, and friends – we actually had *zero* degrees of freedom! There simply weren't any free choices to make at all: we had to say "uh, the only vector in the kernel is $\begin{bmatrix} 0 \\ 0 \end{bmatrix}$ itself. Nothin' much we can do about that."

With that prelude out of the way, it's time for a new term. The **nullity** of a linear operator (square matrix) is *the dimension of its kernel*. The idea of "dimension" here is closely linked to the concept of "degrees of freedom." In Figure 5.9, you can see that all the points in B's kernel are lined up on a straight line. A line is a *one*-dimensional shape: you can specify any point on it with just one coordinate, telling you how far leftwards or rightwards you are. Hence the dimension of B's kernel – or its "nullity" – is 1.

A mere point, on the other hand, is a *zero*-dimensional shape: there's nothing to specify further about it – it's just a point, man. So what this means is that in a 2×2 matrix with linearly *in*dependent

5.5. RANK

columns – like F_h, or $S_{v=\frac{1}{2}, h=2\frac{1}{2}}$, or even the identity matrix I – *the nullity is 0*. Only if the matrix has linearly *de*pendent columns, will its nullity will be greater than 0. In B's case, it is 1. Sometimes you'll see the notation:

$$\text{null } B = 1$$

which means "the nullity of the B operator is 1, which in turn means there's one degree of freedom you get in constructing a vector that will wind up in B's kernel."

5.5 Rank

This in turn is related to yet another new term: the **rank** of a matrix. A square matrix's rank is *the number of linearly independent columns it has*. That's a relatively simple idea. If I give you a 3×3 matrix, you know the rank can't be possibly greater than 3, because there are only three columns in it, period. The question, then, is how many of those columns can be arrived at by linear combinations of the others? If none of them can, then you have a fully healthy yellow domino matrix with three fresh columns that each point in totally different directions. It's a rank 3 matrix. Since it's rank 3 and there are three total columns, it's also sometimes called a **full-rank** matrix.

On the other hand, if some of those columns are linearly dependent on others, then we're in a blue domino situation. Suppose you can get the third column from a linear combination of the other two, but that the first two are indeed independent with respect to each other. Then, we have a rank 2 matrix: it's "one card short of a full deck," as they say. Another term for a matrix whose rank is less than its number of columns is a **rank-deficient** matrix, for obvious reasons.

5.6 The Rank-Nullity Theorem

It turns out that the concepts of rank and nullity are intimately bound up together, and in a very simple way; namely,

rank A + null A = number of columns of A,

for any square matrix A. This is called the **rank-nullity theorem**, and you can take it to the bank.

Let's think about what it means. If you just grab a random square matrix off the shelf at Wal-Mart, it's going to be full rank. For example, if you grab a 3 × 3 matrix, you'd have to have awfully bad luck for one of the columns to be an exact linear combination of the two others. In this case, then, it'll be a full-rank matrix; or put another way, its rank will be 3. And as we've seen in the above examples, the only vector it will map to the origin will be the zero vector itself. That's a zero-dimensional "space," and hence the nullity is 0. And so the formula holds: a rank of 3, plus a nullity of 0, equals 3 columns in our matrix.

If we're unlucky, and we get one column being linearly dependent on the other two, then we have a rank-deficient matrix with blue columns. Since only two of the columns are really "legit," it's a rank 2 matrix. And from the previous analysis, we've seen that such matrices have an entire line in their kernel, not just one point. That one-dimensional line means that their nullity is 1. And again for formula holds: a rank of 2, plus a nullity of 1, equals 3 columns in our matrix.

It turns out some 3×3 matrices are even suckier than that. Suppose we get one that has only *one* linearly independent column – each of the other two are exact (possibly scaled) duplicates of the other one! It's not hard to create such a matrix; how about:

$$S = \begin{bmatrix} 1 & 2 & 3 \\ 2 & 4 & 6 \\ 3 & 6 & 9 \end{bmatrix}.$$

("S" stands for "sucky.") We scratch our head looking at that guy: sure, we've been given permission to go in direction [1 2 3], which is great and all, but the other two columns just give us regurgitated versions of that. There's no additional power in being able to travel in the [2 4 6] direction if you can already go in the [1 2 3] direction, because they're the same direction! And the same is true of the last column as well.

In this case, it turns out to be a rank *1* matrix – only one independent column. And you'll find that its nullity is therefore *2*. There's an entire two-dimensional plane (hanging out in three-dimensional space) any point on which will be in S's kernel. And again, the rank-nullity theorem holds: a rank of 1 plus a nullity of 2 equals 3 columns in the matrix.

This deep relationship holds in any number of dimensions and even in non-real-valued matrices. It's a beautifully descriptive way to capture exactly how much power a matrix has to perform linear transformations.

5.7 Function properties and linear transformations

I'll wrap up this chapter by drawing a connection between linear transformations and the ordinary functions we learned about in *A Cool, Brisk Walk*. Let's review two properties from that book that every function might, or might not, have:

1. **injective** (a.k.a. "one-to-one"): no two elements of the domain map to the same element of the codomain.
2. **surjective** (a.k.a. "onto"): every element of the codomain has at least one element of the domain that maps to it.

For example, consider the function that maps Social Security Numbers (the domain) to the people they belong to (the codomain). This is an injective function, because no two SSNs go with the same person. It's not surjective, though, because there are lots of people in the world that don't have SSNs.

By contrast, consider the function that maps college students to the schools they're enrolled in. This is surjective, since every college has at least *some* students in it. But it's not injective, because of course many students go to the same college.

A function can have both properties, of course, in which case it's called **bijective**. In a twelve-horse race, we might map each horse to its finishing place, which will be an integer from 1 to 12. This function will be injective because no two horses will map to the same number: you can't have two winners, or two sixth-place finishers, for instance. It's also surjective because every number will be mapped to by some horse: we're guaranteed to have a winner, a runner-up, a twelfth-place finisher, and everything in between.

Now what does this all have to do with matrices? Well, if every matrix can be looked at as a linear transformation – which is a function from input vectors to output vectors – we might well ask how its injective-ness and surjective-ness relate to its matrix properties.

Consider first an easy case. Let's say our matrix has more columns than rows. It's tall and skinny, like a 3 × 2. Whatever else may be true, we know that the linear transformation corresponding to such a matrix cannot possibly be surjective. That's because its input vectors are only 2-dimensional, while its output vectors are 3-dimensional. We can't possibly have every single 3-dimensional vector "spoken for" by some 2-dimensional vector: there aren't nearly enough of them. We can map [4 9] to [1 2 3] and [6 3] to [4 5 6], etc....but we're going to run out of 2-dimensional vectors way before we run out of the 3-dimensional outputs we have to map them to. (See Figure 5.10.)

Next think of the opposite case: a fat matrix, like a 2 × 3. Whatever else might be true, we know it can't possibly be *in*jective. It's the mirror image of the previous example. If the outputs are only 2-dimensional, then we can't possibly have every single 3-dimensional input mapped to its very own exclusive output. There just aren't enough of those outputs to go around; some will have to be shared by many different inputs. (Figure 5.11.)

Okay, let's imagine a square matrix then, like a 3 × 3. What can we say about its injective-ness and surjective-ness? The answer turns out to be that *if it's full-rank, its linear transformation will be both injective and surjective (i.e., bijective)*. Every 3-dimensional

5.7. FUNCTION PROPERTIES

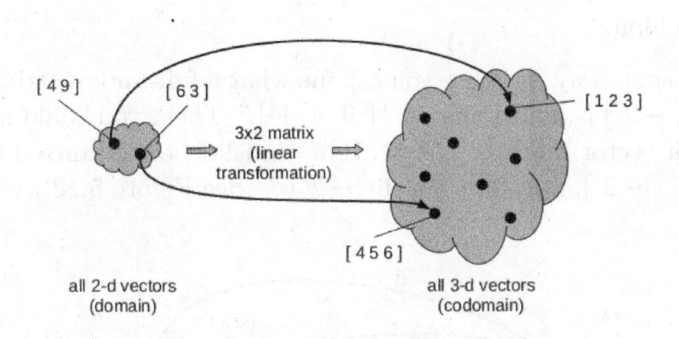

Figure 5.10: A 3 × 2 matrix can't represent a surjective linear transformation – there are far more elements in the codomain than the domain.

input will get mapped to its very own 3-dimensional output, which it exclusively "owns." Furthermore, every possible 3-dimensional output will be accounted for by exactly one input.

The implication is that the linear transformation is **reversible**, like our horse-racing function was. If you ask me for the finishing place of *Sir Winston*, and I tell you "third place," you could then ask me "which horse was in third place?" and I'd be sure to tell you "*Sir Winston*." This is possible because unlike SSNs and college attendance, every input goes with its own output in perfect one-to-

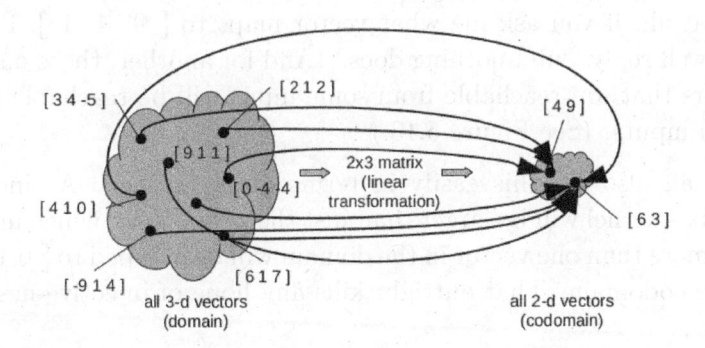

Figure 5.11: A 2 × 3 matrix can't represent an injective linear transformation – there aren't nearly enough elements in the codomain for each element of the domain to get its own.

one fashion.

In the same way, suppose you ask me what a full-rank matrix times [4 6 −2] is, and I answer "[9 4 1]." Then, you could ask me "which vector maps to [9 4 1]?" and I'd be guaranteed to say "[4 6 −2], and *only* [4 6 −2]." (See Figure 5.12.)

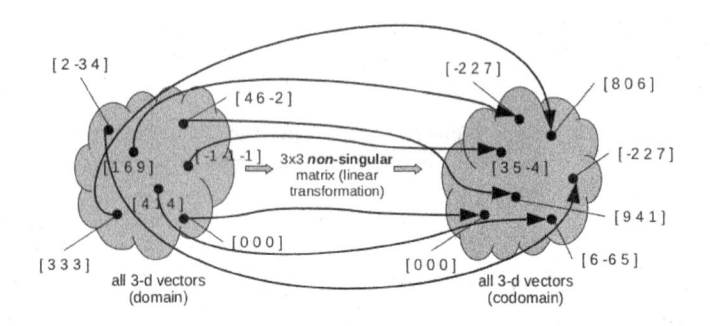

Figure 5.12: A non-singular 3 × 3 matrix's linear transformation. It's both injective and surjective: the domain and codomain are the same size, and every element of the codomain has only *one* incoming arrow. This includes the zero vector, which is mapped to by *only* the zero vector.

Note that this is only true of *full-rank* matrices. If a matrix has some blue dominoes among its columns, this whole guarantee breaks down badly. For one thing, many output vectors won't be reachable at all; if you ask me what vector maps to [9 4 1], I may very well reply, "uh...nothing does." And for another, those output vectors that *are* reachable from some input will be reachable from *many* inputs. (See Figure 5.13.)

You can also see this easily in terms of the kernel. A singular matrix's kernel will be larger than just the zero vector, which means that more than one vector in the domain will be mapped to [0 0 0] in the codomain. That outright kills any hope of injective-ness, of course.

Such linear transformations – and matrices – are non-reversible, and as we'll see in the next chapter, they have no **inverse** matrix at all. Stay tuned.

5.7. FUNCTION PROPERTIES

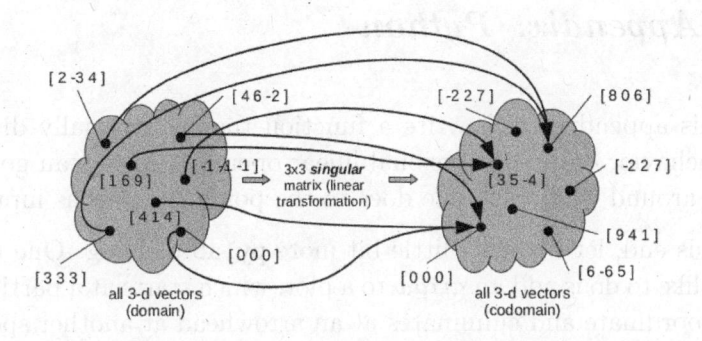

Figure 5.13: A *singular* 3 × 3 matrix's linear transformation. It's a hot mess. Many points in the codomain won't be reachable at all, and the few that are reachable (including the zero vector) will be reachable from a myriad of different inputs.

🐍 *Appendix: Python*

In this appendix, we'll write a function that will visually display the behavior of a 2-dimensional linear operator, so we can get our head around what each one does to the points it takes as input.

To this end, let's learn a little bit more `pylab` plotting. One thing we'd like to do is add an *arrow* to a plot, which starts at a particular x-y coordinate and culminates at an arrowhead at another specific particular x-y coordinate. The (clunky, IMO) command to do this in pylab is this:

> `pylab.arrow(`*from_xValue*, *from_yValue*,
>   *to_xValue* - *from_xValue*, *to_yValue* - *from_yValue*,
>   `head_width=.2, head_length=.5)`

There are six (count 'em) arguments, the first four of which are coordinate-ish things and the last two of which are aesthetic trappings (which you can change to suit your taste). The first four numbers are, in order:

1. The x-coordinate of where the arrow starts.
2. The y-coordinate of where the arrow starts.
3. The length of the arrow in the x direction.
4. The length of the arrow in the y direction.

Because the third and fourth arguments are lengths, instead of coordinates, you have to do some subtraction to compute the right values for them. It's not that big a deal, but I do occasionally resent it.

The second thing to add to our plotting repertoire is the ability to create horizontal and vertical lines, so we can display the axes on a plot. This is simpler; you just call `pylab.axhline(`*some_y_value*`)` or `pylab.axvline(`*some_x_value*`)` to draw a horizontal or vertical line, respectively. If we do simply want to create a pair of axes, then the "*some_x/y_values*" are both 0.

Put this all together, and we can use this code to create Figure 5.14:

5.7. FUNCTION PROPERTIES

```
import pylab
pylab.plot(-5,7,'o')
pylab.arrow(-5,7,8,-4,head_width=.2,head_length=.5)
pylab.axhline(0)
pylab.axvline(0)
pylab.xlim(-10,10)
pylab.ylim(-10,10)
pylab.show()
```

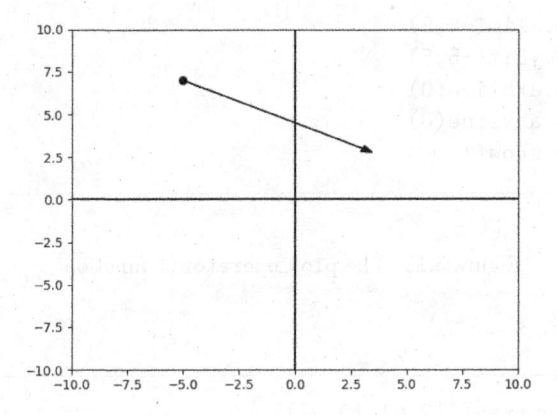

Figure 5.14: Drawing an arrow from point (-5,7) to point (3,3).

Okay. Now let's write a function which will take a 2 × 2 matrix as an argument, generate some random inputs, and plot an arrow (like the one above) for each input showing which point it gets mapped to. The complete code is in Figure 5.15.

The meat of this function is actually all on one line: output_vector = M.dot(input_vector). That's what takes each randomly-generated input vector and performs matrix-vector multiplication on it to yield the corresponding output. Everything else is random number generation and window dressing.

Let's take it for a spin with a few matrices:

```
def plot_operator(M):
    for i in arange(100):
        xval = random.rand() * 10 - 5
        yval = random.rand() * 10 - 5
        input_vector = array([xval, yval])
        pylab.plot(xval, yval, 'o')

        output_vector = M.dot(input_vector)

        pylab.arrow(input_vector[0], input_vector[1],
            output_vector[0] - input_vector[0],
            output_vector[1] - input_vector[1],
            head_width=.2, head_length=.3)

    pylab.xlim(-5,5)
    pylab.ylim(-5,5)
    pylab.axhline(0)
    pylab.axvline(0)
    pylab.show()
```

Figure 5.15: The plot_operator() function.

```
stretch = array([[2,0],[0,2]])
plot_operator(stretch)

flip_horiz_shrink_vert = array([[-1,0],[0,.8]])
plot_operator(flip_horiz_shrink_vert)

rotate_90_ccw = array([[0,1],[-1,0]])
plot_operator(rotate_90_cw)

rad_17 = 17 * pi / 180
rotate_17deg_ccw = array([[cos(rad_17),-sin(rad_17)],
    [sin(rad_17),cos(rad_17)]])
plot_operator(rotate_17deg_ccw)
```

5.7. FUNCTION PROPERTIES

For that last one, we had to first convert 17° to radians (by multiplying by $\frac{\pi}{180}$) and then plug that value into the sines and cosines of the general rotation matrix on p. 124. The results of these four operators are shown in the plots in Figure 5.16.

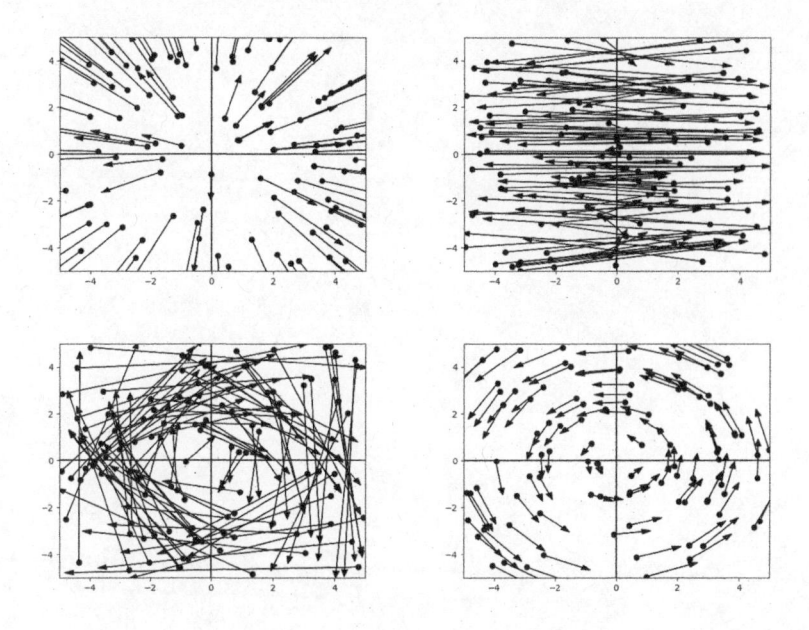

Figure 5.16: The operations of four matrices depicted graphically on random input vectors: `stretch` (upper-left), `flip_horiz_shrink_vert` (upper-right), `rotate_90deg_ccw` (lower-left), and `rotate_17deg_cw` (lower-right).

Chapter 6

Matrix multiplication

So far, we've multiplied scalars by vectors (p. 21), vectors by other vectors (p. 24), scalars by matrices (p. 87), and even matrices by vectors (p. 89). The only thing we haven't done yet is multiply one entire matrix by another. That mysterious operation is the subject of this chapter.

Luckily, we've already set ourselves up for success. As it will turn out, matrix-matrix multiplication is really just matrix-*vector* multiplication "in a loop"; *i.e.*, repeated several times.

6.1 When it's legal and what you get

But let's not get ahead of ourselves. First, let's outline the very curious rules for (1) when two matrices *can* be multiplied at all (often they can't), and (2) if they can, what the dimensions of the result are. These rules will surprise you at first (they certainly did me).

Let's say we have two matrices called A and B. Suppose that A is an $m \times n$ matrix (m rows and n columns), and that B is a $p \times q$ matrix. Visually, here's what we've got:

Here are the rules:

> 1. n must be equal to p, or you can't multiply the matrices at all.
> 2. If n does equal p, then you'll get an $m \times q$ matrix when you multiply them.

Those rules are so strange and unexpected that it's worth taking a long moment to stare at both the matrices and the rules and try to digest them.

Some concrete examples:

1. Can we multiply a 3×2 matrix by a 2×4? Yes, since $n = 2$ and $p = 2$. And our result will be a 3×4:

2. Can we multiply a 2×5 matrix by a 5×3? Yes, since $n = 5$ and $p = 5$. And we get a 2×3:

3. Can we multiply a 4 × 3 matrix by another 4 × 3? No, since $n = 3$ but $p = 4$. Sorry.

$$4\underbrace{\begin{bmatrix} \bullet & \bullet & \bullet \\ \bullet & \bullet & \bullet \\ \bullet & \bullet & \bullet \\ \bullet & \bullet & \bullet \end{bmatrix}}_{3} \cdot 4\underbrace{\begin{bmatrix} \bullet & \bullet & \bullet \\ \bullet & \bullet & \bullet \\ \bullet & \bullet & \bullet \\ \bullet & \bullet & \bullet \end{bmatrix}}_{3} = \text{NOPE.}$$

It's sooo bizarre. Sometimes you multiply two biggish matrices together and get a small one; sometimes you multiply narrow ones and get a tall one; sometimes it seems like you'd get a valid answer and yet there is none.

Anyway, now that we have the ground rules for what the resulting matrix will be shaped like (if there even is one) let's talk about actually calculating the entries. I'm going to give you *three* different ways to think about this, each of which sheds a different light on the operation.

6.2 Way #1: Lather, rinse, repeat

The first way is to view the matrix multiplication $A \cdot B$ as **repeated matrix-vector multiplication**, where the matrix is A and the vectors are the **columns** of B. The final answer is formed by stitching together the results of the individual matrix-vector multiplications.

Let's see it in action. If you remember the procedure on p. 89, you can confirm that if we perform this matrix-vector multiplication:

$$\begin{bmatrix} 2 & 1 & 5 \\ 0 & 3 & -2 \end{bmatrix} \cdot \begin{bmatrix} 0 \\ 0 \\ 7 \end{bmatrix},$$

we'll get the answer

$$\begin{bmatrix} 35 \\ -14 \end{bmatrix}.$$

And if we do this:

$$\begin{bmatrix} 2 & 1 & 5 \\ 0 & 3 & -2 \end{bmatrix} \cdot \begin{bmatrix} 9 \\ 99 \\ 999 \end{bmatrix},$$

we'll get this:

$$\begin{bmatrix} 5112 \\ -1701 \end{bmatrix}.$$

Finally, if we do this:

$$\begin{bmatrix} 2 & 1 & 5 \\ 0 & 3 & -2 \end{bmatrix} \cdot \begin{bmatrix} -13 \\ -13 \\ -13 \end{bmatrix},$$

we'll get this:

$$\begin{bmatrix} -104 \\ -13 \end{bmatrix}.$$

Notice what I did there. I took the *same* 2 × 3 matrix each time, and multiplied it by some vector – a weird one, to help jog your memory in a moment – to get an answer.

All right. Now let's see what happens if I perform the following matrix-*matrix* multiplication:

$$\begin{bmatrix} 2 & 1 & 5 \\ 0 & 3 & -2 \end{bmatrix} \cdot \begin{bmatrix} 0 & 9 & -13 \\ 0 & 99 & -13 \\ 7 & 999 & -13 \end{bmatrix} = \;?$$

Examine the columns of the right-hand matrix: they should ring a bell. Each *column* is one of the *vectors* that we just multiplied our matrix by to get a columnar answer. The result of this operation is achieved by simply putting all those columnar answers together:

$$\begin{bmatrix} 2 & 1 & 5 \\ 0 & 3 & -2 \end{bmatrix} \cdot \begin{bmatrix} 0 & 9 & -13 \\ 0 & 99 & -13 \\ 7 & 999 & -13 \end{bmatrix} = \begin{bmatrix} 35 & 5112 & -104 \\ -14 & -1701 & -13 \end{bmatrix}.$$

See how that works? The result of the multiplication is just the three individual matrix-vector products, all concatenated together in an "answer matrix." The left column of our answer is $\begin{bmatrix} 35 \\ -14 \end{bmatrix}$, which is exactly what we got when we multiplied that left-hand matrix by James Bond. The right column of our answer is $\begin{bmatrix} -104 \\ -13 \end{bmatrix}$, which is what we got when we multiplied the matrix by triple -13's. And the middle column of the answer is the matrix times the stack of nines. So you can see that matrix-*matrix* multiplication is really just repeated matrix-*vector* multiplication.

This way of thinking about matrix multiplication might be the one that resonates most strongly with you. (It did for me.)

6.3 Way #2: All possible dot products

On the other hand, maybe you'll like this one better. Matrix-matrix multiplication can also be viewed as **all possible dot products** between the **rows** of A and the **columns** of B.

Flash back for a moment to *A Cool, Brisk Walk* chapter 6, and the Fundamental Theorem of Counting. Answer this question: "You have two choices of appetizer, and three choices of entrée. How many different dinner combinations are possible?"

The answer is six, since each of the two appetizers can go with any of the three entrées. So you could choose:

1. shrimp cocktail, filet mignon
2. shrimp cocktail, chicken pesto

3. shrimp cocktail, eggplant parmigiana
4. artichoke dip, filet mignon
5. artichoke dip, chicken pesto
6. artichoke dip, eggplant parmigiana

Now back to matrices. If I multiply these two matrices together:

$$\begin{bmatrix} 2 & 1 & 5 \\ 0 & 3 & -2 \end{bmatrix} \text{ and } \begin{bmatrix} 0 & 9 & -13 \\ 0 & 99 & -13 \\ 7 & 999 & -13 \end{bmatrix},$$

how many possible dot products are there between *rows* of A and *columns* of B?

The answer is six, since each of the two A rows can go with any of the three B rows. The possibilities are:

1. [2 1 5] and [0 0 7]
2. [2 1 5] and [9 99 999]
3. [2 1 5] and [-13 - 13 - 13]
4. [0 3 - 2] and [0 0 7]
5. [0 3 - 2] and [9 99 999]
6. [0 3 - 2] and [-13 - 13 - 13]

(Note *very* carefully that we use the *columns* of B, not the rows!)

Very well. Let's compute all those dot products then:

- [2 1 5] · [0 0 7] = 35
- [2 1 5] · [9 99 999] = 5112
- [2 1 5] · [-13 - 13 - 13] = -104
- [0 3 - 2] · [0 0 7] = -14
- [0 3 - 2] · [9 99 999] = -1701
- [0 3 - 2] · [-13 - 13 - 13] = -13

Those six dot products are precisely the entries in our answer matrix:

$$\begin{bmatrix} 35 & 5112 & -104 \\ -14 & -1701 & -13 \end{bmatrix}.$$

The only thing you have to be careful of is which answer goes in which place. The rule is:

> The dot product of row i of A and column j of B goes in row i, column j of the answer.

A sensible arrangement, I think you'll agree. Multiplying row 0 with column 0 will give us the entry in row 0, column 0 of our answer. Multiplying row 14 with column 9 will give us the entry in row 14, column 9 of our answer. And so forth.

In terms of our current example, the reason that the number 5112 goes in the *top middle* of our answer (as opposed to the bottom left, or anywhere else) is that 5112 is the dot product of the *top* row of A ([2 1 5]) with the *middle* column of B ([9 99 999]). Be sure to practice with this so you don't get numbers out of place.

It might help to keep in mind possible applications here. Why would we ever want to compute "all possible dot products?" Well, think back to our matchmaker example. Let's say we have 4 women and 5 men, each of whom has completed a survey. Finding all the compatibilities – *i.e.*, predicting the dating success of all possible pairings – is precisely computing the dot product of every gal with every guy (assuming heterosexuality). That's 20 possible dot products, which we can calculate with a single matrix multiplication.

6.4 Way #3: Several linear combinations

Our third and final way to think about matrix multiplication is in terms of linear combinations. Remember (from p. 92) that every matrix-*vector* multiplication $A \cdot \vec{x}$ is essentially specifying some linear combination of A's *columns*. If we multiply A by the vector $\begin{bmatrix} 3 \\ 5 \end{bmatrix}$, we're saying "I'd like 3 copies of A's first column, plus 5 copies of its second column, please."

Matrix multiplication is simply asking for several *different* linear combinations. If we multiply a matrix A by this one:

$$\begin{bmatrix} 0 & 9 & -13 \\ 0 & 99 & -13 \\ 7 & 999 & -13 \end{bmatrix},$$

we're requesting the following:

> "Hello, I'd like to put in an order for three things. First, I'd like 7 copies of A's third column (ignore the first two). Additionally, I'd like 9 copies of its first column, 99 copies of its second column, and 999 copies of its third column, all added together. Finally, please give me −13 copies of each of its columns, again added together. Thanks! You should have my credit card number on file."

To fulfill this order, we compute each of the three linear combinations requested. Using the same A matrix we've been using ($\begin{bmatrix} 2 & 1 & 5 \\ 0 & 3 & -2 \end{bmatrix}$) this amounts to:

$$\text{First combination: } 7\begin{bmatrix} 5 \\ -2 \end{bmatrix} = \begin{bmatrix} 35 \\ -14 \end{bmatrix}$$

$$\text{Second combination: } 9\begin{bmatrix} 2 \\ 0 \end{bmatrix} + 99\begin{bmatrix} 1 \\ 3 \end{bmatrix} + 999\begin{bmatrix} 5 \\ -2 \end{bmatrix} = \begin{bmatrix} 5112 \\ -1701 \end{bmatrix}$$

$$\text{Third combination: } -13\begin{bmatrix} 2 \\ 0 \end{bmatrix} - 13\begin{bmatrix} 1 \\ 3 \end{bmatrix} - 13\begin{bmatrix} 5 \\ -2 \end{bmatrix} = \begin{bmatrix} -104 \\ -13 \end{bmatrix}$$

Packaging up all those results again gives us:

$$\begin{bmatrix} 35 & 5112 & -104 \\ -14 & -1701 & -13 \end{bmatrix}.$$

Same answer no matter which of the three ways we think about it.

6.5 Outer and inner products

All right. Now for some surprises.

Remember (p. 88) that we will sometimes want to treat a vector as a sort of degenerate matrix: a matrix with only one row, or only one column. And we will sometimes want to do this matrix multiplication thing with two vectors, treating one of them as a row vector and the other as a column vector. Which one is which makes a tremendous difference.

As an illustration, I'm going to define vectors $\vec{x}$ and $\vec{y}$ this way:

$$\vec{x} = \begin{bmatrix} 3 & 1 & 2 \end{bmatrix}, \quad \vec{y} = \begin{bmatrix} 5 \\ 4 \\ -3 \end{bmatrix}.$$

So $\vec{x}$ is a row vector, and $\vec{y}$ is a column vector. Put another way, $\vec{x}$ can be thought of as a 1×3 matrix, and $\vec{y}$ as a 3×1 matrix.

Now if we do treat these as matrices, then performing the operation $\vec{x} \cdot \vec{y}$ gives us:

$$\vec{x} \cdot \vec{y} = \begin{bmatrix} 3 & 1 & 2 \end{bmatrix} \cdot \begin{bmatrix} 5 \\ 4 \\ -3 \end{bmatrix} = 13.$$

It's just the dot product, of course, calculated in the usual way.

Now suppose I swap the order, and compute $\vec{y}$ times $\vec{x}$ instead. What would I get? The answer will surely surprise you:

$$\vec{y} \cdot \vec{x} = \begin{bmatrix} 5 \\ 4 \\ -3 \end{bmatrix} \cdot \begin{bmatrix} 3 & 1 & 2 \end{bmatrix} = \begin{bmatrix} 15 & 5 & 10 \\ 12 & 4 & 8 \\ -9 & -3 & -6 \end{bmatrix}.$$

Hooooooo...wut?! $\vec{x}$ times $\vec{y}$ is the *number* 13, but $\vec{y}$ times $\vec{x}$ is an entire *grid* full of numbers?

Yes it is. Here's why.

Remember our rules from p. 144. First, we can only multiply two matrices if $n = p$. And that's true here whether we do $\vec{x} \cdot \vec{y}$ or $\vec{y} \cdot \vec{x}$. But the second rule tells us that the answer will be a $m \times q$ matrix. If we put $\vec{x}$ on the left, then $\vec{x} \cdot \vec{y}$ will give us a 1×1 matrix. But if we put $\vec{y}$ on the left, then $\vec{y} \cdot \vec{x}$ must give us a 3×3 matrix. Strange but true.

Btw, when we do the first thing – treat the vector on the left-hand side of the multiplication as a row vector, and the other as a column vector – it's called the **inner product** of the two vectors. The other way is called the **outer product**.

6.6 $A \cdot A^\mathsf{T}$ vs. $A^\mathsf{T} \cdot A$

Here's another interesting consequence of our operation. As we've seen, you certainly can't multiply a matrix A by just "any old thing," since rule 1 on p. 144 says that n must equal p.

You can, however, *always* perform the operation $A \cdot A^\mathsf{T}$, no matter what dimensions A is. That's because if A is, say, 17×28, then A^T will be 28×17, and $n = p$ (both are 28) as required. You'll get a 17×17 matrix if you do that.

You also can *always* perform the operation $A^\mathsf{T} \cdot A$. Again, if A is 17×28, then A^T will be 28×17, and so again $n = p$ (both are 17). You'll get a 28×28 matrix if you do that.

Here's an example, smaller so it fits on the page. Let's say A is

$$\begin{bmatrix} 2 & 20 & 3 & -2 & -4 \\ -5 & 1 & 4 & 1 & 9 \end{bmatrix}.$$

The two operations give us:

$$A \cdot A^\mathsf{T} = \begin{bmatrix} 2 & 20 & 3 & -2 & -4 \\ -5 & 1 & 4 & 1 & 9 \end{bmatrix} \cdot \begin{bmatrix} 2 & -5 \\ 20 & 1 \\ 3 & 4 \\ -2 & 1 \\ -4 & 9 \end{bmatrix} = \begin{bmatrix} 433 & -16 \\ -16 & 124 \end{bmatrix},$$

6.6. $A \cdot A^\mathsf{T}$ VS. $A^\mathsf{T} \cdot A$

and

$$A^\mathsf{T} \cdot A = \begin{bmatrix} 2 & -5 \\ 20 & 1 \\ 3 & 4 \\ -2 & 1 \\ -4 & 9 \end{bmatrix} \cdot \begin{bmatrix} 2 & 20 & 3 & -2 & -4 \\ -5 & 1 & 4 & 1 & 9 \end{bmatrix} =$$

$$\begin{bmatrix} 29 & 35 & -14 & -9 & -53 \\ 35 & 401 & 64 & -39 & -71 \\ -14 & 64 & 25 & -2 & 24 \\ -9 & -39 & -2 & 5 & 17 \\ -53 & -71 & 24 & 17 & 97 \end{bmatrix}.$$

Two other intriguing facts are worth noting here, one of which you may have noticed. If you run your eyeballs carefully over those two results, you'll see that both of them are **symmetric matrices**. This is always true of a matrix times its transpose, and that turns out to be important for some applications.

The other fact – certainly not ascertainable to my eyeballs, at least – is that both of these matrices have only *rank 2*. That's not surprising about $A \cdot A^\mathsf{T}$, since it's just a 2×2 anyway. But it is very surprising about $A^\mathsf{T} \cdot A$. That's a 5×5 matrix with only *two* linearly independent columns!

And this is always true. When you multiply a matrix by its transpose, either way you do it, the rank will only be the *lower* of the two dimensions.

The way I think of it is this. When you take a tall matrix (like our 5×2, above) and multiply it by a wide one (the 2×5), yes you're going to get a result with large dimensions. Sure. But in a way, you only put "two columns' worth" of information into the operation. The result is a large 5×5, but that's misleading, because there just isn't enough information present in those 25 entries to represent five independent directions. The 5×5 result is brittle, containing only two columns' worth of information spread out over a large landscape. It's almost as if I wrote a fourteen-sentence paragraph with only three sentences repeated again and again, with the words rescrambled a bit each time. Sure, it looks like a long paragraph at first glance, but try reading it and you'll recognize how little information it really contains.

6.7 Associative, but not commutative

The next surprising thing I'll point out is that matrix multiplication does *not* follow one of the laws of plain-Jane multiplication that you're used to counting on. Namely, matrix multiplication is *not* commutative.

You're so accustomed to this being true that it's positively jarring. Ever since Mrs. Jones taught you in second grade, you've safely relied on the fact that:

$$115 \cdot 272 = 272 \cdot 115.$$

It might be a pain to work out the answer, but at least you've know without even thinking that it doesn't matter which order you do the multiplication in.

But *oh!* this totally does not work with matrix multiplication. Taking two matrices at random:

$$A = \begin{bmatrix} 4 & 2 \\ 2 & 3 \end{bmatrix}, B = \begin{bmatrix} 1 & -1 \\ 2 & 0 \end{bmatrix}$$

$$A \cdot B = \begin{bmatrix} 8 & -4 \\ 8 & -2 \end{bmatrix},$$

$$B \cdot A = \begin{bmatrix} 2 & -1 \\ 8 & 4 \end{bmatrix} \text{ surprise!}$$

Not even close to the same thing. And in general, matters are even worse because you normally can't even *do* the operation both ways! (If A were a 2×4, for example, and B a 4×3, then $A \cdot B$ would give you a 2×3 matrix but $B \cdot A$ is impossible.) You actually have

6.7. ASSOCIATIVE, BUT NOT COMMUTATIVE

to really work at it to come up with two matrices whose product is the same both ways.

Nothing much to say here except to stay on your toes.

Another "given," however, *is* true of matrices, and a good thing, too. That's the **associative** property. This means that if you're multiplying together a string of matrices, it doesn't matter which multiplication you perform first. In other words, for any three matrices A, B, and C:

$$(A \cdot B) \cdot C = A \cdot (B \cdot C).$$

Again, an example to illustrate:

$$A = \begin{bmatrix} 4 & 2 \\ 2 & 3 \end{bmatrix}, B = \begin{bmatrix} 1 & -1 \\ 2 & 0 \end{bmatrix}, C = \begin{bmatrix} 3 & 4 \\ 1 & 5 \end{bmatrix}$$

$$(A \cdot B) \cdot C = \begin{bmatrix} 8 & -4 \\ 8 & -2 \end{bmatrix} \cdot \begin{bmatrix} 3 & 4 \\ 1 & 5 \end{bmatrix} = \begin{bmatrix} 20 & 12 \\ 22 & 22 \end{bmatrix},$$

$$A \cdot (B \cdot C) = \begin{bmatrix} 4 & 2 \\ 2 & 3 \end{bmatrix} \cdot \begin{bmatrix} 2 & -1 \\ 6 & 8 \end{bmatrix} = \begin{bmatrix} 20 & 12 \\ 22 & 22 \end{bmatrix}. \checkmark$$

And this always works.

One reason this is nice has to do with linear operators. Recall from section 5.2 (pp. 117–125) that we can create operators to scale, flip, and rotate points in the Cartesian plane. To review:

$\begin{bmatrix} 2 & 0 \\ 0 & 2 \end{bmatrix}$ stretch points twice as far from the origin

$\begin{bmatrix} .866 & -.5 \\ .5 & .866 \end{bmatrix}$ rotate points 30° counterclockwise

$\begin{bmatrix} -1 & 0 \\ 0 & 1 \end{bmatrix}$ flip points horizontally across the y-axis

Multiplying any of these matrices by a vector has the desired effect.

Now suppose we wanted to perform *several* of these operations on a vector. For example, take a random point $(8.5, 19)$. To stretch, rotate, *and* flip it, we'd do this:

$$\begin{bmatrix} 2 & 0 \\ 0 & 2 \end{bmatrix} \cdot \begin{bmatrix} .866 & -.5 \\ .5 & .866 \end{bmatrix} \cdot \begin{bmatrix} -1 & 0 \\ 0 & 1 \end{bmatrix} \cdot \begin{bmatrix} 8.5 \\ 19 \end{bmatrix}.$$

This works out to $\begin{bmatrix} -33.722 \\ 24.408 \end{bmatrix}$ if you're keeping score at home.

Now often instead of transforming a single point, we want to transform an entire image, which contains multiple points. Imagine calculating every pixel of Bowser as his Kart trips over a green shell and spins towards the side of the screen. We can take advantage of the associativity of matrix multiplication to pre-compute a *single* matrix that will stretch/flip/rotate/squish/whatever any point we care to multiply it by:

$$T = \begin{bmatrix} 2 & 0 \\ 0 & 2 \end{bmatrix} \cdot \begin{bmatrix} .866 & -.5 \\ .5 & .866 \end{bmatrix} \cdot \begin{bmatrix} -1 & 0 \\ 0 & 1 \end{bmatrix} = \begin{bmatrix} -1.732 & -1 \\ -1 & 1.732 \end{bmatrix}.$$

This makes our game engine run a lot faster, since we don't have to do all those calculations separately for every point in the image. Instead, we calculate our T matrix (for **t**ransformation) just once, and then multiply it by every point.

In fact, if we have all of Bowser's pixels in a 2×1000 matrix:

$$B = \begin{bmatrix} 18 & 19 & 22 & 32 & 34 & \cdots & 195 \\ 9 & 9 & 11 & 14 & 19 & \cdots & 212 \end{bmatrix},$$

then we can compute what pixels to draw in the next frame with just one operation: $T \cdot B$!

$$B_{\text{next}} = T \cdot B = \begin{bmatrix} -1.732 & -1 \\ -1 & 1.732 \end{bmatrix} \cdot \begin{bmatrix} 18 & 19 & 22 & 32 & 34 & \cdots & 195 \\ 9 & 9 & 11 & 14 & 19 & \cdots & 212 \end{bmatrix}.$$

You gotta admit, that's pretty neat.

6.8 The "identity" matrix

Remember back on p. 98 how we defined "identity matrices?" They looked like this:

$$\begin{bmatrix} 1 & 0 & 0 \\ 0 & 1 & 0 \\ 0 & 0 & 1 \end{bmatrix}$$

They could be any size, but they were always square, and they always had 1's on the diagonal and 0's everywhere else.

I promised to tell you why this kind of matrix was called an "identity" matrix, and now's the time. It's simply because when you multiply it by any matrix, you get that same matrix back. Let's try it:

$$\begin{bmatrix} 1 & 0 & 0 \\ 0 & 1 & 0 \\ 0 & 0 & 1 \end{bmatrix} \cdot \begin{bmatrix} 7 & 7 & 9 & 4 \\ -10 & -5 & 5 & 3 \\ 17 & 16 & 14 & 13 \end{bmatrix} = \begin{bmatrix} 7 & 7 & 9 & 4 \\ -10 & -5 & 5 & 3 \\ 17 & 16 & 14 & 13 \end{bmatrix}.$$

Yep, it works. And you can put the identity matrix on either the left side or the right of the multiplication, and it still works.

Because of this property, the identity matrix plays the same role as the number zero in addition (0 plus any number is that same number) and the number one in multiplication (1 times any number is that same number). Those numbers are called the "identity elements" for those operations, since you get the "identical" number back when you use them. Same reasoning here.

6.9 The "inverse" of a matrix

In high school (or maybe middle school) you learned what the **reciprocal** of a number was: namely, the number that you had to multiply it by to get 1. So the reciprocal of 3 was $\frac{1}{3}$, since $3 \cdot \frac{1}{3} = 1$. Similarly, the reciprocal of $-\frac{1}{5}$ was -5 and the reciprocal of $-\frac{\pi}{8}$ was $-\frac{8}{\pi}$. Easy.

Another name for the reciprocal of a number, by the way, is the "multiplicative **inverse**." If you want to "invert" the number 3, you use $\frac{1}{3}$; this sends 3 back to 1, which the identity element for multiplication. (Similarly, the "*additive* inverse" of 3 is -3, since if you're *adding* instead of multiplying, that's the number you use to send 3 back to 0, which is the identity element for addition.)

Now how do you think this concept would apply to *matrix* multiplication? I give you a square matrix A, and I ask you to find its "reciprocal" – that is, its **inverse**. The answer I'm looking for is *the matrix you'd multiply by A to get the identity matrix*. Ooo, deep.

Now there are many differently-sized identity matrices, but you can probably guess that I'm referring to the one of the same dimensions as A. In other words, if I give you:

$$A = \begin{bmatrix} 5 & 6 & 7 \\ 2 & 1 & 2 \\ 9 & 8 & -2 \end{bmatrix},$$

I'm asking for the matrix that we can multiply by A and get:

$$\begin{bmatrix} 1 & 0 & 0 \\ 0 & 1 & 0 \\ 0 & 0 & 1 \end{bmatrix},$$

since that one's the right size.

Incidentally, the notation we use for A's inverse is not $\frac{1}{A}$, as you might expect, but A^{-1}. It's pronounced "A inverse."

Now it's not at all obvious that (1) there even *is* an inverse matrix for A, nor that (2) there's only *one* inverse matrix for A. And in fact we'll see in the next section that sometimes there is no inverse for a matrix A (although there's never more than one, as it happens). But usually there is exactly one, as it turns out. And that will be good news.

Why good news? Why do we care?

6.9. THE "INVERSE" OF A MATRIX

Simultaneous equations

There are several important reasons why we care, as it happens. In this section I'm going to talk about only one of them, and it'll seem at first as if I've veered off-topic into something that has nothing to do with linear algebra at all. But stay with me.

From your pre-college days, you undoubtedly remember solving **simultaneous equations**. For example, faced with this:

$$2x - 3y = 1$$
$$3x + y = 7,$$

you could use a variety of different techniques to work out that $x = 2$ and $y = 1$. For me, the least hateful way of solving those problems was to use substitution: get one variable in terms of the other (like fiddling with that first equation to get $x = \frac{1+3y}{2}$, then plugging $\frac{1+3y}{2}$ in for x in the second equation). But you may have done the thing where you multiply one of the entire equations by some number and add it to the other one, or maybe you learned yet another way. As long as you don't screw up any of your math, you'll get the same answer regardless of technique.

The reason these are called "simultaneous equations," by the way, is that you're looking for values of x and y that *simultaneously* make both equations true. It's easy to just eyeball it and find an x and a y that make just one of the equations true. But getting values that satisfy both equations simultaneously is the trick.

You may have done more than just "two equations, two unknowns" in high school, like this problem that has three of each:

$$6x + 2y - 4z = -4$$
$$x + y + 2z = 8$$
$$2x - 2y + 8z = 4.$$

(*Shudder*) With enough laborious steps, and enough caffeine, you'll manage to crank out the correct answer which is $x = -1$, $y = 5$, $z = 2$.

It probably won't surprise you to learn that it's also possible to solve five equations in five unknowns, or a hundred equations in a hundred unknowns, *etc.* It may surprise you to learn that there are situations where we actually need to *do* that, because the equations stand for real relationships between real quantities and solving simultaneous equations is how we figure out the real values.

Luckily for the human race, all that error-prone algebraic manipulation required to solve a hundred simultaneous equations this way (or even a few thousand) is utterly unnecessary. Matrices come brilliantly to our rescue.

Let me recast the first problem above,

$$2x - 3y = 1 \tag{6.1}$$
$$3x + y = 7, \tag{6.2}$$

in the following way:

$$\begin{bmatrix} 2 & -3 \\ 3 & 1 \end{bmatrix} \cdot \begin{bmatrix} x \\ y \end{bmatrix} = \begin{bmatrix} 1 \\ 7 \end{bmatrix}. \tag{6.3}$$

Whoa. Sudden leap from high school back to college. But do you see the connection? Stare hard at the matrices in equation 6.3 and compare them with the original equations 6.1 and 6.2. You'll realize that the matrix entries are the *coefficients* of the equations, and the right-most vector has the values from the equations' right-hand-sides.

A light bulb will go on for you as soon as you realize that the matrix equation is *exactly the same* as the two ordinary equations! That's because when we do matrix-vector multiplication, we do two separate things: (1) take the dot product of the top matrix row and the $\begin{bmatrix} x \\ y \end{bmatrix}$ vector, and (2) take the dot product of the *bottom* matrix row and the $\begin{bmatrix} x \\ y \end{bmatrix}$ vector. When we do this, we get:

$$\begin{bmatrix} 2x - 3y \\ 3x + 1 \end{bmatrix} = \begin{bmatrix} 1 \\ 7 \end{bmatrix}.$$

6.9. THE "INVERSE" OF A MATRIX

This is just another way of saying *exactly* the same thing that 6.1 and 6.2 do.

Okay, so why is this important? Here's why. Suppose we could find the *inverse* of the left matrix in equation 6.3. We'll call it A^{-1}. Now if we multiply both sides of that equation by A^{-1} we'd get:

$$A^{-1} \cdot \begin{bmatrix} 2 & -3 \\ 3 & 1 \end{bmatrix} \cdot \begin{bmatrix} x \\ y \end{bmatrix} = A^{-1} \cdot \begin{bmatrix} 1 \\ 7 \end{bmatrix}$$

$$\begin{bmatrix} 1 & 0 \\ 0 & 1 \end{bmatrix} \cdot \begin{bmatrix} x \\ y \end{bmatrix} = A^{-1} \cdot \begin{bmatrix} 1 \\ 7 \end{bmatrix}$$

$$\begin{bmatrix} x \\ y \end{bmatrix} = A^{-1} \cdot \begin{bmatrix} 1 \\ 7 \end{bmatrix}$$

See how that works? Multiplying the matrix by its inverse makes it disappear entirely from the left-hand side. That's because a matrix times its inverse is the identity matrix, and the identity matrix times any vector is just that vector. So we've reduced the problem of solving these simultaneous equations the high school way to just (1) finding A's inverse and (2) multiplying it by our $\begin{bmatrix} 1 \\ 7 \end{bmatrix}$ vector.

Great, so how do we compute A^{-1}? Answer: ask a computer. Any programming language worth its salt (including Python) can figure it out lickety-split with one line of code. Here, I'm just going to tell you the answer I got, and see if you can verify it:

$$\text{Stephen asserts that } A^{-1} = \begin{bmatrix} \frac{1}{11} & \frac{3}{11} \\ -\frac{3}{11} & \frac{2}{11} \end{bmatrix}.$$

Crazy, right? Yeah. Let's multiply it out to be sure:

$$A \cdot A^{-1} = \begin{bmatrix} 2 & -3 \\ 3 & 1 \end{bmatrix} \cdot \begin{bmatrix} \frac{1}{11} & \frac{3}{11} \\ -\frac{3}{11} & \frac{2}{11} \end{bmatrix} =$$

$$\begin{bmatrix} 2 \cdot \frac{1}{11} - 3 \cdot (-\frac{3}{11}) & 2 \cdot \frac{3}{11} - 3 \cdot \frac{2}{11} \\ 3 \cdot \frac{1}{11} + 1 \cdot (-\frac{3}{11}) & 3 \cdot \frac{3}{11} + 1 \cdot \frac{2}{11} \end{bmatrix} = \begin{bmatrix} 1 & 0 \\ 0 & 1 \end{bmatrix} \checkmark$$

Remarkable. Our answer to the simultaneous equations, then, is:

$$\begin{bmatrix} x \\ y \end{bmatrix} = \begin{bmatrix} \frac{1}{11} & \frac{3}{11} \\ -\frac{3}{11} & \frac{2}{11} \end{bmatrix} \cdot \begin{bmatrix} 1 \\ 7 \end{bmatrix} = \begin{bmatrix} 2 \\ 1 \end{bmatrix}.$$

So we confirm that $x = 2$ and $y = 1$, just as whatever hellacious algebra you used on p. 159 told you.

The deal is, this approach is scalable to any number of equations and unknowns you like, with no algebraic manipulation required. As long as you have a programming language to compute the inverse for you, you can crank out your answer in no time. Here's the answer to the three-equation example I showed earlier:

$$6x + 2y - 4z = -4$$
$$x + y + 2z = 8$$
$$2x - 2y + 8z = 4,$$

so

$$\begin{bmatrix} 6 & 2 & -4 \\ 1 & 1 & 2 \\ 2 & -2 & 8 \end{bmatrix} \cdot \begin{bmatrix} x \\ y \\ z \end{bmatrix} = \begin{bmatrix} -4 \\ 8 \\ 4 \end{bmatrix}.$$

Ask Python, "what's the inverse of $\begin{bmatrix} 6 & 2 & -4 \\ 1 & 1 & 2 \\ 2 & -2 & 8 \end{bmatrix}$?"

Python replies: "$\begin{bmatrix} \frac{3}{20} & -\frac{1}{10} & \frac{1}{10} \\ -\frac{1}{20} & \frac{7}{10} & -\frac{1}{5} \\ -\frac{1}{20} & \frac{1}{5} & \frac{1}{20} \end{bmatrix}$!"

Therefore: $\begin{bmatrix} x \\ y \\ z \end{bmatrix} = \begin{bmatrix} \frac{3}{20} & -\frac{1}{10} & \frac{1}{10} \\ -\frac{1}{20} & \frac{7}{10} & -\frac{1}{5} \\ -\frac{1}{20} & \frac{1}{5} & \frac{1}{20} \end{bmatrix} \cdot \begin{bmatrix} -4 \\ 8 \\ 4 \end{bmatrix} = \begin{bmatrix} -1 \\ 5 \\ 2 \end{bmatrix}.$

Problem solved.

6.10 An amazing (and useful) fact

Recall our friends the "ortho**gonal** matrices" from p. 101. (And remember that Stephen thought they should be named "ortho**normal** matrices" instead, but that he was not yet – and still isn't – King of the World.) An orthogonal matrix is one whose columns are all orthogonal to each other, and all have a norm of 1.

Now here's an incredible fact about orthogonal matrices which blew my mind when I first heard it. If O is an orthogonal matrix, then *its inverse is the same as its transpose*; namely, $O^\mathsf{T} = O^{-1}$.

What?!

This is astounding. When we learned the *transpose* operation on p. 88, it was so simple a kindergartner could do it. All you do is turn the matrix on its side: the rows become the columns and the columns become the rows. It's trivial.

But the *inverse* operation is a horse of an entirely different color. It's messy enough that I haven't even told you how to calculate it: I've just said, "ask Python." And when you looked at the inverses of some pretty simple matrices (like on the previous page), you probably thought "smh, how did Python ever come up with *that?*"

So it's truly astonishing that a quick and painless operation like transpose could ever coincide with a gnarly and perplexing one like inverse. But they do, if the matrix is orthogonal. And you can see why, if you think about matrix multiplication in "Way #2" (p. 147).

Suppose I take the transpose of a matrix O and multiply that by O itself. So I'm computing $O^\mathsf{T} \cdot O$. Then, I'll get *every column of O dot-product-ed with every column of O*. See how that works? Taking the transpose of the matrix on the left-hand side flips the rows and columns. So when we take the dot product of the first row of O^T with the first column of O, we're really doing the dot product of O^T's first column *with itself*. And when we multiply the first row of O^T by the *second* column of O, we're really multiplying the first column of O by the second column of O. And so forth. Every entry in our final $O^\mathsf{T} \cdot O$ answer will be the result of multiplying some column of O by some other column of O.

Now consider what we know about orthogonal matrices:

- If O is orthogonal, then each of its columns has a norm of 1. That means that multiplying any column of O by itself will give a dot product of 1. (If you have trouble seeing this, you might peek back to p. 36 where we thought about the dot product in terms of the cosine of the angle between vectors. A vector times itself has an angle θ of 0, of course, and so $\cos 0 = 1$. If the vector itself is already of length 1, then $1 \cdot 1 = 1$, duh.)

- If O is orthogonal, then each of its columns is orthogonal to all the others. Which in turn means that each column has a *zero* dot product with any of the others.

So if O is a 3 × 3, say, computing $O^\mathsf{T} \cdot O$ gives us this:

$$O^\mathsf{T} \cdot O =$$

$$\begin{bmatrix} \text{column 1} \cdot \text{column 1} & \text{column 1} \cdot \text{column 2} & \text{column 1} \cdot \text{column 3} \\ \text{column 2} \cdot \text{column 1} & \text{column 2} \cdot \text{column 2} & \text{column 2} \cdot \text{column 3} \\ \text{column 3} \cdot \text{column 1} & \text{column 3} \cdot \text{column 2} & \text{column 3} \cdot \text{column 3} \end{bmatrix}$$

$$= \begin{bmatrix} 1 & 0 & 0 \\ 0 & 1 & 0 \\ 0 & 0 & 1 \end{bmatrix} \quad !$$

Look at that! Multiplying O times its transpose gave us *the identity matrix*. And that, of course, is the definition of "inverse": "the matrix you can multiply by to get the identity matrix." And so we've just proven that for orthogonal matrices, the inverse is the same as the transpose.

This will save us a lot of work in the future, when working with **orthonormal bases**, which have an interesting connection to symmetric matrices that we'll see. So file this useful tip away.

6.11 Change-of-basis matrices (*from* standard)

I left you hanging back on p. 95 when we converted Ron's $\vec{r}$ vector from the "domino basis" to the standard basis, but couldn't go in the reverse direction with Hermione's $\vec{h}$ vector. Now we can.

You can probably guess how to do this: all we have to do is compute the *inverse* of the $COB_{B_d \to B_s}$ change-of-basis matrix, and we'll get the corresponding $COB_{B_s \to B_d}$ change-of-basis matrix.

$$\text{Hey Python, "what's the inverse of } \begin{bmatrix} 1 & 4 \\ 2 & 4 \end{bmatrix}?"$$

$$\text{Python replies: } "\begin{bmatrix} -1 & 1 \\ \frac{1}{2} & -\frac{1}{4} \end{bmatrix}!"$$

So:

$$COB_{B_s \to B_d} = \begin{bmatrix} -1 & 1 \\ \frac{1}{2} & -\frac{1}{4} \end{bmatrix},$$

and since Hermione was $\begin{bmatrix} 5 \\ 2 \end{bmatrix}$ in standard coordinates, we convert her to the domino basis as follows:

$$\vec{h}_{B_d} = \begin{bmatrix} -1 & 1 \\ \frac{1}{2} & -\frac{1}{4} \end{bmatrix} \cdot \vec{h}_{B_s} = \begin{bmatrix} -1 & 1 \\ \frac{1}{2} & -\frac{1}{4} \end{bmatrix} \cdot \begin{bmatrix} 5 \\ 2 \end{bmatrix}_{B_s} = \begin{bmatrix} -3 \\ 2 \end{bmatrix}_{B_d}.$$

This means that Hermione, in addition to being expressible as "five $\begin{bmatrix} 1 \\ 0 \end{bmatrix}$'s and two $\begin{bmatrix} 0 \\ 1 \end{bmatrix}$'s," is equally expressible as "negative three $\begin{bmatrix} 1 \\ 2 \end{bmatrix}$'s and two $\begin{bmatrix} 4 \\ 4 \end{bmatrix}$'s." Multiply it out if you doubt me.

6.12 "Singular" matrices

All right. Time for the last concept in what has been a hefty chapter.

Rewind for a moment and think about reciprocals of ordinary numbers again. The reciprocal of 4 is $\frac{1}{4}$, the reciprocal of $-\frac{3}{7}$ is $-\frac{7}{3}$, yadda yadda. A number's reciprocal is simply the number you can multiply it by to get 1.

No matter what the number is, you can get its reciprocal just by taking "one over" it. Right?

Almost right. But there's one number for which that doesn't work. And that's the number zero. Quick: what can you multiply *zero* by and get 1? Answer: nothing. It's the one and only number that has no multiplicative inverse.

Now we've been drawing this parallel between regular old numbers and square matrices. The analog of "reciprocal" in Numbers Land is "matrix inverse" in Linear Algebra Land. So what's the analog to the number zero, then?

The answer is a **singular matrix.** "Singular" is a word I mostly associate with Sir Arthur Conan Doyle's original Sherlock Holmes mysteries: Holmes was always saying, "what a singular discovery, Watson!" That word struck me as so odd in Doyle's short stories that I had to look it up. Turns out, it basically means "incredibly weird, so much so that it's practically one-of-a-kind."[1]

Very well, then: a "singular matrix" is essentially a "weird matrix." But what does that mean? Simply this: *it has no inverse.* Just like the number zero, you can't take the reciprocal of it.

A few observations about this. First of all, as in Number Land, the "normal case" is for a matrix to *not* be singular. If you pick a number at random, the odds are incredibly high that it *will* have a reciprocal. The only way to get unlucky is to draw the number 0 exactly. Similarly, if you pick a matrix at random, it will almost

---

[1] The word singular is *not* a synonym for the word "single," as many a college student has mistakenly supposed.

6.12. "SINGULAR" MATRICES

certainly not be a singular one.

However, unlike in Number Land, there's not just *one* singular matrix, either. And there's not just one of each size, either. In fact, for any size you like (say, 4 × 4) there are infinitely many different singular matrices. It might seem like a contradiction to say "there are infinitely many of them, yet there's a very low probability you'll get one at random," but it's really not. It's no more of a contradiction than saying "there are infinitely many integers, but if you choose a real number at random there's a very low probability it'll be an integer."[2]

Now by this point, a question might have occurred to you. Above, I outlined a very simple procedure for solving simultaneous equations: convert the equations to an equivalent matrix, take the inverse of it, and multiply it by the constants on the right-hand side. But what if it's a singular matrix, you ask? How then can we find the solution?

The important answer is: *you can't*. And this isn't because the linear algebra shortcut broke down. It's because a singular matrix implies that *there is no solution*.

Here's an example. Suppose I gave you these two simultaneous equations:

$$2x + 3y = 8$$
$$4x + 6y = 11.$$

At first glance, nothing looks out of the ordinary. But look closer and you'll see the fatal flaw. The first equation says "$2x + 3y$ equals something." The second one says "$4x + 6y$ equals something else." But wait a minute! No matter what the right-hand sides may say, $4x + 6y$ has to be *exactly double* what $2x + 3y$ is. (Think about it: multiply $2x+3y$ by 2 and you get $4x+6y$.) So if $2x+3y$ is 8 – as the first equation claims – then $4x + 6y$ *has* to be 16. It can't possibly be 11 or anything else, or the wheels would fall off the universe.

---

[2]This is really the same sort of difference as "countably infinite" vs. "uncountably infinite" sets that I alluded to in Chapter 2 of *Cool Brisk Walk*.

You'll notice that if you try to solve this using your high school tools, you will also fall into a pit:

$2x = 8 - 3y$ (subtract $3y$ from both sides of 1st equation)

$x = \dfrac{8 - 3y}{2}$ (divide both sides by 2)

$4(\dfrac{8-3y}{2}) + 6y = 11$ (plug expression for x into 2nd equation)

$2(8 - 3y) + 6y = 11$ (divide 4 by 2)

$16 - 6y + 6y = 11$ (multiply out the 2)

$16 = 11$??!

Don't worry, 16 doesn't really equal 11. We just tried to solve two equations which were mutually contradictory, and it predictably produced nonsense.

In Linear Algebra Land, the above equations correspond to this:

$$\begin{bmatrix} 2 & 3 \\ 4 & 6 \end{bmatrix} \cdot \begin{bmatrix} x \\ y \end{bmatrix} = \begin{bmatrix} 8 \\ 11 \end{bmatrix},$$

which of course is fatally flawed in exactly the same way. The fatal flaw is that this matrix:

$$\begin{bmatrix} 2 & 3 \\ 4 & 6 \end{bmatrix}$$

is *singular*.

Now I want you to look carefully at that matrix and make a discovery. Consider the matrix's *columns*. Does anything strike you as unusual about them?

If you can't spot the weirdness, let me redraw them this way:

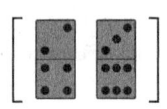

6.12. "SINGULAR" MATRICES

That's right: those columns are *blue dominoes*.

It turns out that the definition of **singular** is *a matrix in which the columns are not linearly independent.* Such a matrix is "broken" in exactly the same way that blue dominoes are broken: its columns don't each branch out in a brand new direction, and so no matter what linear combination of them you try to take, you can't reach most points.

If you think about it, that's exactly what we're trying to do here. The above matrix equation is essentially saying "find me a linear combination of $\begin{bmatrix} 2 \\ 4 \end{bmatrix}$ and $\begin{bmatrix} 3 \\ 6 \end{bmatrix}$ that will land me at the point $\begin{bmatrix} 8 \\ 11 \end{bmatrix}$." But there is no such linear combination. I can't take x copies of the first vector and y copies of the second and get to $\begin{bmatrix} 8 \\ 11 \end{bmatrix}$, because those vectors point in the same dog-gone direction.

By the way, it might have occurred to you that it's possible to get extremely lucky. If we tweak the second of our equations ever so slightly:

$$2x + 3y = 8$$
$$4x + 6y = \mathbf{16},$$

then suddenly it's not only possible to get *a* solution, but *zillions* of different solutions. All of these work:

$x = 1$	$x = 4$	$x = -2$	$x = 3$	$x = 16$	...
and	and	and	and	and	and
$y = 2$	$y = 0$	$y = 4$	$y = \frac{2}{3}$	$y = -8$	...

That's because any pair of numbers that work in the first equation are automatically going to also work in the second. So it's not quite correct to say "a singular matrix means there are no solutions," since in very rare cases it can instead mean *"too many* solutions."

Lastly, let's complete the connection from section 5.7 (p. 133). You'll recall that if a square matrix is full-rank, then its linear transformation will be both injective and surjective (and hence, bijective). Every input vector will be mapped to its *own* output vector (not sharing that output with any other input vector), and every possible output vector will have an input that maps to it.

This is precisely true for *non-singular* matrices. And here's why: only non-singular matrices have inverses. A bijective function is reversible: not only is there a unique output for every input, but there's a unique input for every output. And so it makes sense that there would be an inverse matrix that "undoes" the mapping from input to output. Singular matrices, on the other hand, do not correspond to bijective transformations at all. Many inputs will map to the same output, and some outputs won't have any input mapping to them at all. Thus it's perfectly expected that there be no inverse for such matrices, because the presence of an inverse implies that we can do the mapping in both directions.

6.13 The Central Dogma of square matrices

I've mentioned several times how all of these different ideas are tied together. Let me now be explicit and complete about that.

Suppose you have a square matrix A. There are two possibilities: either its columns are all linearly independent of each other, or else they aren't. Which of those two things are true puts A in one of two big categories. I'm going to call the first type of matrix a "yellow matrix" and the second type a "blue matrix," to match our definitions about the linear independence (or lack thereof) of dominoes.

6.13. THE CENTRAL DOGMA OF SQUARE MATRICES

The following things are all true for **yellow** matrices:

- A is a **non-singular** square matrix.
- A has *all linearly independent* columns (yellow dominoes).
- A is "full rank." (The rank is equal to the dimension of the matrix.)
- The kernel of A has only the zero vector in it.
- The nullity of A is 0.
- A has an **inverse** matrix, which we can call A^{-1}.
- A represents a system of equations which can be solved (and which has exactly one solution.)
- A represents a linear transformation that is bijective.

On the flip side, the following are all true for **blue** matrices:

- A is a **singular** square matrix.
- A's columns are *not* linearly independent (blue dominoes).
- A is "rank-deficient." (The rank is less than the dimension of the matrix.)
- The kernel of A has *more* than just the zero vector in it.
- The nullity of A is greater than 0.
- There is *no* inverse matrix of A.
- A represents a system of equations which either can't be solved, or which has infinitely many solutions.
- A represents a linear transformation that is neither injective nor surjective.

Either all the stuff in the first box is true, or all the stuff in the second box. There is no in between.

🐍 *Appendix: Python*

Matrix multiplication in Python is easy peasy. In fact, it's exactly the same as vector multiplication, and matrix-vector multiplication: all three operations use the same .dot() syntax. Reproducing the example on p. 155:

```
A = array([[4,2],[2,3]])
B = array([[1,-1],[2,0]])
C = array([[3,4],[1,5]])

print("A times B is:")
print(A.dot(B))
print("B times C is:")
print(B.dot(C))

print("(A times B) times C is:")
print(A.dot(B).dot(C))

print("A times (B times C) is:")
print(A.dot(B.dot(C)))
```

```
A times B is:
[[ 8 -4]
 [ 8 -2]]

B times C is:
[[ 2 -1]
 [ 6  8]]

(A times B) times C is:
[[20 12]
 [22 22]]

A times (B times C) is:
[[20 12]
 [22 22]]
```

6.13. THE CENTRAL DOGMA OF SQUARE MATRICES 173

Matrix inverse with NumPy

Many times this chapter (*e.g.*, p. 161, p. 162, p. 165) I've told you that Python can magically find the inverse of a matrix for us, and that this is so easy I'm not even going to go through how to compute it by hand. Now's the time for me to follow through on that promise. To find the inverse of a matrix, you simply call "`linalg.inv()`" and pass the matrix as an argument.

Here are the examples from this chapter:

```
amazing = array([[6,2,-4],[1,1,2],[2,-2,8]])
print(linalg.inv(amazing))
```

```
[[ 0.15 -0.1   0.1 ]
 [-0.05  0.7  -0.2 ]
 [-0.05  0.2   0.05]]
```

If that truly is the inverse of `amazing`, then we'd better be able to multiply it by `amazing` and get the identity matrix back, right?

```
print(amazing.dot(linalg.inv(amazing)))
```

```
[[ 1.00000000e+00  0.00000000e+00  5.55111512e-17]
 [ 2.77555756e-17  1.00000000e+00  1.38777878e-17]
 [ 5.55111512e-17 -2.22044605e-16  1.00000000e+00]]
```

Believe it or not, that's the right answer. At first you might cry foul that this looks very different from this:

$$\begin{bmatrix} 1 & 0 & 0 \\ 0 & 1 & 0 \\ 0 & 0 & 1 \end{bmatrix}$$

But actually it's not. Look again. The "e-16"s and "e-17"s at the end of some of the entries are Python's way of displaying **scientific notation**. "e-17" actually means "times 10^{-17}," a number which is $\frac{1}{10^{17}}$ or .00000000000000001 if you prefer. That means that when you see `5.55111512e-17` as a matrix entry, Python is really telling you that it's the number .00000000000000000555111512, which I think you'll agree is about zero. Similarly, the value `1.00000000e+00` just means 1×10^0, which equals one. So the matrix above actually *is* the identity matrix, to a very high degree of precision.[3] very close to an identity matrix.

If you try to take the inverse of a singular matrix, of course, you'll get an error (after all, you can't divide by zero no matter how pure your intentions):

```
singular = array([[2,4,6],[-1,2,9],[1,2,3]])
print(linalg.inv(singular))
```

| LinAlgError: Singular matrix

Ouch! We got told.

Finally, let me mention that if you actually want to solve a system of simultaneous equations a la p. 159, it's best to not take the inverse with `linalg.inv()` and multiply it by the vector. This is because doing so accumulates more round-off error of the type mentioned above. It turns out to be more precise (and faster besides) to use the `linalg.solve()` function for this. This function takes two arguments – the matrix of coefficients, and the vector of constants from the right-hand-sides of the equals signs – and computes the answer all in one go. Here are the answers we found earlier (on p. 162):

---

[3]This behavior happens very often with computer programs, and there's really no way around it. Every time a computer stores a number, it's really storing an approximation to that number given a certain amount of storage (in bits) that it has been given to store it. This leads to tiny round-off errors that can result in things being very very close to, but not exactly, the correct value.

6.13. THE CENTRAL DOGMA OF SQUARE MATRICES

```
twoM = array([[2,-3],[3,1]])
twoV = array([1,7])
print(linalg.solve(twoM,twoV))

threeM = array([[6,2,-4],[1,1,2],[2,-2,8]])
threeV = array([-4,8,4])
print(linalg.solve(threeM,threeV))
```

[2. 1.]

[-1. 5. 2.]

Bada. Boom.

Chapter 7

Applications

I was going to make this chapter the finale of the book, but found I just couldn't wait. This is what I love about linear algebra: not the abstract manipulation of meaningless numbers in grids, but the ways in which the whole topic of matrices applies beautifully and usefully to real-world scenarios.

This chapter doesn't begin to cover *all* the applications of linear algebra! Those are vast, and probably innumerable. But here are three of my favorites presented in capsule form so you can get a taste for why it's useful to do all this stuff.

Leslie matrices

Our first example will deal with modeling population growth in communities of organisms, whether butterflies, ferns, zombies (okay, maybe not zombies), or people. In these cases, we have a system whose properties evolve over time, and our interest is in predicting how those properties will change in the future.

L1. "Systems" and "states"

The word "**system**" is kind of vague, but really all we mean by it is some complex phenomenon whose rules of behavior are at least partly known. Examples of systems are natural habitats, economies, schools, rocket engines, and sports leagues. Each of these examples contains interacting parts that influence each other in complicated ways, and has various things about them we could measure through time.

We'll often talk about the **state** of a system, which is a pretty vague word too. You can think of a system's state as a collection of all the relevant things that characterize its situation at a moment in time. If our system is an economy, this would include things like the number of workers in different job sectors, the average wage of those workers, and the total amount of inventory in all warehouses and stores. If our system is a habitat, it would include the number of each different type of animal currently living in it, possibly together with its sex and age.

I think of a system's state as "all the things you'd have to write down and remember if you wanted to pause the system and restart it later." Think of a game. If you're playing chess, and get interrupted, you and your opponent will need to write down the current locations of all the pieces on the board, plus whose turn it is. If you're playing Monopoly, there's a whole lot more to remember: how much money every player has, who owns which properties, what board space each token is on, who has a Get Out Of Jail Free card, and whether the current player has already rolled doubles (and if so, whether once or twice).

Interestingly, we most often use a *vector* to model the current state of a system. Just imagine a vector in which the first element was the number of Monopoly dollars that player 1 has, the second through fourth elements are player 2's through 4's money, the fifth element is the space number of player 1's token, and so forth. Or, imagine an economy with five different industries, whose state is represented by a ten-dimensional vector giving the current number of workers and current demand for products in each industry.

Systems are often studied as though time marched forwards in fixed intervals. (Sometimes these are called "discrete-time systems.") Each "time step" marks the evolution from one system state to another, as a result of that amount of time elapsing. In our Monopoly example, the time step would be one player's turn: each time a player rolls and moves, the state of the system changes slightly. For the economy, we might measure it in time steps of one week, in which every industry gains or loses employees and/or inventory each week.

Starting from an initial state and working out how future states will unfold is called "simulating" the system, and a computer program that does this is called a **simulation**.

L2. The Markov property

One interesting type of system that arises – and the one we'll study here – is one in which *the state at the next time step depends only on the state at the current time step*. This is accurate for, say, the game of chess. When you're considering your move, all you need to know is the *current* state; *i.e.*, where all the pieces currently are. You don't need to know what happened in the past to get the game to the current position. Questions like "how did the black queen *get* to square e7, anyway?" and "which piece was the one that captured the missing white knight?" are irrelevant.

A system whose next state depends only on its current state is said to have the **Markov property**, a term we will revisit in Chapter 9.

L3. The bunny rabbit state vector

Let's say we'd like to study a local population of bunny rabbits. For reasons that will become clear later, we're only going to count *female* rabbits. We'll make our time step be one year, and say that in each year, there are some number of baby girl rabbits (0 years old), some number of 1-year-old girl rabbits, some number of 2-year-old girl rabbits, and some number of 3-year-old girl rabbits. To keep things manageable, we'll also say that the maximum lifespan of a rabbit is 3 years, after which all rabbits go to heaven.

Thus our state vector will be a four-dimensional vector of four numbers: namely, the total population of female rabbits of each of the four ages. Perhaps at "time 0" (the current year, say) our state vector is:

$$\overrightarrow{\text{pop}_0} = \begin{bmatrix} 67 \\ 115 \\ 23 \\ 5 \end{bmatrix}$$

This indicates that when we begin our study, there are 67 baby rabbits, 115 one-year-olds, 23 two-year-olds, and only 5 three-year-olds. We call this vector $\overrightarrow{\text{pop}_0}$ because it contains the rabbit populations at year number 0.

L4. The Leslie matrix for population prediction

We're now going to define a matrix, traditionally named L, called a **Leslie Matrix** after ecologist Patrick Leslie. Leslie matrices have the following very strict form, so study it carefully:

$$L = \begin{bmatrix} f_0 & f_1 & f_2 & f_3 \\ s_0 & 0 & 0 & 0 \\ 0 & s_1 & 0 & 0 \\ 0 & 0 & s_2 & 0 \end{bmatrix}.$$

LESLIE MATRICES

Leslie matrices can be any (square) size. Here I've chosen 4 × 4 because we're keeping track of four different age brackets of bunny rabbits.

Notice that most of the entries are zero. The only ones that can be nonzero are (1) the top row, and (2) the first "subdiagonal" – meaning, the diagonal going from row 1, column 0 down to row 4, column 3. (Or, in a general $n \times n$ Leslie matrix, from row 1, column 0 down to row n, column $n - 1$.)

So what's the method to this madness? Here's what:

- "f" stands for **fecundity**. That's a fancy ecology word for "fertility." The f entries stand for – get this – the number of babies on average that each female rabbit of a certain age will give birth to. So if f_2 is .9, for instance, that means that every two-year-old mommy rabbit will, on average, give birth to .9 baby rabbits. Obviously some two-year-old females will have fewer babies than others, but $f_2 = .9$ means that on average each mom will produce .9 of them.

    Now you can see why I said we only need to keep track of the female rabbit population. Females – the child-bearers – are the limiting factor. As long as there are a few males (or even one) running around the population to perform the fertilization task, the number of males won't really matter to the long-term survival of the species.

    By the way, if any of the f entries are 0, that simply means that female rabbits of that age are infertile. (In many species, of course, only females within a certain age range can bear children.)

- "s" stands for **survival**. These s entries represent the probabilities that a rabbit of each age will survive another year. For example, if s_0 is .8, that means that every (female) baby rabbit has an 80% chance of surviving to become a one-year-old. If $s_2 = .5$, then only half of the two-year-olds will survive to become three-year-olds. Notice that there is no s_3 in the matrix; that's because we assumed that 3 years is the maximum age of a rabbit, and so none of the three-year-olds will survive anyway.

All the other entries in L have to be zero, and I think you can see the reason. If you're a one-year-old rabbit, there's only two possibilities for you: you can either survive to become a two-year-old next year, or else you can die. There's no possibility that you'll jump over age 2 and become a three-year-old next year, nor is there a chance that you'll "fail" grade 1 and have to be a one-year-old again next year.

Notice also that the s entries must be between 0 and 1 (they're survival *probabilities*, after all), although the f entries need not be. (Some species have very high birth rates, and a female of child-bearing age can easily produce more than just one offspring per year on average.)

To be concrete, let's whip up a random Leslie matrix and look at it:

$$L = \begin{bmatrix} .1 & .6 & .4 & .2 \\ .4 & 0 & 0 & 0 \\ 0 & .8 & 0 & 0 \\ 0 & 0 & .6 & 0 \end{bmatrix}.$$

Upon inspection, we can see that in this population, the following things are true:

- Baby rabbits rarely – but sometimes – have offspring. On average, for every ten baby rabbits in our population in a given year, they'll produce one new baby rabbit the next year.
- Rabbits reach peak fertility as one-year-olds ($\frac{6}{10}$ babies per mother). This fertility then declines each year thereafter until death.
- Baby rabbits have a hard time surviving: less than half of them (40%) survive their inaugural year.
- Both one-year-old and two-year-old rabbits have better than even odds of survival, though this survival rate does decline from year two to year three.

L5. Projecting forwards: matrix multiplication

Now let's look at our Leslie matrix in action. Earlier, we started out our hypothetical female rabbit population with these values:

$$\overrightarrow{\text{pop}_0} = \begin{bmatrix} 67 \\ 115 \\ 23 \\ 5 \end{bmatrix}$$

Now how many rabbits can we expect in each of these age groups next year?

That might seem like a complicated question, but the answer is actually staring you in the face. It's just matrix multiplication:

$$\overrightarrow{\text{pop}_1} = L \cdot \overrightarrow{\text{pop}_0}.$$

Wow! Really? Why does that work?

Well, think about what matrix multiplication actually does. First, each of our female rabbits, regardless of age, will contribute something to the expected number of newborn rabbits next year. Our current babies will contribute on average only .1 of a newborn each, while one-year-olds will produce .6 newborns each, two-year-olds .4 newborns each, and three-year-olds .2 newborns each. That's *exactly* the dot product of the top row of L (the fecundity row) times the current population vector!

Then, for each of the other age groups, the number of rabbits next year will simply be the number of rabbits *one year younger* this year, multiplied by the survival rate of that age group. For example, 67 babies this year will result in about 26.8 one-year-olds next year, since only 40% of them will survive. This, too, turns out to be a dot product: the survival row for that age times the number of rabbits of that age.

Check it out:

$$\begin{bmatrix} .1 & .6 & .4 & .2 \\ .4 & 0 & 0 & 0 \\ 0 & .8 & 0 & 0 \\ 0 & 0 & .6 & 0 \end{bmatrix} \cdot \begin{bmatrix} 67 \\ 115 \\ 23 \\ 5 \end{bmatrix} = \begin{bmatrix} .1 \cdot 67 + .6 \cdot 115 + .4 \cdot 23 + .2 \cdot 5 \\ .4 \cdot 67 \\ .8 \cdot 115 \\ .6 \cdot 23 \end{bmatrix} = \begin{bmatrix} 85.9 \\ 26.8 \\ 92.0 \\ 13.8 \end{bmatrix}.$$

Don't get too freaked out by the idea of "85.9 baby rabbits." These are just averages based on the various probabilities. In real life, there would of course not be any partial rabbits out there.

Once you see the previous calculation, it won't surprise you that

$$\overrightarrow{\text{pop}_2} = L \cdot \overrightarrow{\text{pop}_1},$$
$$\overrightarrow{\text{pop}_3} = L \cdot \overrightarrow{\text{pop}_2},$$
$$\overrightarrow{\text{pop}_4} = L \cdot \overrightarrow{\text{pop}_3},$$
etc.

These work out to:

$$\overrightarrow{\text{pop}_2} = \begin{bmatrix} .1 & .6 & .4 & .2 \\ .4 & 0 & 0 & 0 \\ 0 & .8 & 0 & 0 \\ 0 & 0 & .6 & 0 \end{bmatrix} \cdot \begin{bmatrix} 85.9 \\ 26.8 \\ 92.0 \\ 13.8 \end{bmatrix} = \begin{bmatrix} 64.23 \\ 34.36 \\ 21.44 \\ 55.2 \end{bmatrix},$$

$$\overrightarrow{\text{pop}_3} = \begin{bmatrix} .1 & .6 & .4 & .2 \\ .4 & 0 & 0 & 0 \\ 0 & .8 & 0 & 0 \\ 0 & 0 & .6 & 0 \end{bmatrix} \cdot \begin{bmatrix} 64.23 \\ 34.36 \\ 21.44 \\ 55.2 \end{bmatrix} = \begin{bmatrix} 46.66 \\ 25.69 \\ 27.5 \\ 12.86 \end{bmatrix},$$

$$\overrightarrow{\text{pop}_4} = \begin{bmatrix} .1 & .6 & .4 & .2 \\ .4 & 0 & 0 & 0 \\ 0 & .8 & 0 & 0 \\ 0 & 0 & .6 & 0 \end{bmatrix} \cdot \begin{bmatrix} 46.66 \\ 25.69 \\ 27.5 \\ 12.86 \end{bmatrix} = \begin{bmatrix} 33.65 \\ 18.67 \\ 20.55 \\ 16.49 \end{bmatrix},$$

and so on out to eternity.

Also, since matrix multiplication is commutative, we can carry out the products in any order. We can start at the beginning (year 0) and multiply L by itself the requisite number of times to compute

LESLIE MATRICES

any future year. So, computing the fourth generation after the starting state can be written as:

$$\overrightarrow{\text{pop}_4} = L \cdot L \cdot L \cdot L \cdot \overrightarrow{\text{pop}_0},$$

and the thirtieth generation as:

$$\overrightarrow{\text{pop}_{30}} = L^{30} \cdot \overrightarrow{\text{pop}_0},$$

(where L^{30} means "L multiplied by itself 30 times," of course).

Sadly for the rabbits, this works out to:

$$\overrightarrow{\text{pop}_{30}} = \begin{bmatrix} 0.0123 \\ 0.0066 \\ 0.0071 \\ 0.0057 \end{bmatrix},$$

which means that in their present environment, this rabbit colony's days are numbered. Maybe Hazel and Fiver will come up with a migration plan that increases their survival rates...

Hamming codes

Our next example is about **error-correcting codes**, extremely useful in the transfer of electronic data. These "codes," by the way, have nothing to do with the *secret* codes used in cryptography, which conceal and reveal hidden messages. (Those are a different application, which also rely on linear algebra, by the way!)

The particular error-correcting code we'll learn is called the **Hamming code**, invented by mathematician Richard Hamming. I hope you find it as amazing as I do.

H1. Doing "arithmetic mod 2"

One thing we need to get out of the way first is a little bookkeeping matter. With Hamming codes, we're going to be dealing exclusively with **binary** data. As you'll remember from *Cool Brisk Walk* chapter 7, binary numbers are base 2, with only 0 and 1 as the digits.

Although this may sound like a limitation, it's not: every single piece of information that's transferred between computers or is stored on one *must* be represented in binary form anyway. This is true not only of numeric data, but also text documents, MP3 audio files, GIF or JPG image files, and even videos. Representing every kind of information as a long sequence of 0's and 1's is a solved problem, so it's no big deal for our error-correcting scheme to assume that the messages it works with are in binary. It could hardly be any other way.

Binary digits thus really aren't that weird. What's slightly more weird is doing our arithmetic "modulo 2," which the Hamming code will require. What this means is that every time we perform an addition or a multiplication operation, we're only going to keep *the least-significant bit of the answer*. Mathematically, this amounts to taking our result modulo 2 – which means "divide the answer by 2 and take the remainder." You'll quickly see that this means all we care about is whether our answer is even or odd; if it's even, our result is 0, and if it's odd, our result is 1.

Here are the complete addition and multiplication tables for one-bit binary numbers. There's only one surprise, and that's in the lower left:

$$0 + 0 = 0 \qquad 0 \cdot 0 = 0$$
$$0 + 1 = 1 \qquad 0 \cdot 1 = 0$$
$$1 + 0 = 1 \qquad 1 \cdot 0 = 0$$
$$1 + 1 = \mathbf{0} \qquad 1 \cdot 1 = 1$$

Everything else is what you learned in elementary school. But remember that in "arithmetic mod 2," one plus one equals *zero*. In terms of *Cool Brisk Walk* chapter 7, we have $1_2 + 1_2 = 10_2$, but since we only want to keep the least-significant bit of the answer, we throw away the 1 in 10_2 which leaves us with 0_2.

To test your understanding, compute this dot product mod 2:

$$\begin{bmatrix} 1 & 1 & 0 & 1 & 0 & 1 & 1 \end{bmatrix} \cdot \begin{bmatrix} 0 \\ 1 \\ 0 \\ 1 \\ 1 \\ 1 \\ 0 \end{bmatrix}$$

The answer should turn out to be:

$$1 \cdot 0 + 1 \cdot 1 + 0 \cdot 0 + 1 \cdot 1 + 0 \cdot 1 + 1 \cdot 1 + 1 \cdot 0 =$$
$$0 + 1 + 0 + 1 + 0 + 1 + 0 = 1.$$

There are an odd number of 1–1 pairs when lining up those vectors element by element, and therefore the dot product is 1.

H2. Noisy channels

Okay, down to business. The setting for the Hamming Code is the sending of information over a so-called **noisy channel**. A noisy channel is a transmission path through which data can be sent, but because it is "noisy," some of the information is likely to be **corrupted** along the way. A corrupted bit is simply one that is transmitted incorrectly: the sender tried to send a 0 but the receiver erroneously got a 1, or vice versa.

Figure 7.1: A binary message sent through a noisy channel. Seven out of the eight bits were transmitted and received correctly.

This setting is depicted in Figure 7.1. The sender in the picture tried to transmit an eight-bit digital message to the receiver, and was successful in doing so...almost. That fifth bit is the problem: the sender sent a 1, but the receiver got a 0. This is life on a noisy channel.

Why would this happen? Interference, distortion, literal "noise": these all play a role in our big chaotic imperfect world. You've all experienced your cell phone getting bad service or your radio getting bad reception. That's the information getting slightly (or perhaps majorly) corrupted in transmission, to the point where you get a garbled version of what the cell tower transmitted or the radio station broadcast.

And of course the frustrating thing is not merely that some bits were corrupted, but that the receiver doesn't *know* whether any were corrupted. She received a string of bits, most of which are probably correct, but a few of which might not be. The bad ones are indistinguishable from the good ones, so she doesn't have any way of knowing which ones to trust.

Or does she?

H3. The Hamming code scheme

Enter the Hamming code. The sender and receiver will cooperate in an amazing way such that – within certain limits – bits that are corrupted in-transit can be *detected* as such by the receiver, and then *corrected* without the receiver even needing to asking the sender to repeat himself.

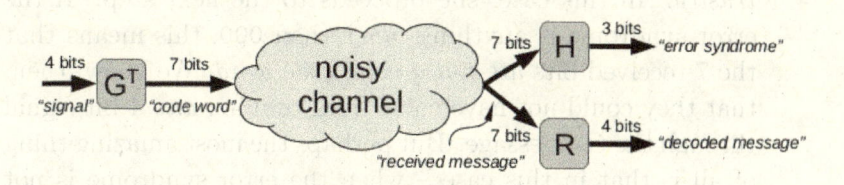

Figure 7.2: The Hamming code error-correction scheme.

The overall scene is shown in Figure 7.2. Study it carefully. Here are the key points:

1. Each of the gray boxes – mysteriously labeled G^T, H, and R in the figure – is a *linear transformation.*

2. The sender begins by carving up his message into consecutive 4-bit pieces. As you may remember from *Cool Brisk Walk*, these 4-bit chunks are called **nibbles**. Each nibble is sent separately. For purposes of understanding this system, we'll just consider "the entire message" to be a single nibble. (Longer messages simply repeat the whole process once per nibble.) This 4 bits of information that the sender is trying to communicate is called the **signal**.

3. The sender begins by running those 4 signal bits through the G^T linear transformation, which maps them to a 7-dimensional vector. Those 7 bits are called a **code word**. The code word is what's actually sent through the noisy channel, not the original signal.

4. On the other end of the wire, the receiver gets 7 bits of information. These *may* be identical to the code word that

was sent, but of course they may instead contain one or more corrupted bits.

5. The receiver proceeds to do two things with these 7 bits. First, she runs them through the H linear transformation to produce a 3-bit string called the **error syndrome**. This is the key to the whole scheme. *If the error syndrome is exactly 000, that means that the 7 bits were uncorrupted and can be trusted.* In this case, she proceeds to the next step. If the error syndrome is anything *other* than 000, this means that the 7 received bits are *not a valid code word*. We know, then, that they could not have come from running *any* 4-bit signal through the G^T message. But perhaps the most amazing thing of all is that in this case – when the error syndrome is not 000 – it will incredibly spell out a binary number telling her *exactly which bit was corrupted!*

For instance, if the error syndrome is 110, which is the binary number six, then she knows bit number 6 (out of 7) was corrupted, and she needs to flip it from a 0 to a 1 or from a 1 to a 0. If the error syndrome is 001, which is a binary one, then she knows to flip the *first* bit of the received message.

6. Finally, the receiver takes the 7 bits – corrected if necessary, based on the error syndrome – and runs them through the R linear transformation. This produces the 4-bit nibble that the sender originally sent.

The reason all this works is that Hamming carefully designed the G^T, H, and R linear transformations so that everything works out as described. I'm sure you'd like to look at those now. You already know something about them, because of the number of bits they take as inputs and outputs:

- G^T must be a 7×4 matrix, since it maps a 4-bit vector to a 7-bit vector.
- H must be a 3×7 matrix, since it transforms each 7-bit vector into a 3-bit vector.
- Finally, R must be a 4×7, since it maps 7 bits into 4 bits.

. HAMMING CODES

Here they are in all their glory:[1]

$$G^\mathsf{T} = \begin{bmatrix} 1 & 0 & 1 & 1 \\ 1 & 1 & 0 & 1 \\ 0 & 0 & 0 & 1 \\ 1 & 1 & 1 & 0 \\ 0 & 0 & 1 & 0 \\ 0 & 1 & 0 & 0 \\ 1 & 0 & 0 & 0 \end{bmatrix}$$

$$H = \begin{bmatrix} 0 & 0 & 0 & 1 & 1 & 1 & 1 \\ 0 & 1 & 1 & 0 & 0 & 1 & 1 \\ 1 & 0 & 1 & 0 & 1 & 0 & 1 \end{bmatrix}$$

$$R = \begin{bmatrix} 0 & 0 & 0 & 0 & 0 & 0 & 1 \\ 0 & 0 & 0 & 0 & 0 & 1 & 0 \\ 0 & 0 & 0 & 0 & 1 & 0 & 0 \\ 0 & 0 & 1 & 0 & 0 & 0 & 0 \end{bmatrix}$$

You can stare at these for a while if you want, and try to figure out the method in the madness. I confess, it seems like a lot of voodoo magic to me, especially G^T. The H matrix actually has a very reliable pattern: if you look at the columns, you'll recognize that from left to right they are the binary numbers 1 through 7!

H4. Examples

All right, let's work through this scheme for a couple of actual examples.

Example 1: no corruption

Our sender desires to transmit the 4-bit message **1110** to the receiver. So **1110** is the signal. He multiplies G^T by it to get:

---

[1] Incidentally, in Hamming's original design all of these matrices had seven columns, including "G", which was a 4 × 7. However, since we always use the transposed-version-of-G when we multiply a vector by it, the accepted convention has become to just call it "G^T" and treat it as a 7 × 4 matrix, as I'm doing here.

$$\begin{bmatrix} 1 & 0 & 1 & 1 \\ 1 & 1 & 0 & 1 \\ 0 & 0 & 0 & 1 \\ 1 & 1 & 1 & 0 \\ 0 & 0 & 1 & 0 \\ 0 & 1 & 0 & 0 \\ 1 & 0 & 0 & 0 \end{bmatrix} \cdot \begin{bmatrix} 1 \\ 1 \\ 1 \\ 0 \end{bmatrix} = \begin{bmatrix} 0 \\ 0 \\ 0 \\ 1 \\ 1 \\ 1 \\ 1 \end{bmatrix}.$$

So he sends 0001111 into the noisy channel.

(Time passes.)

On the other side of the world, the receiver picks up a 7-bit message: 0001111. She first asks herself: "is this message legit? Is it a valid code word?" To find out, she multiplies it by H:

$$\begin{bmatrix} 0 & 0 & 0 & 1 & 1 & 1 & 1 \\ 0 & 1 & 1 & 0 & 0 & 1 & 1 \\ 1 & 0 & 1 & 0 & 1 & 0 & 1 \end{bmatrix} \cdot \begin{bmatrix} 0 \\ 0 \\ 0 \\ 1 \\ 1 \\ 1 \\ 1 \end{bmatrix} = \begin{bmatrix} 0 \\ 0 \\ 0 \end{bmatrix}.$$

Good news: the error syndrome is all zeroes! This means that the 7 bits she received are in fact what was sent. All that remains is to run them through the R transformation to uncover the original message:

$$\begin{bmatrix} 0 & 0 & 0 & 0 & 0 & 0 & 1 \\ 0 & 0 & 0 & 0 & 0 & 1 & 0 \\ 0 & 0 & 0 & 0 & 1 & 0 & 0 \\ 0 & 0 & 1 & 0 & 0 & 0 & 0 \end{bmatrix} \cdot \begin{bmatrix} 0 \\ 0 \\ 0 \\ 1 \\ 1 \\ 1 \\ 1 \end{bmatrix} = \begin{bmatrix} 1 \\ 1 \\ 1 \\ 0 \end{bmatrix}.$$

Ta da!

HAMMING CODES

Example 2: one-bit corruption

Our sender desires to transmit 0011 to the receiver. He transforms it using G^T by it to get:

$$\begin{bmatrix} 1 & 0 & 1 & 1 \\ 1 & 1 & 0 & 1 \\ 0 & 0 & 0 & 1 \\ 1 & 1 & 1 & 0 \\ 0 & 0 & 1 & 0 \\ 0 & 1 & 0 & 0 \\ 1 & 0 & 0 & 0 \end{bmatrix} \cdot \begin{bmatrix} 0 \\ 0 \\ 1 \\ 1 \end{bmatrix} = \begin{bmatrix} 0 \\ 1 \\ 1 \\ 1 \\ 1 \\ 0 \\ 0 \end{bmatrix}.$$

The sender thus puts the code word 0111100 into the noisy channel.

(Time passes...but something goes wrong! Little do the sender or receiver know, but the fourth bit of this code word hits a glitch and is flipped to a 0!)

On the other side of the world, the receiver picks up a 7-bit message: 0110100. She first asks herself: "is this message legit? Is it a valid code word?" To find out, she multiplies it by H:

$$\begin{bmatrix} 0 & 0 & 0 & 1 & 1 & 1 & 1 \\ 0 & 1 & 1 & 0 & 0 & 1 & 1 \\ 1 & 0 & 1 & 0 & 1 & 0 & 1 \end{bmatrix} \cdot \begin{bmatrix} 0 \\ 1 \\ 1 \\ 0 \\ 1 \\ 0 \\ 0 \end{bmatrix} = \begin{bmatrix} 1 \\ 0 \\ 0 \end{bmatrix}.$$

Egads! Our error syndrome raises a red flag. It's not all zeroes, so something must have gone amiss.

But all is not lost, since Hamming magic tells us exactly *what* went amiss. The error syndrome 100 corresponds to the binary number 4. Therefore, bit number 4 of the received message is what was corrupted. Our friend must not have sent 0110100, but rather 0111100!

The receiver thus confidently plugs this corrected vector into the R matrix to yield:

$$\begin{bmatrix} 0 & 0 & 0 & 0 & 0 & 0 & 1 \\ 0 & 0 & 0 & 0 & 0 & 1 & 0 \\ 0 & 0 & 0 & 0 & 1 & 0 & 0 \\ 0 & 0 & 1 & 0 & 0 & 0 & 0 \end{bmatrix} \cdot \begin{bmatrix} 0 \\ 1 \\ 1 \\ 1 \\ 1 \\ 0 \\ 0 \end{bmatrix} = \begin{bmatrix} 0 \\ 0 \\ 1 \\ 1 \end{bmatrix},$$

which is exactly the signal our sender intended. Amazing!

H5. The one fly in the ointment

Some things are too good to be true. That's not the case with the Hamming code: it is good, and it is true. But it does have a limitation, which I alluded to earlier and will now spell out.

The Hamming code can only deal with **single-bit errors**. As long as only *one* of the 7 bits transmitted as a code word is corrupted, the receiver can intelligently detect the error and even figure out which bit to correct. But if more than one bit is corrupted in a single batch-of-seven, all bets are off.

The reason is this. Hamming designed the G^T matrix (and its counterpart, R) so that *any two code words are at least two bits apart*. This calls for some explanation.

Remember from *Cool Brisk Walk* that there are 2^4, or 16, possible 4-bit patterns. This is our vocabulary when using the Hamming code: we can say any of sixteen different "things" each time we send a message. Now the G^T matrix transforms those 4 bits into 7 bits. How many possible 7-bit sequences are there? Answer: 2^7, or *128*.

Think about that for a minute. There are 128 different 7-bit strings, yet only 16 of them are valid code words. That means that if you picked a random 7-bit string out of a hat, the probability is pretty small that you'd actually hit upon a code word: $\frac{16}{128} = \frac{1}{8} = .125$,

HAMMING CODES 195

to be precise. This is what gives the Hamming code its detective power: you have to get pretty "lucky" to fool it. Over 87% of the time, your choice of 7-bits is instantly exposed as a fraud by the H matrix.

And if we consider only the 16 valid code words out of those 128, you'll see that Hamming designed it so that you can't get to any one of them from any of the others without changing at least *two* bits. This means that two separate, independent errors would have to occur in order for one valid code word (representing a particular 4-bit signal) to be corrupted into another valid code word (representing a *different* 4-bit signal). As long as only one bit gets flipped, you're guaranteed that the code word will be corrupted into a *non*-code word, and thus be exposed to the light.

There are actually whole families of error correcting codes with various properties, some of which are more intricate and can detect and even correct multi-bit errors. The Hamming code was just the first, and what a great insight it gave us.

Graph analysis

The last application I'll present in this chapter deals with **graph-based** data. We covered graphs extensively in Chapter 5 of *Cool Brisk Walk*, but now we'll bring our matrix skills to bear on our analysis, and with striking effect.

Recall that a **graph**, in discrete math terms, is not an x-y plot, which is what most people think of when they hear the term. Instead, it's a special kind of data structure for organizing data. A graph consists of **vertices** (singular: **vertex**) connected by **edges**. Here's an example:

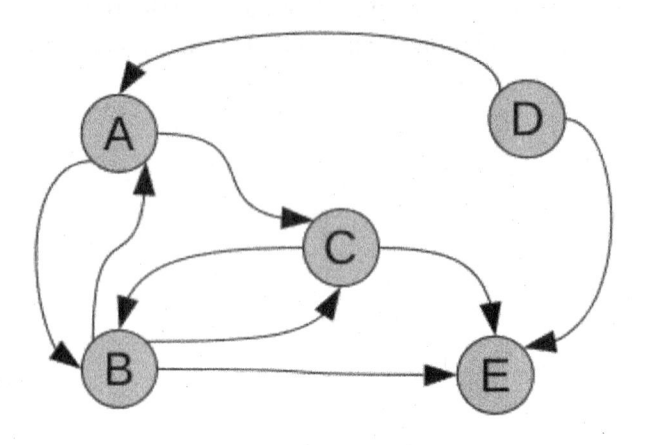

Figure 7.3: A directed graph.

Each vertex represents some entity (say, a computer on a network, or a user on social media) and the edges represent relationships between them (network connections, for example, or "followings"). As graphs go, this one is minuscule; the Facebook graph, in which vertices are users and edges are friendships, has well over a billion vertices. But it will serve our purposes for illustration.

G1. Graph terms

Here's a refresher on some important graph terms, most of which are repeats from *Cool Brisk Walk* Chapter 5:

order/size. Colloquially, researchers sometimes refer to the number of vertices in a graph as its **order**, and the number of its edges as its **size**. (The ratio of these quantities becomes a subject of interest as well.) Figure 7.3 has order 5 and size 9.

adjacent. If two vertices have an edge directly connecting them, they are called "adjacent." In Figure 7.3, vertices A and D are adjacent, but *not* A and E. (Even though you can get from A to E, you must do so indirectly, through D.)

directed/undirected. In Figure 7.3, the edges have arrowheads. This is called a **directed** graph, and means that there is a meaningful directionality to the edges: the information that A points to C does not imply that C also points to A.

Sometimes, though, we don't care about which "way" the edge goes, and so we draw the graph with lines only, no arrowheads. This is true of Figure 7.4 on p. 198, which is thus an **undirected** graph.

Facebook is real-life example of an undirected graph (if I'm friends with you, then you're friends with me, always) but Twitter is a directed graph (if I follow you, that doesn't necessarily mean you also follow me).

path. A **path** is a sequence of consecutive edges that takes you from one vertex to the other. In Figure 7.3, there is a path from A to E, which goes through C. By contrast, there is no path at all from G to J in Figure 7.4.

traverse. We use the verb "**traverse**" to mean "follow an edge from one vertex to another." This often comes up in the context of searching for data in the graph, or finding a path through the graph with certain features.

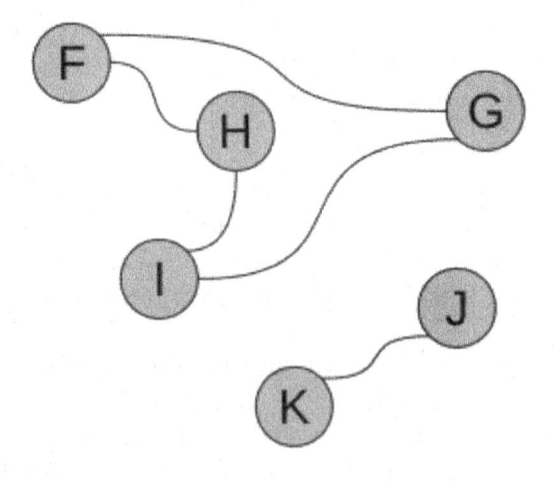

Figure 7.4: An undirected graph.

weighted. Sometimes, the edges in the graph are unlabeled. But we frequently want to associate a *number* with each edge, in order to represent the length of a road between cities, say, or the relative importance of a friendship. This number is called the **weight** of the edge, and a graph with such weights is called a **weighted graph**.

degree. A vertex's "degree" is simply the number of other vertices that are adjacent to it. In Figure 7.4, vertices J and K have degree 1, and the others have degree 2. For a directed graph, we distinguish between the number of incoming edges, called the "**in-degree**," and the number of outgoing edges, or "**out-degree**." So vertex B in Figure 7.3 has an in-degree of 2 and an out-degree of 3, while D has an in-degree of 0 and an out-degree of 2.

connected/disconnected. A graph is **connected** (sometimes called "**fully connected**," which means the same thing) if every vertex is "reachable" from every other vertex by traversing its edges. Otherwise, it's **disconnected**. Figure 7.4 is clearly not connected, since we can't get to J/K from the others.

What about Figure 7.3? Well, that depends on how we define the term "connected." If we say a directed graph is **strongly connected**, that means that every vertex can be reached from every other even if you only follow the arrows' directions. If it's merely **weakly connected** if you can reach every vertex when *ignoring* the edge directions. So the A-B-C-D-E graph is weakly connected, but not strongly connected.

cycle. In a graph, a **cycle** is a group of vertices that are connected in a ring: you can start at one, traverse edges to the others, and then return to where you started. A→B→A is a cycle in our first graph, and F–H–I–G is a cycle in the second graph.

DAG. Finally, if a graph is directed and contains *no* cycles, we called it a "**DAG**," or "directed, acyclic graph." Certain kinds of directed graphs must inherently be cycle-free to even make sense. For instance, if each vertex represents an action item in a project plan, and a directed edge indicates that one item must be completed before another can begin, there must be no cycles or else the project could never be completed!

An example DAG is given in Figure 7.5 (p. 200), which shows part of the computer science curriculum at UMW. Each vertex is a required course – CPSC 284, in fact, is our Applied Discrete Mathematics course, which you are currently reading the book for. The directed edges represent prerequisites: you must complete CPSC 110 before beginning CPSC 284, for instance. You should take a moment and verify that there are no cycles in this graph, because if there are, it would spell doom for computer science majors.

G2. The adjacency matrix

Okay, so that's a bunch of stuff about graphs. Now let's talk about how to *represent* a graph in a computer program. Clearly, it would be a poor choice to store an image file with a bunch of circles and lines. We need something much simpler and more flexible, which will capture the essence of what the graph *is*, not how it is drawn.

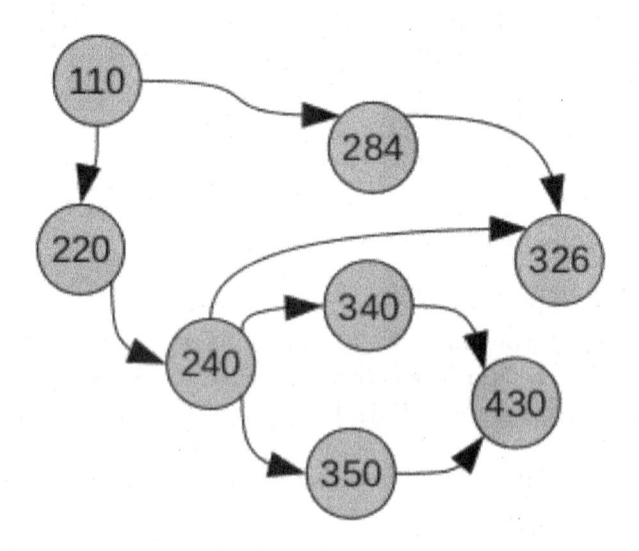

Figure 7.5: A DAG (directed, acyclic graph).

One very common way to do this is with an **adjacency matrix**. A graph's adjacency matrix is simply a square matrix where every row (and column) corresponds to one vertex. A "1" in row i, column j means "yes, vertex i and vertex j are adjacent." Otherwise, they're not.

We often use the letter A to denote the adjacency matrix. Here's the adjacency matrix for Figure 7.3 (p. 196):

$$A_{7.3} = \begin{array}{c} \\ A \\ B \\ C \\ D \\ E \end{array} \begin{array}{c} \begin{array}{ccccc} A & B & C & D & E \end{array} \\ \left[\begin{array}{ccccc} 0 & 1 & 1 & 0 & 0 \\ 1 & 0 & 1 & 0 & 1 \\ 0 & 1 & 0 & 0 & 1 \\ 1 & 0 & 0 & 0 & 1 \\ 0 & 0 & 0 & 0 & 0 \end{array} \right] \end{array}$$

Stick your finger in p. 196 and flip back and forth between the graph and the matrix to ensure it's correct. The top row is [0 1 1 0 0], because vertex A has an outgoing edge to B and to C, but not to

GRAPH ANALYSIS

D or to E. Also, vertex A has *incoming* edges from B and D (but neither from C nor E), which is why its left column is:

$$\begin{bmatrix} 0 \\ 1 \\ 0 \\ 1 \\ 0 \end{bmatrix}.$$

Notice that the diagonal terms are zero, which means that none of the vertices has "an edge to itself," which is what we normally do.

When you've convinced yourself that you understand that adjacency matrix, test your skills by verifying this one as well, for the undirected graph in Figure 7.4 (p. 198):

$$A_{7.4} = \begin{array}{c} \\ F \\ G \\ H \\ I \\ J \\ K \end{array} \begin{array}{c} \begin{array}{cccccc} F & G & H & I & J & K \end{array} \\ \begin{bmatrix} 0 & 1 & 1 & 0 & 0 & 0 \\ 1 & 0 & 0 & 1 & 0 & 0 \\ 1 & 0 & 0 & 1 & 0 & 0 \\ 0 & 1 & 1 & 0 & 0 & 0 \\ 0 & 0 & 0 & 0 & 0 & 1 \\ 0 & 0 & 0 & 0 & 1 & 0 \end{bmatrix} \end{array}$$

G3. Adjacency matrix properties

I almost named this section "stupid adjacency matrix tricks" (after David Letterman's "stupid dog tricks" skit) but I decided to play it straight. In it, we're going to make some deep connections between the properties of any graph (we'll call it G) and its adjacency matrix A. This is just the tip of the iceberg, believe me; more is coming in Chapter 9 when we cover eigenvalues.

Undirected $G \Leftrightarrow$ symmetric A

The first one you might already have noticed from your study of p. 200. And that is that if the graph is *un*directed, its adjacency matrix will be *symmetric*. If you didn't see this before, run your eyeballs over those two matrices again, and notice how the F–G–H–I–J–K matrix is a mirror image of itself across the main diagonal, whereas the A–B–C–D–E matrix is not.

This is, of course, a natural consequence of what "undirected" means. If a graph has no arrowheads, then every time you can go from X to Y, you can also go from Y to X. So if A's entry at row X and column Y is a 1, then the entry at row Y and column X must also be a 1. And that's what makes a matrix symmetric.

DAG $G \Leftarrow$ upper-triangular A

I haven't yet given you an adjacency matrix for the DAG in Figure 7.5 (p. 200). Here you go:

$$A_{\text{DAG}} = \begin{array}{c} \\ 110 \\ 220 \\ 240 \\ 340 \\ 284 \\ 350 \\ 326 \\ 430 \end{array} \begin{array}{c} \begin{array}{cccccccc} 110 & 220 & 240 & 340 & 284 & 350 & 326 & 430 \end{array} \\ \left[\begin{array}{cccccccc} 0 & 1 & 0 & 0 & 1 & 0 & 0 & 0 \\ 0 & 0 & 1 & 0 & 0 & 0 & 0 & 0 \\ 0 & 0 & 0 & 1 & 0 & 1 & 1 & 0 \\ 0 & 0 & 0 & 0 & 0 & 0 & 0 & 1 \\ 0 & 0 & 0 & 0 & 0 & 0 & 1 & 0 \\ 0 & 0 & 0 & 0 & 0 & 0 & 0 & 1 \\ 0 & 0 & 0 & 0 & 0 & 0 & 0 & 0 \\ 0 & 0 & 0 & 0 & 0 & 0 & 0 & 0 \end{array} \right] \end{array}.$$

As always, take a minute to verify the entries. And then, recognize that this matrix is *upper-triangular*.

Why should that be? Think of it this way. The graph is a DAG, which means it has no cycles, which in turn means that there must be *some* order in which a student could complete the courses in the curriculum and not violate any prerequisites. One such ordering is:

CPSC 110, 220, 240, 340, 284, 250, 326, 430.

(That's not the only such ordering; 110, 284, 220, 240, 350, 340, 430, 326 would work just as well.)

GRAPH ANALYSIS

Now suppose I create the adjacency matrix with the rows (and columns) in that order. The first column *must* have all zeroes, because by definition the first course you take in the sequence must have no prerequisites. The second column must also have all zeroes...with the possible exception of the first row, because the first course (and *only* the first course) might be required in order to take the second course. This goes on down the line: each course we take may have as prerequisites any of the previous courses, but none of the future courses. And so the matrix will have all zeroes below the main diagonal, which is the definition of "upper-triangular." Ka-ching.

The order of the rows (and columns) is of course the key. It's easy to make a *non*-upper-triangular adjacency matrix for a DAG, just by shuffling the rows and columns in a different order. Here's one:

$$A_{\text{DAG}_2} = \begin{array}{c} \\ 326 \\ 350 \\ 284 \\ 340 \\ 240 \\ 430 \\ 110 \\ 220 \end{array} \begin{array}{c} \begin{array}{cccccccc} 326 & 350 & 284 & 340 & 240 & 430 & 110 & 220 \end{array} \\ \left[\begin{array}{cccccccc} 0 & 0 & 0 & 0 & 0 & 0 & 0 & 0 \\ 0 & 0 & 0 & 0 & 0 & 1 & 0 & 0 \\ 1 & 0 & 0 & 0 & 0 & 0 & 0 & 0 \\ 0 & 0 & 0 & 0 & 0 & 1 & 0 & 0 \\ 1 & 1 & 0 & 1 & 0 & 0 & 0 & 0 \\ 0 & 0 & 0 & 0 & 0 & 0 & 0 & 0 \\ 0 & 0 & 1 & 0 & 0 & 0 & 0 & 1 \\ 0 & 0 & 0 & 0 & 1 & 0 & 0 & 0 \end{array} \right] \end{array}.$$

Nothing upper-triangular about that one. So the implication only holds in one direction: if your adjacency matrix is upper-triangular, this implies that the graph will be a DAG, but not necessarily vice versa. There will, however, always be *some* way to get an upper-triangular A from a DAG, if you order the rows in the "correct" way.

Disconnected $G \Leftarrow$ block diagonal A

Lastly, here's kind of a mind-blowing one. Suppose we have a disconnected graph, like the one in Figure 7.4 (p. 198). This disconnectedness is apparent from the adjacency matrix, because it is – get this – block diagonal!

$$A_{7.4} = \left[\begin{array}{cccc|cc} 0 & 1 & 1 & 0 & 0 & 0 \\ 1 & 0 & 0 & 1 & 0 & 0 \\ 1 & 0 & 0 & 1 & 0 & 0 \\ 0 & 1 & 1 & 0 & 0 & 0 \\ \hline 0 & 0 & 0 & 0 & 0 & 1 \\ 0 & 0 & 0 & 0 & 1 & 0 \end{array}\right]$$

The ordering-of-the-adjacency-matrix-rows thing comes into play here, just as it did with upper-triangular matrices and DAGs. We would clearly shuffle the order around and get a non-block-diagonal matrix. But there will be some ordering that gives us a block diagonal, and here's why: a disconnected graph is separable into isolated subgraphs.[2] None of the subgraphs have any connections to any of the others. So, if we order our adjacency matrix rows (and columns) such that we list all the vertices in one subgraph, then the next, then the next, we *must* have zeroes everywhere except the blocks on the diagonal. Neat!

G4. Using the adjacency matrix

The adjacency matrix view of a graph lets us calculate a number of insightful properties. Some of these we won't get to until Chapter 9, but some we can look at now.

Here's a simple one. Suppose we multiply the adjacency matrix by a vector of all 1's?

---

[2] This is a **partition**, if you remember your set theory from *Cool Brisk Walk*.

$$\begin{array}{c} \begin{array}{ccccc} A & B & C & D & E \end{array} \\ \begin{array}{c} A \\ B \\ C \\ D \\ E \end{array}\begin{bmatrix} 0 & 1 & 1 & 0 & 0 \\ 1 & 0 & 1 & 0 & 1 \\ 0 & 1 & 0 & 0 & 1 \\ 1 & 0 & 0 & 0 & 1 \\ 0 & 0 & 0 & 0 & 0 \end{bmatrix} \cdot \begin{bmatrix} 1 \\ 1 \\ 1 \\ 1 \\ 1 \end{bmatrix} = \begin{bmatrix} 2 \\ 3 \\ 2 \\ 2 \\ 0 \end{bmatrix}\begin{array}{c} A \\ B \\ C \\ D \\ E \end{array} \end{array}$$

That might seem like a mindless operation, until you realize what it produced. The result is a vector of the *out-degrees* of each vertex! Double check it with p. 196 if you don't believe me. Vertex A has two outgoing arrows, B has three, C and D each have two, and E has none.

A similar trick can be performed by *left*-multiplying the adjacency matrix by a *row* of 1's:

$$\begin{bmatrix} 1 & 1 & 1 & 1 & 1 \end{bmatrix} \cdot \begin{array}{c} \begin{array}{ccccc} A & B & C & D & E \end{array} \\ \begin{array}{c} A \\ B \\ C \\ D \\ E \end{array}\begin{bmatrix} 0 & 1 & 1 & 0 & 0 \\ 1 & 0 & 1 & 0 & 1 \\ 0 & 1 & 0 & 0 & 1 \\ 1 & 0 & 0 & 0 & 1 \\ 0 & 0 & 0 & 0 & 0 \end{bmatrix} \end{array} = \begin{array}{c} \begin{array}{ccccc} A & B & C & D & E \end{array} \\ \begin{bmatrix} 2 & 2 & 2 & 0 & 3 \end{bmatrix} \end{array}.$$

This gives us the in-degrees. Of course, for an undirected graph – and a symmetric matrix – these two results will be the same.

Path counting

One thing that turns out to be very important about graphs is the number of paths between various nodes. In fact, the whole Google search engine (and all its imitators) are essentially based on this principle, which we will further unpack in Chapter 9. If vertices are Web pages and edges are hyperlinks between them, then the "importance" of a page is intimately related to *how many other pages have paths to it.*[3]

We could take a first, very rough cut at this just by looking at the in-degrees we computed in the previous section. Which of our A–B–C–D–E pages is the "most important?" Well, I guess we'd say that E is. Its in-degree is 3, more than any other vertex, which means that three of the other pages in our mini-web link to it. No other page is so popular.

A more sophisticated analysis involves looking at paths, not just single edges. If you think about it, the adjacency matrix itself gives us the number of "paths of length 1" between each pair of vertices. For short, we use the term "1-path." Our p. 196 graph has one 1-path between B and C, but no 1-paths between D and B, which is why the adjacency matrix has a 1 in one place but a 0 in another.

Now what if we wanted to count the number of 2-paths? Glancing back at p. 196, you can see that it's certainly possible to count these, but it's kind of a pain in the neck. There's *one* 2-path between A and B (A→C→B), but *two* 2-paths between A and E (A→B→E and A→C→E). Clearly this is error-prone, as well as tedious, to count manually. And if I asked you to stare at that graph and tell me how many *50*-paths there were from A to C, you'd tell me to jump in the lake.

Is there a way to automate such computations? Of course, or I wouldn't be telling you all this. It's amazingly elegant, too. Would you believe that the number of 2-paths *from* every vertex *to* every vertex is just:

$$A \cdot A$$

?!!

Holy smokes, that actually *works*? Yes! Check it out:

---

[3] I'm slightly oversimplifying things, but only a bit. The main principle is bedrock, and this explanation will hold us over until we get to the PageRank algorithm itself near the end of the book.

$$A^2 = \begin{bmatrix} 0 & 1 & 1 & 0 & 0 \\ 1 & 0 & 1 & 0 & 1 \\ 0 & 1 & 0 & 0 & 1 \\ 1 & 0 & 0 & 0 & 1 \\ 0 & 0 & 0 & 0 & 0 \end{bmatrix} \cdot \begin{bmatrix} 0 & 1 & 1 & 0 & 0 \\ 1 & 0 & 1 & 0 & 1 \\ 0 & 1 & 0 & 0 & 1 \\ 1 & 0 & 0 & 0 & 1 \\ 0 & 0 & 0 & 0 & 0 \end{bmatrix} = \begin{bmatrix} 1 & 1 & 1 & 0 & 2 \\ 1 & 2 & 1 & 0 & 1 \\ 1 & 0 & 1 & 0 & 1 \\ 0 & 1 & 1 & 0 & 0 \\ 0 & 0 & 0 & 0 & 0 \end{bmatrix}.$$

Spot check that result. It says that there is one 2-path from A to C, and two 2-paths from A to E, both of which we already figured out. It also says that there's *no* 2-path from B to A, even though there was a 1-path from B to A. Examining Figure 7.3, we see that's true as well. And of course the fourth column and fifth row of $A \cdot A$ have all zeroes, just as A itself did, since there's no 2-path (or any length path) that starts at E nor that terminates at D.

Even more amazingly, by repeatedly multiplying A by itself like this, we can repeat this result to get the number of paths of *any* length: 3-paths, 4-paths, 5-paths...

$$A^3 = \begin{bmatrix} 0 & 1 & 1 & 0 & 0 \\ 1 & 0 & 1 & 0 & 1 \\ 0 & 1 & 0 & 0 & 1 \\ 1 & 0 & 0 & 0 & 1 \\ 0 & 0 & 0 & 0 & 0 \end{bmatrix}^3 = \begin{bmatrix} 1 & 2 & 2 & 0 & 2 \\ 2 & 1 & 2 & 0 & 3 \\ 0 & 2 & 1 & 0 & 1 \\ 1 & 1 & 1 & 0 & 2 \\ 0 & 0 & 0 & 0 & 0 \end{bmatrix},$$

$$A^4 = \begin{bmatrix} 0 & 1 & 1 & 0 & 0 \\ 1 & 0 & 1 & 0 & 1 \\ 0 & 1 & 0 & 0 & 1 \\ 1 & 0 & 0 & 0 & 1 \\ 0 & 0 & 0 & 0 & 0 \end{bmatrix}^4 = \begin{bmatrix} 2 & 3 & 3 & 0 & 4 \\ 1 & 4 & 3 & 0 & 3 \\ 2 & 1 & 2 & 0 & 3 \\ 1 & 2 & 2 & 0 & 2 \\ 0 & 0 & 0 & 0 & 0 \end{bmatrix},$$

$$A^5 = \begin{bmatrix} 0 & 1 & 1 & 0 & 0 \\ 1 & 0 & 1 & 0 & 1 \\ 0 & 1 & 0 & 0 & 1 \\ 1 & 0 & 0 & 0 & 1 \\ 0 & 0 & 0 & 0 & 0 \end{bmatrix}^5 = \begin{bmatrix} 3 & 5 & 5 & 0 & 6 \\ 4 & 4 & 5 & 0 & 7 \\ 1 & 4 & 3 & 0 & 3 \\ 2 & 3 & 3 & 0 & 4 \\ 0 & 0 & 0 & 0 & 0 \end{bmatrix} \cdots$$

Truly amazing. That last result, for instance, has a 3 in the upper-left. That means that there must be exactly three 5-paths from A back to A. Can you spot them in Figure 7.3?[4] And how about the 6 in the upper-right? Can you find all six 5-paths from A to E?[5]

Oh, and the number of 50-paths? No sweat:

$$A^{50} = \begin{bmatrix} 7{,}778{,}742{,}049 & 12{,}586{,}269{,}025 & 12{,}586{,}269{,}025 & 0 & 15{,}557{,}484{,}098 \\ 7{,}778{,}742{,}048 & 12{,}586{,}269{,}026 & 12{,}586{,}269{,}025 & 0 & 15{,}557{,}484{,}097 \\ 4{,}807{,}526{,}977 & 7{,}778{,}742{,}048 & 7{,}778{,}742{,}049 & 0 & 9{,}615{,}053{,}953 \\ 4{,}807{,}526{,}976 & 7{,}778{,}742{,}049 & 7{,}778{,}742{,}049 & 0 & 9{,}615{,}053{,}952 \\ 0 & 0 & 0 & 0 & 0 \end{bmatrix}.$$

So apparently there are exactly 12,586,269,025 different paths of length 50 between vertices A and B, and just one more (12,586,269,026, to be exact) from B back to itself. Don't worry, I won't make you figure out all 12 billion in either case.

Okay, but why does any of this work? What possible connection could there be between multiplying an adjacency matrix by itself repeatedly and counting the number of paths in the graph?

Well, consider first the 2-path question. To find the number of 2-paths from (say) A to E, we need the following two things to be true:

1. We need an edge from A to "something else."
2. We need an edge from that "something else" to E.

Now the way we got the number "2" in the upper-right corner of A^2 (top of p. 207) was by taking the dot product of the top row (vertex A's row) with the right column (E's column):

---

[4]The solutions are: A→C→B→A→B→A, A→B→A→C→B→A, and A→C→B→C→B→A.
[5]I believe they are A→B→A→B→C→E, A→B→A→C→B→E, A→B→C→B→C→E, A→C→B→A→B→E, A→C→B→A→C→E, and A→C→B→C→B→E. Whew!

GRAPH ANALYSIS

$$\begin{matrix} A & B & C & D & E \\ [0 & 1 & 1 & 0 & 0] \end{matrix} \cdot \begin{matrix} A \\ B \\ C \\ D \\ E \end{matrix} \begin{bmatrix} 0 \\ 1 \\ 1 \\ 1 \\ 0 \end{bmatrix} = 0 \cdot 0 + 1 \cdot 1 + 1 \cdot 1 + 0 \cdot 1 + 0 \cdot 0 = 2.$$

Look at that calculation and see the magic. To get from A to E, there are two possible "something elses": B, and C. Each one can serve as a waystation on your two-step journey from A to E. Accordingly, the two terms in our dot product that multiplied to 1 were the B and C entries. Putting it all together: since there's one way to get from A to B, and one way to get from B to E, that's one possible 2-path; and since there's one way to get from A to C, and one way to get from C to E, that's the other possible 2-path.

For larger numbers, it's just more of the same. Let's say we've figured out the number of 9-paths from each vertex to each other one:

$$A^9 = \begin{bmatrix} 0 & 1 & 1 & 0 & 0 \\ 1 & 0 & 1 & 0 & 1 \\ 0 & 1 & 0 & 0 & 1 \\ 1 & 0 & 0 & 0 & 1 \\ 0 & 0 & 0 & 0 & 0 \end{bmatrix}^9 = \begin{bmatrix} 21 & 34 & 34 & 0 & 42 \\ 22 & 33 & 34 & 0 & 43 \\ 12 & 22 & 21 & 0 & 25 \\ 13 & 21 & 21 & 0 & 26 \\ 0 & 0 & 0 & 0 & 0 \end{bmatrix}.$$

Now we want to know how many 10-paths there are. All we need to do is multiply by A one more time:

$$A^{10} = A^9 \cdot A = \begin{bmatrix} 21 & 34 & 34 & 0 & 42 \\ 22 & 33 & 34 & 0 & 43 \\ 12 & 22 & 21 & 0 & 25 \\ 13 & 21 & 21 & 0 & 26 \\ 0 & 0 & 0 & 0 & 0 \end{bmatrix} \cdot \begin{bmatrix} 0 & 1 & 1 & 0 & 0 \\ 1 & 0 & 1 & 0 & 1 \\ 0 & 1 & 0 & 0 & 1 \\ 1 & 0 & 0 & 0 & 1 \\ 0 & 0 & 0 & 0 & 0 \end{bmatrix}.$$

Let's again consider the upper-right entry, with paths from A to E. To get the number of 10-paths, we take the dot product of A's row with E's column:

$$\begin{array}{ccccc}A & B & C & D & E\\ [21 & 34 & 34 & 0 & 42]\end{array}\cdot \begin{array}{c}A\\B\\C\\D\\E\end{array}\begin{bmatrix}0\\1\\1\\1\\0\end{bmatrix} = 21\cdot 0+34\cdot 1+34\cdot 1+0\cdot 1+42\cdot 0 = 68.$$

Here's the rationale. We can get from B directly to E. That means that any 9-path from A to B will give us a 10-path from A to E! And since there are 34 such paths, that's 34 possible A-to-E paths with B as their second-to-last step. Similar reasoning for C as the penultimate vertex gives us our total. The entire answer for 10-paths, if you're curious, works out to:

$$A^{10} = \begin{bmatrix} 34 & 55 & 55 & 0 & \mathbf{68} \\ 33 & 56 & 55 & 0 & 67 \\ 22 & 33 & 34 & 0 & 43 \\ 21 & 34 & 34 & 0 & 42 \\ 0 & 0 & 0 & 0 & 0 \end{bmatrix}.$$

One final thing before I go. What if we wanted to know not how many paths of *exactly* length 7, but how many paths of *length 7 or less*? Easy. Any such path has 7 or fewer edges. So we can just add the number of 1-paths, the number of 2-paths, the number of 3-paths...all the way up to the number of 7-paths. Simple matrix addition gives us that answer:

$$A + A^2 + A^3 + A^4 + A^5 + A^6 + A^7 = \sum_{i=1}^{7} A^i = \begin{bmatrix} 20 & 33 & 33 & 0 & 40 \\ 21 & 32 & 33 & 0 & 41 \\ 12 & 21 & 20 & 0 & 25 \\ 13 & 20 & 20 & 0 & 25 \\ 0 & 0 & 0 & 0 & 0 \end{bmatrix}.$$

So exactly 33 paths of 7 edges or fewer from B to C. This tells us that there's quite a bit of information-travel potential between these two vertices, whether they represent computers or people or something else. Applying such logic to a social network can tell us a great deal about who the movers and shakers are in an online community. Stay tuned for more.

Chapter 8

Eigenanalysis

The title of this chapter alone is enough to make one's blood run cold. You might be thinking, "even if I could pronounce this, would I want to?"

In German, the root *eigen* (pronounced EYE-gun) means something like "one's own, inherent thing." As we'll see, in studying the eigenvectors and eigenvalues of a matrix – a process called eigenanalysis – we're examining its deepest, innermost properties. We're peering deep within all the flesh to see its skeleton. And it turns out this is the key to the most profound understanding of what a given matrix is and does.

Just look at all the nifty words we'll learn:

- **eigenvector**
- **eigenvalue**
- **eigendecomposition**
- **eigenbasis**

These are all involved in the **eigenanalysis** of a matrix.

8.1 The resonant frequency

We could come at this subject in a bunch of different ways, but let me start with the first thing that clicked for me when I learned it. At the time, I was reminded of the phenomenon of a "resonant frequency" that some systems exhibit.

You'll remember this effect if you've ever been on a playground swing. When somebody pushes you (or when you pump your legs to "push" yourself) you have to do it at the right time and at the right pace. The swing has a natural frequency of oscillation, and it resists being pushed faster or slower than that. If you find you're swinging from back to front every two seconds, you'll have to pump your legs every two seconds. Period. Even if you have thighs like Dwayne Johnson, trying to pump once every 1.5 seconds – or even furiously at 5 times a second – will do you no good. Timing it so you pump your legs at exactly the swing's resonant frequency is the only way to go higher and higher.

There are other famous examples of the resonant frequency phenomenon. Perhaps you've heard of the Tacoma Narrows Bridge (if you've never seen it, check out the video on YouTube). It was a beautiful double-lane suspension bridge in Washington State that crossed the Puget Sound – at the time, the third-largest suspension bridge in the world. Incredibly, on November 7th, 1940, it began to wobble with increasing intensity as crosswinds dangerously amplified its internal structural vibrations. It looked like a 3,000-foot-long undulating Slinky.[1] Moments later, the concrete cracked and split and the entire bridge completely collapsed and fell into

---

[1] The classic "Slinky" toy, by the way, is another example of a system that has a resonant frequency. You can't make it go down the stairs any faster or slower than it wants to go.

the water. Luckily, drivers had wisely stopped crossing it minutes before, and the only actual casualty was a cocker spaniel.

The reasons for the Tacoma Bridge catastrophe are a bit complex, but a key contributing factor was that a very specific rate of oscillation – a "sweet spot," though it was hardly sweet for those involved – caused the fluctuations to build on each other instead of being dampened. It's as if the Tacoma Bridge *wanted* to vibrate at a certain frequency, just like a playground swing has an intrinsic rhythm that the child can't speed up or slow down.

Yet another example: every non-percussive musical instrument. A piano or guitar string tuned to middle C has a certain length and tension, which causes it to resist vibrations at any frequency other than exactly 262 per second. Thus, when you strike it, only the 262 Hz[2] tone gains any traction, and the instrument sounds a clear, pure note.

8.2 Linear operators, revisited

Okay, so what does all this have to do with linear algebra? Well, consider the linear operators we learned about in Section 5.2 (p. 117). Remember that a linear operator is a square matrix that transforms one vector into another one of the same dimension when you left-multiply that vector by the matrix. Let's look at this one:

---

[2] "Hz," pronounced "hertz," is a unit meaning "cycles (backs-and-forths) per second." Every musical note is defined by a particular frequency. The lowest key on the piano is 27.5 Hz, and the highest is 4,186 Hz.

$$M = \begin{bmatrix} 1\frac{1}{2} & -1 \\ -\frac{1}{2} & 1 \end{bmatrix},$$

and take it for a spin. If we multiply it by, say, $\begin{bmatrix} 1 \\ 2 \end{bmatrix}$, we get:

$$\begin{bmatrix} 1\frac{1}{2} & -1 \\ -\frac{1}{2} & 1 \end{bmatrix} \cdot \begin{bmatrix} 1 \\ 2 \end{bmatrix} = \begin{bmatrix} -\frac{1}{2} \\ 1\frac{1}{2} \end{bmatrix}, \quad \text{so} \quad \begin{bmatrix} 1 \\ 2 \end{bmatrix} \rightarrow \text{maps to} \rightarrow \begin{bmatrix} -\frac{1}{2} \\ 1\frac{1}{2} \end{bmatrix}.$$

For the input $\begin{bmatrix} 2 \\ 1 \end{bmatrix}$, we get:

$$\begin{bmatrix} 1\frac{1}{2} & -1 \\ -\frac{1}{2} & 1 \end{bmatrix} \cdot \begin{bmatrix} 2 \\ 1 \end{bmatrix} = \begin{bmatrix} 2 \\ 0 \end{bmatrix}, \quad \text{so} \quad \begin{bmatrix} 2 \\ 1 \end{bmatrix} \rightarrow \begin{bmatrix} 2 \\ 0 \end{bmatrix}.$$

And M maps the input $\begin{bmatrix} -3 \\ 5 \end{bmatrix}$ to:

$$\begin{bmatrix} 1\frac{1}{2} & -1 \\ -\frac{1}{2} & 1 \end{bmatrix} \cdot \begin{bmatrix} -3 \\ 5 \end{bmatrix} = \begin{bmatrix} -9\frac{1}{2} \\ 6\frac{1}{2} \end{bmatrix}, \quad \text{so} \quad \begin{bmatrix} -3 \\ 5 \end{bmatrix} \rightarrow \begin{bmatrix} -9\frac{1}{2} \\ 6\frac{1}{2} \end{bmatrix}.$$

See a pattern? Me neither. It seems to be all over the place, mapping each input to some random output with no real rhyme or reason. All of these mappings are depicted in Figure 8.1 (p. 215).

Hitting a matrix's resonant frequency

None of that was very special. Random-looking stuff gets mapped to other random-looking stuff. But now here comes the plot twist. Let's strike this bad boy at its *resonant frequency*.

$$\begin{bmatrix} 1\frac{1}{2} & -1 \\ -\frac{1}{2} & 1 \end{bmatrix} \cdot \begin{bmatrix} -1 \\ \frac{1}{2} \end{bmatrix} = \begin{bmatrix} -2 \\ 1 \end{bmatrix}, \quad \text{so} \quad \begin{bmatrix} -1 \\ \frac{1}{2} \end{bmatrix} \rightarrow \begin{bmatrix} -2 \\ 1 \end{bmatrix}.$$

8.2. LINEAR OPERATORS, REVISITED

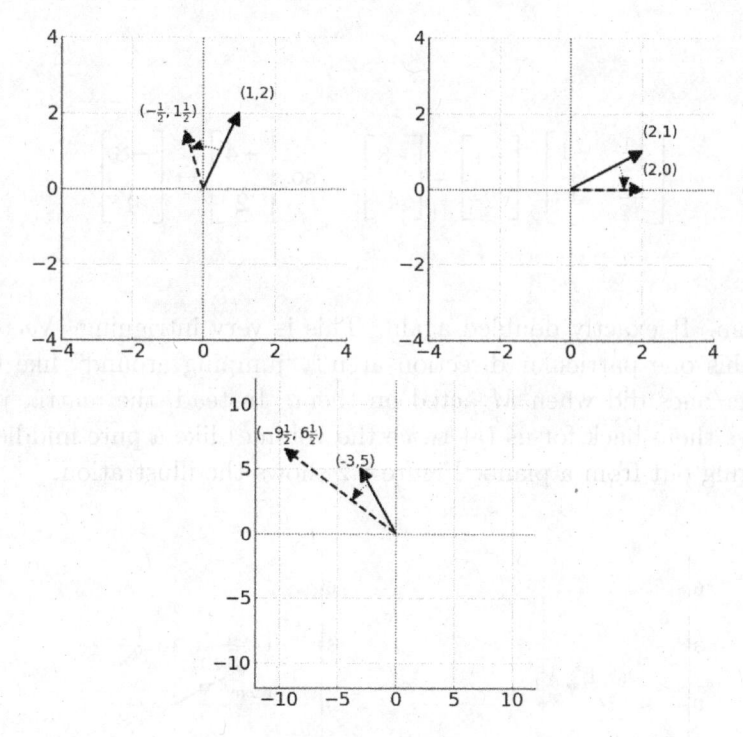

Figure 8.1: The M matrix's operation. Three randomly-chosen input vectors (solid) are mapped to crazy output vectors (dashed).

It's easy to miss the significance of that, so if nothing jumped out at you, look again. What we just discovered is that the vector $\begin{bmatrix} -1 \\ \frac{1}{2} \end{bmatrix}$ is sort of magic: if we feed it as input to M, the output is *a scaled version of the same vector*. In fact, it exactly doubled in size.

Let's try that again, with the $\begin{bmatrix} -2 \\ 1 \end{bmatrix}$ we just got back:

$$\begin{bmatrix} 1\frac{1}{2} & -1 \\ -\frac{1}{2} & 1 \end{bmatrix} \cdot \begin{bmatrix} -2 \\ 1 \end{bmatrix} = \begin{bmatrix} -4 \\ 2 \end{bmatrix}, \quad \text{so} \quad \begin{bmatrix} -2 \\ 1 \end{bmatrix} \rightarrow \begin{bmatrix} -4 \\ 2 \end{bmatrix}.$$

Boom. It exactly doubled again. And if we then feed it $\begin{bmatrix} -4 \\ 2 \end{bmatrix}$:

$$\begin{bmatrix} 1\frac{1}{2} & -1 \\ -\frac{1}{2} & 1 \end{bmatrix} \cdot \begin{bmatrix} -4 \\ 2 \end{bmatrix} = \begin{bmatrix} -8 \\ 4 \end{bmatrix}, \quad \text{so} \quad \begin{bmatrix} -4 \\ 2 \end{bmatrix} \rightarrow \begin{bmatrix} -8 \\ 4 \end{bmatrix}.$$

Boom. It exactly doubled again. This is very intriguing. Vectors in this one particular direction aren't "jumping around" like the other ones did when M acted on them. Instead, the matrix just plays them back for us (at twice the volume) like a pure middle C singing out from a piano. Figure 8.2 shows the illustration.

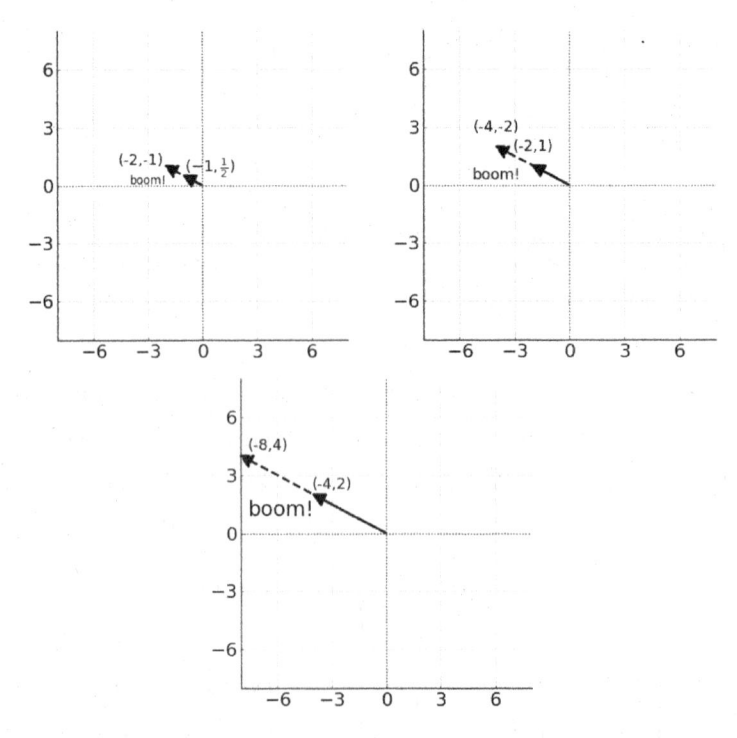

Figure 8.2: The M matrix's operation when applied to one of its eigenvectors. The input (solid) is mapped to the *same* vector, but scaled (dashed).

8.2. LINEAR OPERATORS, REVISITED

Big concept: the vector $\begin{bmatrix} -1 \\ \frac{1}{2} \end{bmatrix}$ (and all its multiples, like $\begin{bmatrix} -2 \\ 1 \end{bmatrix}$, $\begin{bmatrix} -4 \\ 2 \end{bmatrix}$, $\begin{bmatrix} -8 \\ 4 \end{bmatrix}$, ...) is called an **eigenvector** of M. Here's what that means:

> An **eigenvector** of a matrix A is any vector that gets mapped to a scaled version of *itself* – i.e., to a vector in the same direction – when muliplied by A. In symbols, if $\vec{x}$ is an eigenvector of A, then
> $$A\vec{x} = \lambda\vec{x}$$
> for some number λ. And that number λ is called an **eigenvalue** of A.

In this case, the eigenvalue λ is 2, since any vector in the $\begin{bmatrix} -1 \\ \frac{1}{2} \end{bmatrix}$ direction gets multiplied by 2.

Alternate resonant frequencies

You might be curious: are there any *other* "magic" vectors for our M matrix? It turns out there are. Try $\begin{bmatrix} 4 \\ 4 \end{bmatrix}$:

$$\begin{bmatrix} 1\frac{1}{2} & -1 \\ -\frac{1}{2} & 1 \end{bmatrix} \cdot \begin{bmatrix} 4 \\ 4 \end{bmatrix} = \begin{bmatrix} 2 \\ 2 \end{bmatrix}, \text{ so } \begin{bmatrix} 4 \\ 4 \end{bmatrix} \to \begin{bmatrix} 2 \\ 2 \end{bmatrix}.$$

So giving $\begin{bmatrix} 4 \\ 4 \end{bmatrix}$ to the M linear operator produces a *shrunken* version of the input: exactly half as long. And of course this pattern repeats for any vector in the $\begin{bmatrix} 4 \\ 4 \end{bmatrix}$ direction:

$$\begin{bmatrix} 1\frac{1}{2} & -1 \\ -\frac{1}{2} & 1 \end{bmatrix} \cdot \begin{bmatrix} 2 \\ 2 \end{bmatrix} = \begin{bmatrix} 1 \\ 1 \end{bmatrix}, \text{ so } \begin{bmatrix} 2 \\ 2 \end{bmatrix} \to \begin{bmatrix} 1 \\ 1 \end{bmatrix},$$

and so forth. This means that $\begin{bmatrix} 4 \\ 4 \end{bmatrix}$ (and every other vector in the same direction) is also an eigenvector of M, this time with eigenvalue $\lambda = \frac{1}{2}$.

Wow, okay. And does M have still other eigenvectors in store for us as well? The somewhat surprising answer turns out to be ***no***. There's only those two. This is an important fact we'll return to in a moment.

To recap, then, our matrix M has two eigenvectors: $\begin{bmatrix} -1 \\ \frac{1}{2} \end{bmatrix}$ (and any multiple of it) and $\begin{bmatrix} 4 \\ 4 \end{bmatrix}$ (and any multiple of it). The first of these has eigenvalue 2, and the second has eigenvalue $\frac{1}{2}$. Also, we have a special name for the $\begin{bmatrix} -1 \\ \frac{1}{2} \end{bmatrix}$ vector: it's called the **dominant eigenvector**, for reasons you'll see in a moment. A matrix's dominant eigenvector is simply the eigenvector with the highest eigenvalue.

Magnetic pull

Now assuming you followed all that, this next thing is sure to absolutely blow your mind. I know it did mine. I'm going to feed a *random* vector in as an input to our M matrix, and then repeatedly put its output back in to M and see where it goes. Remember that if I do this with an *eigenvector*, I'll keep getting back progressively scaled copies of the input vector. But let's see what happens when I pass in just an ordinary, non-special, non-eigen vector.

I'll choose $\begin{bmatrix} 1 \\ 2\frac{1}{2} \end{bmatrix}$ just for giggles, and call it $\vec{r}$ for "random." If I keep multiplying $\vec{r}$ by M, here's what I get:

$$\vec{r} = \begin{bmatrix} 1 \\ 2\frac{1}{2} \end{bmatrix}, \quad \textbf{❶}$$

$$\begin{bmatrix} 1\frac{1}{2} & -1 \\ -\frac{1}{2} & 1 \end{bmatrix} \cdot \begin{bmatrix} 1 \\ 2\frac{1}{2} \end{bmatrix} = \begin{bmatrix} -1 \\ 2 \end{bmatrix}, \quad \textbf{❷}$$

$$\begin{bmatrix} 1\frac{1}{2} & -1 \\ -\frac{1}{2} & 1 \end{bmatrix} \cdot \begin{bmatrix} -1 \\ 2 \end{bmatrix} = \begin{bmatrix} -3\frac{1}{2} \\ 2\frac{1}{2} \end{bmatrix}, \quad \textbf{❸}$$

$$\begin{bmatrix} 1\frac{1}{2} & -1 \\ -\frac{1}{2} & 1 \end{bmatrix} \cdot \begin{bmatrix} -3\frac{1}{2} \\ 2\frac{1}{2} \end{bmatrix} = \begin{bmatrix} -7\frac{3}{4} \\ 4\frac{1}{4} \end{bmatrix} \cdots \quad \textbf{❹}$$

8.2. LINEAR OPERATORS, REVISITED

You might ask "what's the big deal?" until you look at the upper left of Figure 8.3, where I've plotted this sequence of vectors with the circled numbers ❶, ❷, ❸, and ❹. I've also plotted *the dominant eigenvector* (which was in the direction $\begin{bmatrix} -1 \\ \frac{1}{2} \end{bmatrix}$, as you recall) *as a dotted line* on this plot. Look at what happens: every time we multiply by M, that random old vector is pulled towards M's dominant eigenvector like a magnet! And incredibly, this happens with *any* vector I start with. The other panes of Figure 8.3 shows what happens when I start with $\begin{bmatrix} -2 \\ -1 \end{bmatrix}$, $\begin{bmatrix} -1 \\ -2 \end{bmatrix}$, and $\begin{bmatrix} 2 \\ \frac{1}{2} \end{bmatrix}$. Resonant frequency indeed!

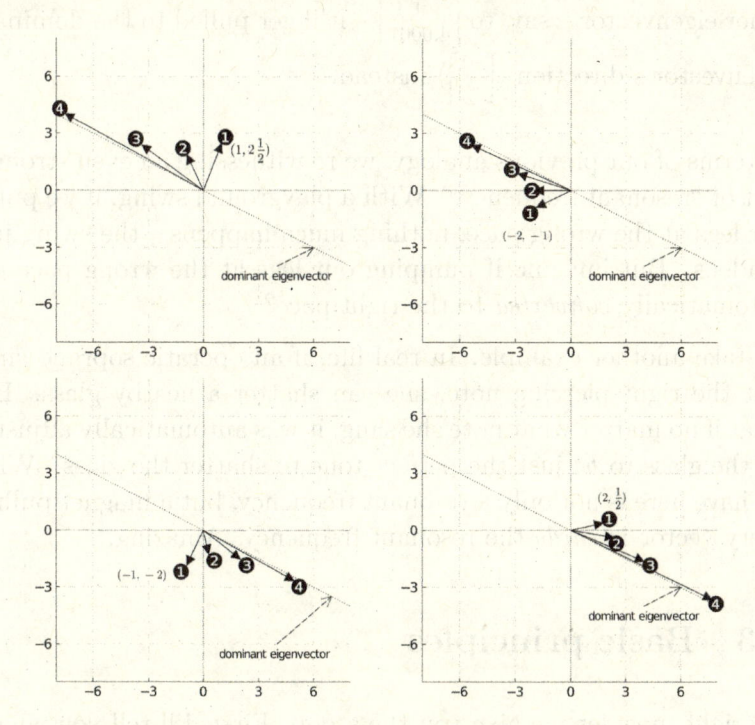

Figure 8.3: Holy cow – repeatedly applying the M operator by any vector at all drags it progressively to the dominant eigenvector!

So we see that "dominant" eigenvector is an apt term. The matrix somehow *wants* to map its inputs to the direction of the dominant eigenvector. If you keep multiplying by that matrix, you'll always be drawn there. And that's true *no matter what vector you started with*. This fact will have immense repercussions when we look at things like Markov chains and the PageRank algorithm in the next chapter.

In fact, the only vector I can start with and not get dragged to the dominant eigenvector is one that is *exactly* in the direction of the *other* eigenvector. As noted previously, if we give M the input $\begin{bmatrix} 4 \\ 4 \end{bmatrix}$ (or anything in that direction), it will stay locked in that direction (a 45° angle counterclockwise from the x-axis) and shrink by half each time. But if we nudge that vector even slightly away from that other eigenvector – say, to $\begin{bmatrix} 4 \\ 4.0001 \end{bmatrix}$ – it'll get pulled to the dominant eigenvector's direction ($\begin{bmatrix} -1 \\ \frac{1}{2} \end{bmatrix}$) instead.

In terms of our previous analogy, we're witnessing an even stronger sort of "resonant frequency." With a playground swing, if we pump our legs at the wrong pace, nothing much happens – the swing just deadens. But imagine if pumping our legs at the wrong pace got automatically *converted* to the right pace?

Or take another example. In real life, if an operatic soprano sings just the right piercing note, she can shatter a nearby glass. But what if no matter what note she sang, it was automatically adjusted by the glass to *be* just the perfect tone to shatter the glass? What we have here is not only a resonant frequency, but a magnet pulling every vector *towards* the resonant frequency. Amazing.

8.3 Basic principles

All right, now let me give you the scoop. First, I'll tell you what's true 99.99% of the time. Then, I'll say a few words about the other 0.01%.

In 99.99% of cases, **an $n \times n$ matrix has n different eigenvectors.** Furthermore, each eigenvector will be linearly independent of all the others. Each one has its own eigenvalue, and the eigenvector with the highest eigenvalue is called the matrix's dominant

8.3. BASIC PRINCIPLES

eigenvector. This is exactly what we saw with the M matrix we've been using since p. 214: it was 2×2, and had two eigenvectors ($\begin{bmatrix}-1\\\frac{1}{2}\end{bmatrix}$ and $\begin{bmatrix}4\\4\end{bmatrix}$) with eigenvalues $\lambda = 2$ and $\lambda = \frac{1}{2}$, respectively. So $\begin{bmatrix}-1\\\frac{1}{2}\end{bmatrix}$ is the dominant one.[3]

It's almost always this simple. The 0.01% cases occur only in the weird situation when we have a "repeated eigenvalue" and thus a "duplicate eigenvector." For example, the innocent-looking but ultimately weird matrix

$$W = \begin{bmatrix}-2 & 1\\-1 & 0\end{bmatrix},$$

is an example of this. Its "two eigenvectors" turn out to be the *same*: $\begin{bmatrix}1\\1\end{bmatrix}$. And each one of them has eigenvalue -1. (Multiply out $W \cdot \begin{bmatrix}1\\1\end{bmatrix}$ to verify that this produces $\begin{bmatrix}-1\\-1\end{bmatrix}$.) This scenario is very uncommon, and is unlikely to come up for you in practical situations.

While you're building your understanding of this material, my advice is to simply blow off the 0.01% stuff. It's just a footnote. What's important is the big takeaway: except in certain diabolically choreographed cases, the number of eigenvectors is the width/height of the matrix, and each of them has its own eigenvalue.

Finding the eigenvectors/eigenvalues

By the way, so far I've just stated to you what the eigenvectors are, and you might wonder how I figured that out. The answer is that I simply gave the matrix to Python and asked it for the eigenvectors and eigenvalues. We'll see the code to do that at the end of the chapter. This is how you'll always do it in practice.

---

[3] Note that when specifying the eigenvectors, we could use *any* vectors that point in the same directions as these. For instance, it would also be correct to say that M's two eigenvectors are $\begin{bmatrix}-2\\1\end{bmatrix}$ and $\begin{bmatrix}1\\1\end{bmatrix}$, or even $\begin{bmatrix}-50\\25\end{bmatrix}$ and $\begin{bmatrix}-1.73\\-1.73\end{bmatrix}$. Multiplying a vector by any constant, remember, doesn't change its direction. And the eigen*value* of a scaled eigenvector doesn't change; the eigenvalues here are still 2 and $\frac{1}{2}$ no matter how we might scale the vectors.

8.4 The Spectral Theorem

And now I present to you a fundamental eigenvalue equation that has $E = mc^2$ level significance. It goes by several names: **The Spectral Theorem**, the **eigendecomposition**, and **diagonalizing** a matrix. It forms the foundation of much of the advanced math that all this eigenstuff is based on.

Here it is:

If A is a $n \times n$ matrix, it can almost always[4] be decomposed into the product of three other $n \times n$ matrices: $V \cdot \Lambda \cdot V^{-1}$, where V has the (normalized) eigenvectors of A as its columns, and Λ is a diagonal matrix with the corresponding eigenvalues on the diagonal. For example, for a 4×4:

$$A = \begin{bmatrix} | & | & | & | \\ \vec{x_1} & \vec{x_2} & \vec{x_3} & \vec{x_4} \\ | & | & | & | \end{bmatrix} \begin{bmatrix} \lambda_1 & 0 & 0 & 0 \\ 0 & \lambda_2 & 0 & 0 \\ 0 & 0 & \lambda_3 & 0 \\ 0 & 0 & 0 & \lambda_4 \end{bmatrix} \begin{bmatrix} | & | & | & | \\ \vec{x_1} & \vec{x_2} & \vec{x_3} & \vec{x_4} \\ | & | & | & | \end{bmatrix}^{-1}$$

where the $\vec{x_k}$'s are the eigenvectors and the λ_k's are the corresponding eigenvalues.

Terminology: decomposing a matrix A into these three matrices – the first of which has the eigenvectors and the second of which has the eigenvalues – is called the **eigendecomposition** of the matrix. We also say that we have "**diagonalized**" A because the middle matrix of the three (called Λ, which is an upper case λ "lambda") is a diagonal matrix. Finally, this whole fact is also sometimes called **the Spectral Theorem** for square matrices.

---

[4] 99.99% of the time. (See p. 221.)

8.4. THE SPECTRAL THEOREM

Example

Let's verify the Spectral Theorem for our M matrix from p. 214. I told you that the eigenvectors were $\begin{bmatrix} -1 \\ \frac{1}{2} \end{bmatrix}$ and $\begin{bmatrix} 4 \\ 4 \end{bmatrix}$, but for the eigendecomposition we need them to have Euclidean norm 1. So we normalize them (recall p. 43) to get:

$$\vec{x_1} = \frac{\begin{bmatrix} -1 \\ \frac{1}{2} \end{bmatrix}}{\left\| \begin{bmatrix} -1 \\ \frac{1}{2} \end{bmatrix} \right\|_2} = \frac{\begin{bmatrix} -1 \\ \frac{1}{2} \end{bmatrix}}{\sqrt{(-1)^2 + (\frac{1}{2})^2}} = \begin{bmatrix} -.894 \\ .447 \end{bmatrix}$$

$$\vec{x_2} = \frac{\begin{bmatrix} 4 \\ 4 \end{bmatrix}}{\left\| \begin{bmatrix} 4 \\ 4 \end{bmatrix} \right\|_2} = \frac{\begin{bmatrix} 4 \\ 4 \end{bmatrix}}{\sqrt{(4)^2 + (4)^2}} = \begin{bmatrix} .707 \\ .707 \end{bmatrix}$$

It's important to note that these normalized versions of our eigenvectors point in the *same* directions that the original ones did ($\begin{bmatrix} -1 \\ \frac{1}{2} \end{bmatrix}$ and $\begin{bmatrix} 4 \\ 4 \end{bmatrix}$). We just scaled them so that they have length 1 (according to the Euclidean norm). But they're still the same eigenvectors.

Okay. Now if the Spectral Theorem is correct, M should be equal to its eigendecomposition. First, let's put together our V matrix (with eigenvectors as columns):

$$V = \begin{bmatrix} -.894 & .707 \\ .447 & .707 \end{bmatrix}$$

Then, let's find its inverse (using Python):

$$V^{-1} = \begin{bmatrix} -.746 & .746 \\ .471 & .943 \end{bmatrix}$$

Next, stick the eigenvalues on the diagonal of an otherwise-all-zeroes matrix:

$$\Lambda = \begin{bmatrix} 2 & 0 \\ 0 & \frac{1}{2} \end{bmatrix}$$

and finally, multiply it all out:

$$V \quad \cdot \quad \Lambda \quad \cdot \quad V^{-1} \quad = \quad M?$$

$$\begin{bmatrix} -.894 & .707 \\ .447 & .707 \end{bmatrix} \cdot \begin{bmatrix} 2 & 0 \\ 0 & \frac{1}{2} \end{bmatrix} \cdot \begin{bmatrix} -.746 & .746 \\ .471 & .943 \end{bmatrix} = \begin{bmatrix} -1.5 & -1 \\ -.5 & 1 \end{bmatrix} \checkmark$$

which indeed equals our M from p. 214.

8.5 The "natural" basis

Now think back all the way to p. 69 when we talked about the notion of a **basis**: a linearly independent set of vectors that spans some space. You'll recall our friends Ron and Hermione, whose vectors $\vec{r}$ and $\vec{h}$ we expressed in both the standard basis {[1 0], [0 1]}, and in a "domino basis" {[1 2], [4 4]}. Importantly, if you have a basis, every vector in the space can be expressed as a linear combination of the basis vectors in exactly one way.

I'm now going to argue that in an important sense, the eigenvectors of a linear operator matrix form the most "natural" basis for it. We call this set of eigenvectors the **eigenbasis** of the matrix. Let me explain why it's the most natural one.

First of all, realize that multiplying any matrix by a *diagonal* one is super easy. All you're doing is taking multiples of each column.

8.5. THE "NATURAL" BASIS

To illustrate, consider the following scattershot matrix, which I chose at random and will call S:

$$S = \begin{bmatrix} 3 & 4 & 2 & 1 \\ 5 & 5 & -7 & 8 \\ 1 & 1 & 1 & 2 \\ 3 & 4 & 6 & 8 \end{bmatrix}.$$

Now think about this. If I told you to multiply (by hand) S times the matrix below, you'd probably cry:

$$\begin{bmatrix} 3 & 4 & 2 & 1 \\ 5 & 5 & -7 & 8 \\ 1 & 1 & 1 & 2 \\ 3 & 4 & 6 & 8 \end{bmatrix} \cdot \begin{bmatrix} 3 & 2 & 1 & 9 \\ 6 & 2 & -2 & 9 \\ 1 & 9 & -3 & 9 \\ 7 & 9 & 4 & 9 \end{bmatrix} = \text{HARD} = ?? \ \odot$$

But if I told you to compute *this* operation by hand, you wouldn't cry:

$$\begin{bmatrix} 3 & 4 & 2 & 1 \\ 5 & 5 & -7 & 8 \\ 1 & 1 & 1 & 2 \\ 3 & 4 & 6 & 8 \end{bmatrix} \cdot \begin{bmatrix} 3 & 0 & 0 & 0 \\ 0 & 2 & 0 & 0 \\ 0 & 0 & -3 & 0 \\ 0 & 0 & 0 & 9 \end{bmatrix} = \text{easy!} = \begin{bmatrix} 9 & 8 & -6 & 9 \\ 15 & 10 & 21 & 72 \\ 3 & 2 & -3 & 18 \\ 9 & 8 & -18 & 72 \end{bmatrix}!$$

The reason this operation is easy is that each column of the right-hand-side matrix has all zero entries but one. Consider its first (leftmost) column, $[\ 3\ 0\ 0\ 0\ ]^\mathsf{T}$. That says, "for the first column of my answer, I'd like three of S's first column, and none of the others." So the first column of our answer is simply $[\ 9\ 15\ 3\ 9\ ]^\mathsf{T}$: we just multiply each entry by 3. Its second column is $[\ 0\ 2\ 0\ 0\ ]^\mathsf{T}$, which means "for the second column of my answer, I'd like two of S's second column, and none of the others." So the second column of the answer is $[\ 8\ 10\ 2\ 8\ ]^\mathsf{T}$. And so on.

In fact, if you think of the columns of the S matrix as a basis, the diagonal matrix is doing nothing more than telling us *how much of each basis vector we want*. It's scaling each basis vector by a certain amount, and adding them all together. And that's the key to seeing the eigenbasis' "naturalness."

Recall (from p.94) that if we have a vector expressed in some basis B, and we want to convert it to the *standard* basis, we can multiply it by the appropriate change-of-basis matrix. And that matrix simply has the basis vectors of B as its columns.

Recall further (from p.165) that if we want to go the other way – if we have a vector expressed in the standard basis, and we want to convert it to some other basis – our change-of-basis matrix is the *inverse* of the one from the previous paragraph.

Now, let's put it all together. Suppose we wanted to take a linear operator A for a test drive; that is, we want to multiply a square matrix A by some vector $\vec{x}$ to perform a linear transformation $A \cdot \vec{x}$.

Look carefully at the spectral theorem formula again:

$$A = V \cdot \Lambda \cdot V^{-1}.$$

This tells us that multiplying $\vec{x}$ by A is the same as multiplying it by those three matrices:

$$A \cdot \vec{x} = V \cdot \Lambda \cdot V^{-1} \cdot \vec{x}.$$

Let's take these multiplications one at a time from the right.[5] Consider what each of them does:

1. Multiplying $\vec{x}$ by V^{-1} converts $\vec{x}$ from the standard basis to the eigenbasis. (!)
2. Then, multiplying by Λ is a trivial operation which gives us "a certain amount" of each eigenvector. (The "amount" is the eigenvalue corresponding to that eigenvector, which effectively tells us how important that eigenvector is to the result.)
3. Finally, multiplying $\vec{x}$ by V converts our answer from the eigenbasis back to the standard basis. (!)

Dissected in this way, we get a super deep insight into what linear operators fundamentally *do*. Yes, you can think of them as matrix multiplications. But under the hood, what we're really doing

---

[5] We're free to do it in this order if we want, because as you remember from p. 154, matrix multiplication is associative.

8.5. THE "NATURAL" BASIS

is converting our input vector to a particular basis (the matrix's eigenbasis). Then, in that space, "matrix-vector multiplication" is a simple scaling operation. We then pop back into the standard basis for our final answer.

Just to make this concrete, let's work out an example using our M matrix from before (p. 214). From p. 223, we learned that V, the matrix with normalized eigenvectors as columns, was

$$V = \begin{bmatrix} -.894 & .707 \\ .447 & .707 \end{bmatrix}.$$

As I explained above, this is really none other than the change-of-basis matrix from M's eigenbasis (we'll call that basis B_λ) to the standard basis B_s. And if we take its inverse, we get the change-of-basis matrix going the other way: from B_s to B_λ. So,

$$\text{COB}_{B_\lambda \to B_s} = \begin{bmatrix} -.894 & .707 \\ .447 & .707 \end{bmatrix}, \quad \text{COB}_{B_s \to B_\lambda} = \begin{bmatrix} -.746 & .746 \\ .471 & .943 \end{bmatrix},$$

where

$$B_\lambda = \left\{ \begin{bmatrix} -.894 \\ .447 \end{bmatrix}, \begin{bmatrix} .707 \\ .707 \end{bmatrix} \right\}, \text{ and } B_s = \left\{ \begin{bmatrix} 1 \\ 0 \end{bmatrix}, \begin{bmatrix} 0 \\ 1 \end{bmatrix} \right\}.$$

Now one of our example inputs to the M linear transformation from p. 214 was $\begin{bmatrix} 2 \\ 1 \end{bmatrix}$, which we saw M map to $\begin{bmatrix} 2 \\ 0 \end{bmatrix}$. So let's run $\begin{bmatrix} 2 \\ 1 \end{bmatrix}$ through the assembly line:

$$\text{COB}_{B_\lambda \to B_s} \cdot \Lambda \cdot \text{COB}_{B_s \to B_\lambda} \cdot \begin{bmatrix} 2 \\ 1 \end{bmatrix}$$

$$\begin{bmatrix} -.894 & .707 \\ .447 & .707 \end{bmatrix} \cdot \begin{bmatrix} 2 & 0 \\ 0 & \frac{1}{2} \end{bmatrix} \cdot \begin{bmatrix} -.746 & .746 \\ .471 & .943 \end{bmatrix} \cdot \begin{bmatrix} 2 \\ 1 \end{bmatrix}$$

1. Multiplying our input vector $\begin{bmatrix} 2 \\ 1 \end{bmatrix}$ – whose coordinates are in the standard basis – by V^{-1} converts it to the eigenbasis.

$$\begin{array}{ccccc} \text{COB}_{B_\lambda \to B_s} & & \Lambda & & \downarrow \\ \begin{bmatrix} -.894 & .707 \\ .447 & .707 \end{bmatrix} & \cdot & \begin{bmatrix} 2 & 0 \\ 0 & \frac{1}{2} \end{bmatrix} & \cdot & \begin{bmatrix} -.746 \\ 1.886 \end{bmatrix} \end{array}$$

So $\begin{bmatrix} 2 \\ 1 \end{bmatrix}_{B_s}$ is the same as $\begin{bmatrix} -.746 \\ 1.886 \end{bmatrix}_{B_\lambda}$, and we're now in the "eigenrealm," ready for the next step.

2. We now take that eigenbasis-version of our input and multiply it by our diagonal matrix of eigenvalues.

$$\begin{array}{ccc} \text{COB}_{B_\lambda \to B_s} & & \downarrow \\ \begin{bmatrix} -.894 & .707 \\ .447 & .707 \end{bmatrix} & \cdot & \begin{bmatrix} -1.492 \\ .943 \end{bmatrix} \end{array}$$

We've merely scaled the eigenbasis-form of our input: the first element got doubled from -.746 to -1.492 (since the first eigenvalue is 2) and the second one got halved from 1.886 to .943 (since the second eigenvalue is $\frac{1}{2}$). This was actually the only "transformation" work to do!

3. Now we merely translate our vector out of eigenspace back to standard basis language, by multiplying by the change-of-basis matrix back the other way:

$$\begin{array}{c} \downarrow \\ = \begin{bmatrix} 2 \\ 0 \end{bmatrix} ! \end{array}$$

Exactly as we predicted.

8.5. THE "NATURAL" BASIS

This is seriously one of the most beautiful things I've seen in all of mathematics. It reminds me of an apple tree orchard. When you're wandering through the grounds, it seems like you're in the middle of a chaotic maze of trees planted in random positions. But when you happen upon a certain special spot, boom! All the trees suddenly line up and a perfectly symmetric pattern emerges. In a similar way, multiplying by a matrix looks like a jumble of random numbers, but seen from one special perspective – the eigenbasis – the operation suddenly becomes astonishingly simple and elegant.

Postlude: symmetric matrices and their eigenbases

One last little thing before we end this theoretical chapter and commence with some exciting "eigenapplications" in the next one. It turns out that in many situations, the square matrix A that we're interested in will be *symmetric*. This is true if we're dealing with the adjacency matrix of an undirected graph, for instance (recall the graph applications section beginning on p. 196). In statistical applications, we work with something called a **covariance matrix** a lot, which shows how much each pair of several random variables are correlated with each other. This, too, will be a symmetric matrix.

It turns out that the eigenvectors of a *symmetric* matrix will always form an **orthonormal basis**. This turns out to be convenient, because of the lesson we learned on p. 163: there we discovered that if a matrix is orthogonal, its inverse is simply the same thing as its transpose. And that means in turn that the Spectral Theorem for such matrices reduces from this:

$$A = V \cdot \Lambda \cdot V^{-1}$$

to simply this:

$$A = V \cdot \Lambda \cdot V^{\mathsf{T}}.$$

The symmetric matrix A itself is nothing more than its eigenvectors, eigenvalues, and eigenvectors back-to-back-to-back.

Crisp and elegant, and as sweet smelling as an apple orchard. In our next and final chapter, we'll eat a few of these juicy apples.

🐍 *Appendix: Python*

On p. 221 I mentioned that to actually find the eigenvalues and eigenvectors of a matrix, you can just ask Python. Okay, so how do you do that?

Here's how: `linalg.eig()`. This function takes a matrix as an argument, and returns a vector of two things: the eigenvalues (in their own vector), and the corresponding eigenvectors. The latter come in a matrix where each column is its own eigenvector, and where eigenvalue k corresponds to the eigenvector in column k.

Let's begin with the M matrix (p. 214) we've been using all chapter. I'll save the result from calling `linalg.eig()` (in a variable called "`eigstuff`") and then print out each component separately.

```
M = array([[1.5,-1],[-.5,1]])
eigstuff = linalg.eig(M)
print(eigstuff[0])
print(eigstuff[1])
```

```
[2.  0.5]
[[ 0.89442719  0.70710678]
 [-0.4472136   0.70710678]]
```

The two eigenvalues are 2 and $\frac{1}{2}$, as we knew. Now the numbers in the eigenvector matrix look a little funky, but you just have to realize that they've been normalized. That first eigenvector – which goes with eigenvalue 2 – is:

```
dominant_eigvec = eigstuff[1][:,0]
print(dominant_eigvec)
```

```
[ 0.89442719 -0.4472136 ]
```

(Notice how I did that, by the way. I took `eigstuff`, accessed element 1 of it (the second element) to get the matrix of eigenvectors, and then used ":,0" in the boxies to get all rows of column 0.)

Now [0.894 −0.447]^T may not look familiar, but remember that it only indicates the *direction* of the eigenvector. Any vector in the same direction is also an eigenvector. So if we, say, divided it by the second entry to get an equally good dominant eigenvector:

```
another_eigvec = dominant_eigvec / dominant_eigvec[1]
print(another_eigvec)
```

```
[ -2. 1. ]
```

that should ring a bell. We can do the same with the other eigenvectors, of course, and there's really nothing more to it than that. (Believe me: calculating them by hand is a *major* pain.)

Chapter 9

Eigenapplications

We end this book with a few more ultra-cool real-world applications of linear algebra. Unlike those in Chapter 7, though, these will all involve the **eigenvalue** concepts you learned in Chapter 8. Our new ability to penetrate to the heart of a matrix and understand its inner structure will enable us to do things we could only dream about before.

Video compression

Imagine you owned a business, and you needed to send a 7×7 matrix over the Internet to one of your customers. Say, this matrix:

$$M_1 = \begin{bmatrix} 5 & -1 & 45 & 16 & 16 & 3 & 37 \\ 3 & -9 & 9 & 27 & -100 & 24 & 601 \\ 13 & 0 & 2 & 13 & -18 & 21 & 11 \\ -4 & 33 & 9 & 1 & 4 & 14 & 50 \\ -21 & 51 & 9 & 17 & 5 & 73 & -5 \\ 31 & -5 & 9 & -99 & -22 & 1 & 7 \\ 6 & 8 & 9 & 24 & 8 & 8 & 8 \end{bmatrix}.$$

How many numbers in total would you have to send your customer to communicate the information in this matrix?

Easy question. There are 49 entries in a 7-by-7 matrix, so you need to send 49 numbers. Duh.

Now suppose you wanted to send this matrix instead:

$$M_2 = \begin{bmatrix} 5 & 5 & 10 & -5 & 20 & 500 & 2\frac{1}{2} \\ 3 & 3 & 6 & -3 & 12 & 300 & 1\frac{1}{2} \\ 13 & 13 & 26 & -13 & 52 & 1300 & 6\frac{1}{2} \\ -4 & -4 & -8 & 4 & -16 & -400 & -2 \\ -21 & -21 & -42 & 21 & -84 & -2100 & -10\frac{1}{2} \\ 31 & 31 & 62 & -31 & 124 & 3100 & 15\frac{1}{2} \\ 6 & 6 & 12 & -6 & 24 & 600 & 3 \end{bmatrix}.$$

How many numbers would you have to send this time?

If you answered, "again, 49," take another look. M_2 is way different than M_1, because it has a very regular structure. Look at M_2's first (leftmost) column. Then realize that its second column is identical to the first. Then further realize that its third column is exactly *twice* the first. And its fourth column is *negative* the first. And its

VIDEO COMPRESSION

last three columns are four times, a hundred times, and one-half times the first column, respectively.

So if your customer knew the matrix would have this type of structure, I claim you could send them all the necessary information in just *fourteen* numbers instead of 42. Here's how:

1. First, send them the first column: [5 3 13 −4 −21 31 6]. That's seven numbers.
2. Then, send them the multiplier for each of the other columns. Namely, [1 1 2 −1 4 100 $\frac{1}{2}$]. That, too, is seven numbers.[1]

From these fourteen numbers alone, the customer can reconstruct the original matrix. All they have to do is compute the outer product (recall p. 152) of the two 7-element vectors they received:

$$\begin{bmatrix} 5 \\ 3 \\ 13 \\ -4 \\ -21 \\ 31 \\ 6 \end{bmatrix} \bullet \begin{bmatrix} 1 & 1 & 2 & -1 & 4 & 100 & \frac{1}{2} \end{bmatrix} =$$

$$\begin{bmatrix} 5 & 5 & 10 & -5 & 20 & 500 & 2\frac{1}{2} \\ 3 & 3 & 6 & -3 & 12 & 300 & 1\frac{1}{2} \\ 13 & 13 & 26 & -13 & 52 & 1300 & 6\frac{1}{2} \\ -4 & -4 & -8 & 4 & -16 & -400 & -2 \\ -21 & -21 & -42 & 21 & -84 & -2100 & -10\frac{1}{2} \\ 31 & 31 & 62 & -31 & 124 & 3100 & 15\frac{1}{2} \\ 6 & 6 & 12 & -6 & 24 & 600 & 3 \end{bmatrix}.$$

What's going on here? Simply put, M_2 has *less information* in it than M_1 does, despite the fact that they are ostensibly the same

---

[1] Yeah, yeah, I know we could omit the first "1" in this second set of seven, because the customer will know that the first column should be multiplied by 1 without us having to tell them. That's a detail, and it's actually messier to take advantage of that. Thirteen is unlucky anyway – ask Thorin Oakenshield if you don't believe me.

size. In fact, you may have realized that M_2 is a **rank-1** matrix. It has only one linearly independent column: all the others are simply (scaled) copies of it. This is what a rank-deficient matrix fundamentally is: a matrix that can have some of its entries "squeezed" out of it without losing any information.

M_1 and M_2 represent the far extremes of this phenomenon. M_1 is full rank (rank-7), and M_2 is just rank-1. In general, a 7 × 7 rank-deficient matrix might not be *as* deficient as M_2 is: it could have a rank anywhere from 1 to 6.

Incidentally, 14 numbers might not seem like that big a savings over 49 (it's only 3.5 times fewer entries), but consider what happens as the matrix gets larger. Suppose it were 1920 × 1920. Transmitting a rank-1 matrix of that size would require 1920 + 1920 = 3,840 numbers to go across the wire. But a full-rank matrix of that size would need *3,686,400* entries. That's nearly 1,000 times as much data.

V1. Enter Netflix

Now what's the application here? Well, it's probably one you use every day. Suppose your aforementioned business is a video streaming service, and your customer is watching one of your videos. The matrix we've been talking about is one **frame** of this video. For simplicity, we'll consider images (frames) that are in **gray scale** rather than color. Each **pixel** of the image is represented by a single number on some scale: perhaps 0 indicates a pitch black pixel in the current frame, and 255 is bright white, and all the numbers in between are shades of gray.[2]

If each frame of our movie is a 1920 × 1920-pixel square[3], and we're

---

[2] Why a range of 0 through 255? Because as you may remember from Chapters 6 and 7 of *A Cool Brisk Walk*, that's how many different values can fit in a single byte (8 bits) of data.

[3] At this point it may occur to you that when you watch a movie, your screen typically isn't perfectly square, but rectangular. Its **aspect ratio** (width-to-height) might be, say, 1.875:1, which yields a 1920 × 1024 canvas.

When your matrix isn't square, instead of using the eigenvalue decomposi-

VIDEO COMPRESSION

shoveling 30 frames per second at our viewer, that would be about 105 Megabytes of information *every second* we'd be trying to send. The Internet ain't got no time for that.

So we'd like to instead send a compressed version of each frame: a matrix whose rank is far less than 1,920 and yet which looks pretty close to the original. Our problem thus reduces to: *what matrix, of the same size as the original image's matrix but of at most rank-k (for some number k) is the "closest" to the original?*

V2. Yet another norm

First, we have to settle on what we mean by one matrix being "close" to another. Here, we'll subtract one matrix from the other, and then take the **Frobenius norm** of this difference. Subtracting matrices, of course, is just the inverse of adding them (p. 87): we do it element by element and get a matrix of the differences. The "Frobenius norm" (which always sounded to me like a character from a Willy Wonka story, btw) is just what you would expect it to be: the square-root of the sum of all these squared differences. In fact it's exactly like the Euclidean norm of a vector (p. 36), except that we have a two-dimensional pane of entries to work with instead of just a one-dimensional list.

To be concrete, let's say we have a matrix M, and an "approximation" to matrix M called $\hat{M}$, with the following values:

$$M = \begin{bmatrix} 17 & 2 \\ -3 & 6 \end{bmatrix}, \quad \hat{M} = \begin{bmatrix} 14 & 4 \\ -5 & -1 \end{bmatrix},$$

How "close" are these two matrices to each other? To quantify this, we first subtract one from the other (doesn't matter which order):

$$M - \hat{M} = \begin{bmatrix} 3 & -2 \\ 2 & 7 \end{bmatrix}.$$

---

tion, as we learned last chapter, we can use the **singular value decomposition (SVD)**, a very closely related technique. In fact, the "singular values" and "singular vectors" that the SVD gives you are exactly the same thing as eigenvalues and eigenvectors for a non-square matrix.

And then we take the square-root of the sum of the squared entries to give us the Frobenius norm:

$$\left\| M - \hat{M} \right\|_F = \sqrt{3^2 + -2^2 + 2^2 + 7^2} = 8.124.$$

This measure passes a quick sanity check: the further apart the entries of M and $\hat{M}$ at a particular row and column, the larger the difference that is added towards the Frobenius norm. So this metric gives pairs of matrices whose entries are more similar to each other a lower overall norm, indicating a higher similarity.

V3. Best low-rank matrix approximations

And now for our eigenstuff. Recall (p. 220 and following) that every eigenvector of a matrix has a corresponding eigenvalue, and that we could arrange these eigenvectors by decreasing eigenvalue if we like. The one with the largest eigenvalue had the special name "dominant eigenvector." I'll also refer to "the top eigenvector," "the top two eigenvectors," "the top ten eigenvectors," and so forth, by which I just mean "the k eigenvectors with the highest eigenvalues."

Okay. It turns out that the best rank-1 approximation to a square matrix (where "best" means "closest to the original when using the Frobenius norm") is *the dominant eigenvector, times its eigenvalue, times the transpose of the dominant eigenvector.* To illustrate, let's say we had this 5 × 5 matrix[4]:

$$A = \begin{bmatrix} 12 & 2 & 1 & 9 & 13 \\ 2 & 20 & 12 & 7 & 5 \\ 1 & 12 & 6 & -4 & 5 \\ 9 & 7 & -4 & 8 & 8 \\ 13 & 5 & 5 & 8 & 13 \end{bmatrix},$$

---

[4]You may notice that this example matrix happens to be *symmetric*. Things actually get slightly weird for non-symmetric matrices, in which case you can again turn to the SVD, which is almost the same thing as the eigendecomposition.

and we wanted the best rank-1 approximation to it. We ask Python for its dominant eigenvector, and the corresponding eigenvalue, and get this:

$$\vec{x_1} = \begin{bmatrix} .462 \\ .538 \\ .257 \\ .38 \\ .535 \end{bmatrix}, \quad \lambda_1 = 37.363.$$

Multiplying these out as indicated above, we get:

$$\vec{x_1} \bullet [\lambda_1] \bullet \vec{x_1}^\mathsf{T} =$$

$$\begin{bmatrix} .462 \\ .538 \\ .257 \\ .38 \\ .535 \end{bmatrix} \bullet [37.363] \bullet \begin{bmatrix} .462 & .538 & .257 & .38 & .535 \end{bmatrix} =$$

$$\begin{bmatrix} 7.963 & 9.288 & 4.441 & 6.563 & 9.222 \\ 9.288 & 10.834 & 5.18 & 7.655 & 10.757 \\ 4.441 & 5.18 & 2.477 & 3.66 & 5.143 \\ 6.563 & 7.655 & 3.66 & 5.409 & 7.6 \\ 9.222 & 10.757 & 5.143 & 7.6 & 10.68 \end{bmatrix}.$$

Take careful note to see that *this is actually the* **Spectral Theorem** *in action* (from p. 222) but using only a subset of the eigenvectors/eigenvalues (namely, the top one) instead of all of them. (This is why I put the top eigenvalue, 37.363, into a 1×1 matrix in the equation above – to help you see that connection.)

Now how close is this approximation to our original A matrix? Not that great, actually. If you run your eyes over the entries, and compare to A (p. 238) it doesn't even look like it's trying very hard. The Frobenius norm of the difference between the two, by the way, is a whopping 573.04, which tells you that limiting ourselves to rank-1 isn't producing a very good approximation. We wouldn't want to send such an image to our viewer, even though it would only take 10 bytes instead of 25, because they might not even know whether they were on HBO or the Disney Channel.

Okay, let's move up to rank-2 then. What's the closest rank-2 matrix to our original? Python says the second highest eigenvalue (and its eigenvector) are:

$$\vec{x_2} = \begin{bmatrix} -.458 \\ .658 \\ .448 \\ -.266 \\ -.293 \end{bmatrix}, \quad \lambda_2 = 27.712.$$

Adding this second eigenvector into the mix, we get:

$$\begin{bmatrix} | & | \\ \vec{x_1} & \vec{x_2} \\ | & | \end{bmatrix} \cdot \begin{bmatrix} \lambda_1 & 0 \\ 0 & \lambda_2 \end{bmatrix} \cdot \begin{bmatrix} | & | \\ \vec{x_1} & \vec{x_2} \\ | & | \end{bmatrix}^T =$$

$$\begin{bmatrix} .462 & -.458 \\ .538 & .658 \\ .257 & .448 \\ .38 & -.266 \\ .535 & -.293 \end{bmatrix} \cdot \begin{bmatrix} 37.363 & 0 \\ 0 & 27.712 \end{bmatrix} \cdot \begin{bmatrix} .462 & .538 & .257 & .38 & .535 \\ -.458 & .658 & .448 & -.266 & -.293 \end{bmatrix}$$

$$= \begin{bmatrix} 12.515 & 2.748 & -0.011 & 9.211 & 12.138 \\ 2.748 & 20.231 & 11.577 & 3.849 & 6.567 \\ -0.011 & 11.577 & 6.831 & 1.07 & 2.291 \\ 9.211 & 3.849 & 1.07 & 6.95 & 9.297 \\ 12.138 & 6.567 & 2.291 & 9.297 & 12.548 \end{bmatrix}.$$

Now we're talking. Flip back and forth between those numbers and the original A on p. 238, and you'll see that with just two eigenvectors, we're starting to get a remarkably close approximation. Frobenius just plummeted to 101.62. Repeating this for the best rank-3 approximation, we get:

$$\begin{bmatrix} | & | & | \\ \vec{x_1} & \vec{x_2} & \vec{x_3} \\ | & | & | \end{bmatrix} \cdot \begin{bmatrix} \lambda_1 & 0 & 0 \\ 0 & \lambda_2 & 0 \\ 0 & 0 & \lambda_3 \end{bmatrix} \cdot \begin{bmatrix} | & | & | \\ \vec{x_1} & \vec{x_2} & \vec{x_3} \\ | & | & | \end{bmatrix}^{\mathsf{T}} =$$

$$\begin{bmatrix} .462 & -.458 & .156 \\ .538 & .658 & -.33 \\ .257 & .448 & .525 \\ .38 & -.266 & -.651 \\ .535 & -.293 & .408 \end{bmatrix} \cdot \begin{bmatrix} 37.363 & 0 & 0 \\ 0 & 27.712 & 0 \\ 0 & 0 & 7.6 \end{bmatrix} \cdot \begin{bmatrix} .462 & .538 & .257 & .38 & .535 \\ -.458 & .658 & .448 & -.266 & -.293 \\ .156 & -.33 & .525 & -.651 & .408 \end{bmatrix}$$

$$= \begin{bmatrix} 12.701 & 2.356 & 0.612 & 8.438 & 12.623 \\ 2.356 & 21.06 & 10.259 & 5.484 & 5.542 \\ 0.612 & 10.259 & 8.925 & -1.528 & 3.921 \\ 8.438 & 5.484 & -1.528 & 10.173 & 7.276 \\ 12.623 & 5.542 & 3.921 & 7.276 & 13.815 \end{bmatrix},$$

which is even closer, with a Frobenius norm of just 59.07.

Each time we add another eigenvector, we give our approximation another degree of freedom which it can use to bend closer to the original. And finally, if we use all 5, we of course get the original matrix back:

$$\begin{bmatrix} | & | & | & | & | \\ \vec{x_1} & \vec{x_2} & \vec{x_3} & \vec{x_4} & \vec{x_3} \\ | & | & | & | & | \end{bmatrix} \cdot \begin{bmatrix} \lambda_1 & 0 & 0 & 0 & 0 \\ 0 & \lambda_2 & 0 & 0 & 0 \\ 0 & 0 & \lambda_3 & 0 & 0 \\ 0 & 0 & 0 & \lambda_4 & 0 \\ 0 & 0 & 0 & 0 & \lambda_5 \end{bmatrix} \cdot \begin{bmatrix} | & | & | & | & | \\ \vec{x_1} & \vec{x_2} & \vec{x_3} & \vec{x_4} & \vec{x_5} \\ | & | & | & | & | \end{bmatrix}^{\mathsf{T}} =$$

$$\begin{bmatrix} -0.462 & -0.458 & 0.156 & 0.735 & -0.109 \\ -0.538 & 0.658 & -0.33 & 0.082 & -0.402 \\ -0.257 & 0.448 & 0.525 & 0.105 & 0.668 \\ -0.38 & -0.266 & -0.651 & -0.181 & 0.572 \\ -0.535 & -0.293 & 0.408 & -0.639 & -0.23 \end{bmatrix} \cdot$$

$$\begin{bmatrix} 37.363 & 0 & 0 & 0 & 0 \\ 0 & 27.712 & 0 & 0 & 0 \\ 0 & 0 & 7.599 & 0 & 0 \\ 0 & 0 & 0 & -.151 & 0 \\ 0 & 0 & 0 & 0 & -6.523 \end{bmatrix} \cdot$$

$$\begin{bmatrix} -0.462 & -0.538 & -0.257 & -0.38 & -0.535 \\ -0.458 & 0.658 & 0.448 & -0.266 & -0.293 \\ 0.156 & -0.33 & 0.525 & -0.651 & 0.408 \\ 0.735 & 0.082 & 0.105 & -0.181 & -0.639 \\ -0.109 & -0.402 & 0.668 & 0.572 & -0.23 \end{bmatrix} =$$

$$\begin{bmatrix} 12 & 2 & 1 & 9 & 13 \\ 2 & 20 & 12 & 7 & 5 \\ 1 & 12 & 6 & -4 & 5 \\ 9 & 7 & -4 & 8 & 8 \\ 13 & 5 & 5 & 8 & 13 \end{bmatrix} = A \quad \checkmark$$

by the Spectral Theorem. (And a Frobenius norm of 0.)

Finally, let's look at this work on an actual image. Figure 9.1 shows a 1800 × 1800 gray scale still frame from a movie. At 1 byte (8 bits) per pixel, the entire original image would take 3.24 MBytes to transmit in full. That's a lot of data for one frame of a movie that the viewer will only see for $\frac{1}{30}^{th}$ of a second.

Figure 9.1: A 3,240,000-byte gray scale image.

Let's see if we can do better. Figure 9.2 starts with a lowly rank-1 matrix (using just the dominant eigenvector), and then increases the rank as the images move left-to-right down the page.

VIDEO COMPRESSION 243

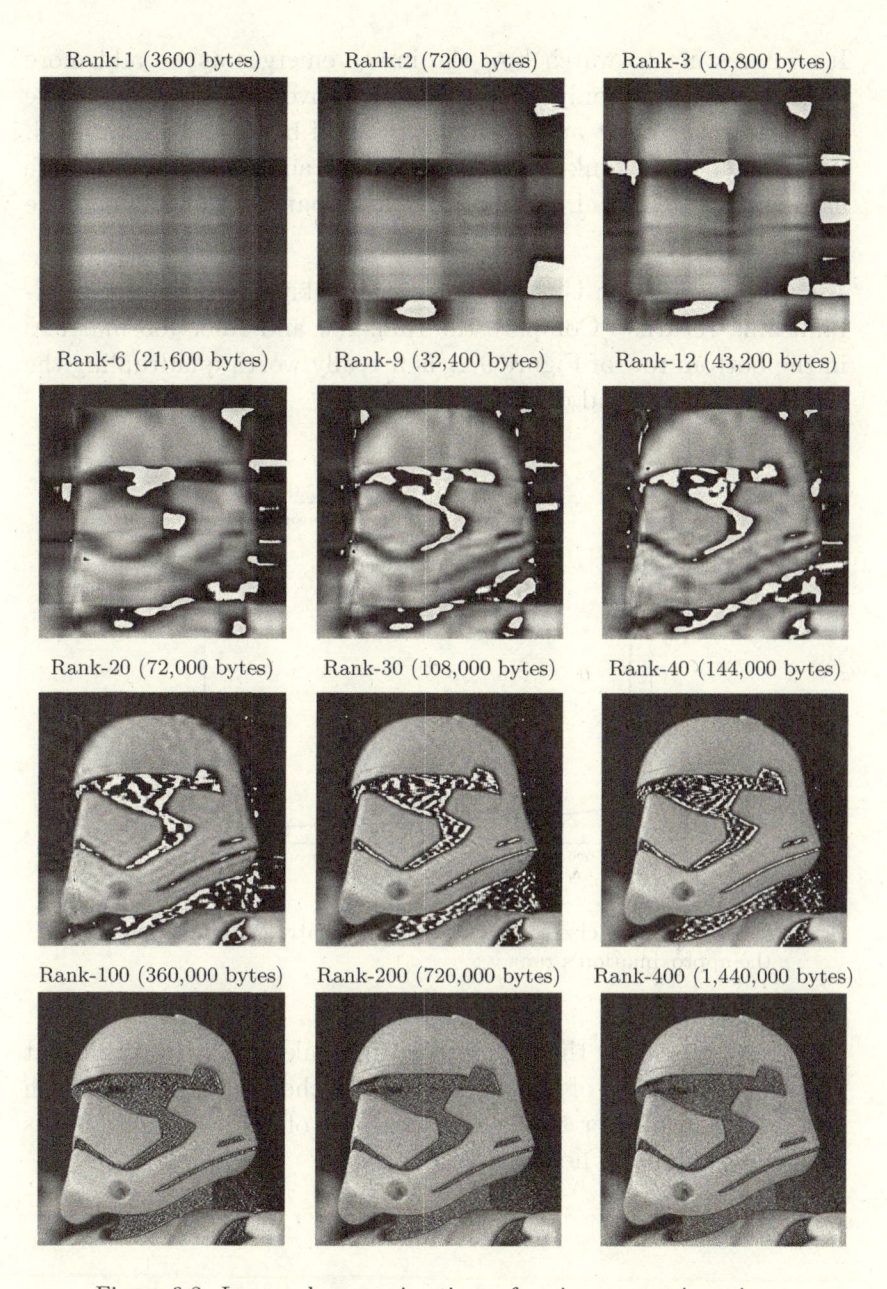

Rank-1 (3600 bytes) Rank-2 (7200 bytes) Rank-3 (10,800 bytes)

Rank-6 (21,600 bytes) Rank-9 (32,400 bytes) Rank-12 (43,200 bytes)

Rank-20 (72,000 bytes) Rank-30 (108,000 bytes) Rank-40 (144,000 bytes)

Rank-100 (360,000 bytes) Rank-200 (720,000 bytes) Rank-400 (1,440,000 bytes)

Figure 9.2: Low-rank approximations of an image matrix, using increasing numbers of eigenvectors (and thus an increasing rank, with increasing storage/transmission costs.)

It's interesting to watch how the image emerges as we add more eigenvectors. With only the dominant eigenvector, all we can make out is a blurry, right-angle-centric splash of black and white. Still, it's not bad for a rank-1 matrix, and after adding just a few more eigenvectors we can already see the basic shape of the helmet come through.

Another observation is that we pretty quickly reach a point of diminishing returns. Compare the rank-100 and rank-400 matrices in the bottom row of Figure 9.2. Is it really worth quadrupling the size to get the second one?

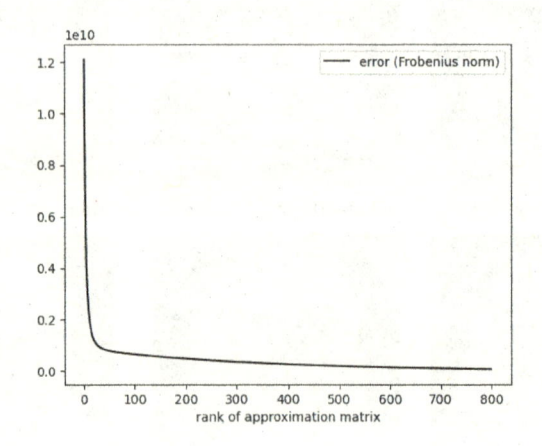

Figure 9.3: The closeness to the original matrix as a function of the approximation's rank.

Figure 9.3 quantifies this by plotting the rank of the matrix against the Frobenius norm of the difference from the original. As you can see, less than fifty or so eigenvectors (out of the total of 1800) is enough to eliminate nearly all the error.

Markov chains

For our next eigenapplication, we'll need to review a few concepts from Chapter 4 of *A Cool Brisk Walk*: probability.

Recall that we can quantify the likelihood of some event happening by assigning it a **probability** between 0 and 1, where 0 means the event is impossible and 1 means it's a certainty. We use the notation "$\Pr(E)$" for this, where E is some event. Sometimes the probability is based on actual counts of past occurrences, and sometimes it is estimated based on intuition and common sense. For instance:

$$\Pr(\text{home team wins in college basketball}) = .6765$$
$$\Pr(\text{worldwide pandemic next year}) = .1$$

You may also recall the notion of **conditional probability**, in which our estimate of an event's likelihood changes based on some other event being known to have (or have not) occurred. We use the notation "$\Pr(A|B)$," pronounced as "the probability of A given B" for this. Examples:

$$\Pr(\text{speeding ticket}) = .05$$
$$\Pr(\text{speeding ticket} \mid \text{driving a red car}) = .15$$

$$\Pr(\text{Jets win tomorrow}) = .7$$
$$\Pr(\text{Jets win tomorrow} \mid \text{starting QB hurt in practice}) = .4$$

In one of these examples the conditional probability is higher than the original, and in the other case it's lower, but either way it's always between 0 and 1.

M1. Systems and states

Now recall from Chapter 7 that we often want to predict how the **state** of some **system** will unfold over its lifetime. A system's "state" is just a way of talking about the (temporary) condition it is in at any one point in time. In this section, we're going to focus on just a single aspect of a system's state, which has a single value at a point in time, not a bunch of stuff like in the Monopoly example. Perhaps our system is the U.S. economy, and in any given quarter its "state" is whether or not it's in a recession. Or maybe we're interested in the system of local weather conditions, for which each day's state is either sunny, cloudy, or rainy.

Let's expand on this last example because we all have so much experience with weather. One way we could get a handle on what tomorrow may bring is to count how many days in the past have been sunny, cloudy, and rainy in our region, and then assume **independence** between days. Remember that if two events are independent, that means that the outcome of one of them has no impact on the other. A Little League player's *jersey color* and *position* are independent of each other: if you tell me Henry's uniform is blue, that doesn't give me any information about whether he's an infielder or a pitcher.

So assuming independence, we could count up the past 100 days in Fredericksburg, and conclude:

$$Pr(sunny) = .5$$
$$Pr(cloudy) = .4$$
$$Pr(rainy) = .1$$

With this simple model, if someone asked us "how likely is it to rain tomorrow?" we'd reply "about a 10% chance," no matter what the weather was today, yesterday, or any other day. We figure that it doesn't matter what happened on those other days, because we're assuming every day is independent of the others.

Now this simplistic response is unsatisfying on several levels. For one, it doesn't take into account the season we're in, mushing all months together into a mediocre gray. But more to the point, it doesn't even take into account the recent past. As we've all observed, weather patterns tend to form and transform on a slower time scale than individual days. If it's hot today, it's pretty likely to remain hot for at least a little while – we're probably not going to get a string of hot, cold, hot, cold, hot, and cold days consecutively.

Remember that when the current state of some system is influenced only by its *previous* state, it has the so-called "Markov property." In this case, we can build a powerful structure called a **first-order Markov chain** to analyze it. Markov chains are named for the brilliant Russian mathematician Andrey Markov, one of the most underrated minds in history, in my opinion. The phrase "first order" here has nothing to do with Kylo Ren or Supreme Leader Snoke; it means that the system's current state depends only on its immediately preceding state, and is conditionally independent of all states longer ago than that.[5] In weather terms, this means knowing that it rained on Tuesday tells you something important about whether it will also rain on Wednesday, but nothing (directly) about Thursday or beyond.

M2. Stochastic matrices

A Markov chain can be modeled as (surprise!) a matrix, which encodes all its *conditional probabilities*. Each one says: "if the previous state is X, here's the probability that the current state will be Y."

For example, maybe it's true that heat waves tend to last longer than a day. If it was sunny yesterday, it's likely to remain sunny today. In symbols, we might say:

$$\Pr(\text{sunny}_k \mid \text{sunny}_{k-1}) = .7$$

The k subscript is just to number the days. This formula says: "the chances of it being sunny on any particular day, given that it was sunny the day before, are 70%."

---

[5] If we said that a system's current state depended on its immediately *two* preceding states, we'd built a second-order Markov chain, and so forth.

Perhaps it's also true in our region that rainstorms tend not to last longer than one day. (Once a storm finally breaks, the atmosphere has "gotten the rain out of its system" and drier days will likely follow.) So we might estimate these quantities:

$$\Pr(\text{rainy}_k \mid \text{rainy}_{k-1}) = .05$$
$$\Pr(\text{cloudy}_k \mid \text{rainy}_{k-1}) = .55$$
$$\Pr(\text{sunny}_k \mid \text{rainy}_{k-1}) = .4$$

We've saying that two rainy days in a row are very unlikely: if it rained yesterday, it's most likely to be cloudy (and dry) today, not wet again.

Note carefully that the above three numbers *add up to exactly 1*, as they must. The weather on day k must either be rainy, cloudy, or sunny in our simple weather model. Since these three possibilities are mutually exclusive and collectively exhaustive, their probabilities must total 1.

If you nodded to the previous paragraph, make sure you also understand that the *following* three numbers do *not* have to add up to 1 (and normally won't):

$$\Pr(\text{cloudy}_k \mid \text{rainy}_{k-1}) = .55$$
$$\Pr(\text{cloudy}_k \mid \text{cloudy}_{k-1}) = .6$$
$$\Pr(\text{cloudy}_k \mid \text{sunny}_{k-1}) = .2$$

Students sometimes get confused here. The three expressions look an awful lot like the ones at the top of the page, yet the bottom three don't represent mutually exclusive and collectively exhaustive options at all. The first of the bottom three says "what's the probability it'll be cloudy today if it was rainy yesterday?" The second asks a question about a completely different circumstance: "what about if it was *cloudy* yesterday? Now how likely are clouds today?" These two numbers (.55 and .6) are unrelated to one another, and not bound by any probability axioms.

And now, the matrix. There are nine different conditional probabilities for this system, and we'll arrange them in a matrix called W (for "weather") as follows:

$$W = \begin{array}{c} \\ \\ \uparrow \\ \text{day}_k \\ \downarrow \end{array} \begin{array}{c} \\ \\ \text{sunny} \\ \text{cloudy} \\ \text{rainy} \end{array} \begin{array}{c} \overleftarrow{} \quad \overrightarrow{\text{day}_{k-1}} \quad \rightarrow \\ \begin{array}{ccc} \text{sunny} & \text{cloudy} & \text{rainy} \end{array} \\ \left[\begin{array}{ccc} .7 & .3 & .4 \\ .2 & .6 & .55 \\ .1 & .1 & .05 \end{array} \right] \end{array}$$

The columns correspond to yesterday's weather, and the rows correspond to today's weather. So if it was cloudy yesterday, the probability of sun today is .3 (top-middle entry). If it was sunny yesterday, the probability of rain today is .1 (bottom-left corner). Take a moment to look at this matrix and verify your understanding of what each entry means. Also verify that the example numbers on the previous couple of pages have all been entered in the right places.

A matrix of the form above goes by many names: some call them **Markov matrices**, others **probability matrices**, still others **transition matrices**, and yet others **substitution matrices**. Me? I like the term **stochastic matrices** (since it sounds cool) so that's what we'll go with here. ("Stochastic," by the way, is a word that basically means "random" or "indeterminate." Any time you're dealing with probability, you have a stochastic system.)

Just like our Leslie matrices from p. 178 did, stochastic matrices have certain constraints they must adhere to in order to join the club. For a matrix to be a stochastic matrix:

1. all its entries must between 0 and 1, and
2. the sum of each of its columns must be exactly 1.

(Notice I wrote "the sum of each *column*," not row, for the same reason I took pains to explain a few paragraphs ago. The rows don't normally sum to 1, and there's no reason they should.)

Before going further, take a moment and verify that the W matrix above is indeed a stochastic matrix.

Then, complete this puzzle. Given the stochastic matrix W, which of the following weeks of weather is most likely to actually occur? And which is least likely? ("S"=sunny, "C"=cloudy, "R"=rainy)

    a. S-R-S-R-S-R-S   c. S-C-S-C-S-C-S
    b. S-R-R-R-S-S-S   d. S-S-S-S-C-C-C

(Answers on p. 265.)

M3. Simulating the Markov chain

The W matrix is square, and thus a linear operator. It can be multiplied by 3×1 column vectors to produce other 3×1 column vectors. Its domain is vectors that represent yesterday's weather, and its codomain is vectors that represent today's weather.

Suppose yesterday – which we'll call "day 1" since it's the first day we'll consider – was a sunny day. We now want to predict what the weather will be today. If we create a column vector for yesterday that has 1 for "sunny" and 0 for the other weather options, all we need to do is multiply it by W, and whammo:

$$W \cdot \overrightarrow{\text{day}_1} = \overrightarrow{\text{day}_2}.$$

By the actual numbers, we get:

$$\begin{array}{c} \\ \text{sunny} \\ \text{cloudy} \\ \text{rainy} \end{array} \begin{array}{ccc} \text{sunny} & \text{cloudy} & \text{rainy} \end{array} \\ \left[\begin{array}{ccc} .7 & .3 & .4 \\ .2 & .6 & .55 \\ .1 & .1 & .05 \end{array} \right] \cdot \left[\begin{array}{c} 1 \\ 0 \\ 0 \end{array} \right] = \left[\begin{array}{c} .7 \\ .2 \\ .1 \end{array} \right].$$

We set $\overrightarrow{\text{day}_1}$ to $[\ 1\ \ 0\ \ 0\ ]^\mathsf{T}$ because we *knew* yesterday's weather. When we set out to make our forecast, we knew that there was a 100% chance it was sunny yesterday, and 0% chance it was either cloudy or rainy.

MARKOV CHAINS

The resulting $\overrightarrow{day_2}$ vector, of course, does not turn out to have only 0's and 1's. That's because the forecast is uncertain. What the $\overrightarrow{day_2}$ vector means is that there will be a 10% chance of rain today, a 20% chance of overcast skies, and a 70% chance of clear blue.

Just like with Leslie matrices, we can run this forward any number of times we want to predict into the distant future. Let's find out what the weather is likely to be on day 4 (the day after tomorrow):

$$W \cdot \overrightarrow{day_1} = \overrightarrow{day_2}$$
$$W \cdot \overrightarrow{day_2} = \overrightarrow{day_3}$$
$$W \cdot \overrightarrow{day_3} = \overrightarrow{day_4}$$

so

$$W^3 \cdot \overrightarrow{day_1} = \overrightarrow{day_4}.$$

That last step takes advantage of the associative property of matrix multiplication. This yields:

$$\begin{array}{c} \text{sunny} \\ \text{cloudy} \\ \text{rainy} \end{array} \begin{bmatrix} \overset{\text{sunny}}{.5455} & \overset{\text{cloudy}}{.4815} & \overset{\text{rainy}}{.49575} \\ .35925 & .42325 & .409125 \\ .09525 & .09525 & .095125 \end{bmatrix} \cdot \begin{bmatrix} 1 \\ 0 \\ 0 \end{bmatrix} = \begin{bmatrix} .5455 \\ .35925 \\ .09525 \end{bmatrix}.$$

Apparently, then, on the day after tomorrow we have only about a 55% chance of sunny weather. That is, if it had been sunny yesterday. What if it had been cloudy yesterday?

$$\begin{array}{c} \text{sunny} \\ \text{cloudy} \\ \text{rainy} \end{array} \begin{bmatrix} \overset{\text{sunny}}{.5455} & \overset{\text{cloudy}}{.4815} & \overset{\text{rainy}}{.49575} \\ .35925 & .42325 & .409125 \\ .09525 & .09525 & .095125 \end{bmatrix} \cdot \begin{bmatrix} 0 \\ 1 \\ 0 \end{bmatrix} = \begin{bmatrix} .4815 \\ .42325 \\ .09525 \end{bmatrix}.$$

Given cloudy weather yesterday, our forecast for the day after tomorrow would look even bleaker: just a 48% chance of sun.

M4.   ...and eigenvectors

Now what does all of this have to do with eigenvectors? So far, all this neat Markov chain material could have been in Chapter 7 before we'd learned about eigenstuff.

Well, if you haven't guessed it, the key insight is related to the diagrams in Section 8.2 ("Magnetic pull," p. 219). Remember that when we took any old vector, and repeatedly multiplied a square matrix by it, the answers we got out were sucked closer and closer to the matrix's dominant eigenvector, as if by magic.

Realize that's exactly what we're doing here with this forecasting-the-future stuff. We started with a vector of 0's and 1's representing the actual weather on a particular day, and we multiplied it by W once for each day we wanted to project our forecast into the future. This means that the further into the future we go, the forecast is going to inevitably be drawn to W's dominant eigenvector.

Python tells us that the dominant eigenvector for our matrix W is:

$$\vec{x_1} = \begin{bmatrix} .5159 \\ .3889 \\ .0952 \end{bmatrix}, \text{ with } \lambda_1 = 1.$$

Believe it or not, this vector gives us **the long-run distribution of the states in the weather system.** Up until now, we've been extrapolating from yesterday's weather out two or three days. But suppose I said, "okay, let's just say a year goes by. What's the probability on any given future day that we'll have sunny, cloudy, or rainy weather?" The answer is given in that magical eigenvector $\vec{x_1}$. On days far in the future, there will be precisely a 51.59% chance of sun, a 38.89% chance of clouds, and a 9.52% chance of showers.

This is the long-run behavior of the Markov chain, dissected and exposed.

It's interesting to think about the fact that it only depends on the W matrix itself, not on the starting vector we used for $\vec{\text{day}_1}$ (such a starting point is often called an **initial condition**). If you think about it, it makes a lot of sense. If we're projecting the long-running behavior of a system, many many days in the future, should it really matter whether *today* happened to be sunny, cloudy, or rainy? Surely predictions way out in the future shouldn't rely any longer on any one observation in the distant past. Its influence has long since faded to nothing. And that's exactly what we find. If you're trying to predict the weather a few days from now, it's worth it to consider what yesterday's weather was and extrapolate out from that. But if you're interested in planning your wedding weekend for next summer, that's just too far out for yesterday's weather to matter. The eigenvector will keep your forecast honest.

Web search

We end this chapter, book, and series with a look at one of the most influential algorithms in world history. It's called "PageRank,"[6] and it's what made Google Google. Like the other applications in this chapter, it's based on eigenvectors. First, though, let's take a look at the state of the art before PageRank.

W1. Web search: pre-Google

It's interesting to study the history of Web search engines, which we don't have time to do here. But one thing you should know is the approach that Google used to dominate the market. Before Google, search engines (like Yahoo!, Excite, and Alta Vista) focused only on returning results that matched your search terms well.

Remember all the way back to the beginning of this book (p. 27 and following), where we discussed a matchmaker dating application for Jezebel, Filbert, and friends. Each person took a survey of interests, and was thereafter represented by a single vector of numbers, which represented how well they liked hiking, candlelight dinners, and so forth. To determine the compatibility between two people, we simply computed the dot product of their two vectors. This worked because in order for a dot product to be large, the two vectors have to have large entries in the same slots of the vector.

One wrinkle with this approach, which we analyzed on pp.44-45, was that it was possible for someone to game the system by simply answering 10 to all the questions. The way to counteract this insidious strategy was to *normalize* everyone's vector before computation. This way, each person effectively only has a certain total "amount" of "interests" which they have to spread among their answers.

Interestingly, this is almost exactly the approach used by Web

---

[6]PageRank was invented by Larry Page and Sergey Brin, the founders of Google. I always wondered if Sergey was jealous that the algorithm wasn't called "BrinRank." Wdyt?

WEB SEARCH

search engines to gauge the similarity between two pages, or the similarity of a page to a search query. Each Web page is represented as a vector of numbers. In place of survey responses as the vector elements, substitute **word counts**. That's right: for every word that appears on any Web page anywhere, a page's vector has an entry for *the number of times that word appears on that page*. So the vector corresponding to (say) cnn.com's home page today might be:

$$\overrightarrow{\texttt{cnn.com}} = [\;\; \underset{a}{105} \quad \underset{\text{aardvark}}{0} \quad \underset{\text{abolish}}{1} \quad \underset{\text{abstention}}{3} \quad \cdots \quad \underset{\text{zoology}}{0} \;\;]$$

This would indicate that the text on cnn.com has 105 instances of the word "a," no "aardvarks," one "abolish," three "abstentions," and so forth: one entry for every possible word.[7] Notice we're deliberately throwing away the information about the *order* words appear on the page. All we care about is how many times each word appears. This is called the **"bag of words"** model, since it's like taking scissors to the page, cutting up all the individual words, and dropping them in a bag. It turns out to work very well in practice.

After forming this vector for a page, we then play the same trick we did on Jezebel & Co., which is to normalize it:

$$\overrightarrow{\texttt{cnn.com}} = [\;\; \underset{a}{.0249} \quad \underset{\text{aardvark}}{0} \quad \underset{\text{abolish}}{.000237} \quad \underset{\text{abstention}}{.000711} \quad \cdots \quad \underset{\text{zoology}}{0} \;\;]$$

This tells us that about 2.5% of all the words on cnn.com today are the word a, .0237% of them are the word abolish, and so on. We're thus summing up the content of the page by saying: "this cnn.com page is 2.5% 'about' the word a, .0237% 'about' the word abolish, *etc.*"

---

[7]This might seem like a prohibitively huge number to you at first, but it's really not. The English language, for instance, only has about half a million words in it, and that's if you count absolutely *everything*, even obscure words that haven't been used since the 15th century. Throw in all the proper nouns, trademarks, slang terms, misspellings, abbreviations, plus the words in every *other* language on earth and you're still just in the low millions. Contrast that with the number of *pages* there are on the Web, which is in the billions.

Now, if I wanted to find "pages with similar content to cnn.com," I'd calculate the dot product of every page's (normalized) vector with CNN's vector, and take the highest results. Or, if a Yahoo! user entered "harry potter the sorcerers stone" in the search box, I'd first make a vector on the fly with a 1 for each of the five words of the query and 0 everywhere else, then normalize it, and finally take its dot product with every page's vector. Effectively, this means I'd be looking for the pages for which the percentage of words that are harry, potter, the, sorcerers, or stone is the highest.

I'm glossing over several other pragmatic steps that search engines take to improve the accuracy of their results. Among them are:

- Getting rid of punctuation, capitalization, and other stuff that doesn't pertain to the root meanings of a word.

- Collapsing all different forms of the same root word to a single entry. In English, this is called **stemming**, because we're finding the word's stem and using it instead of the raw word. The idea here is that the words jump, jumps, jumped, and jumping all reflect the same basic meaning. If we're trying to capture the topics of a Web page, we really don't care which of the specific variants of the word appear, only its root meaning.

- Dropping super-common words altogether. Words like "a," "the," and "of" don't actually hold any meaningful content, because every page has zillions of them regardless of what it's about. Search engines use a **stop list** of common words to discard.

- Scaling the importance of each word by how common it is. This is a gentler version of the previous item, but it's very important. The idea is that the more common a word is, the less about the page it tells you by being present on it.

  Consider these two words, for example: dollar, and Jedi. If I chose a random Web page and told you only that it contained the word dollar, how much would you know about its content? Some, but not much. But if I told you that it contained the word `Jedi`, how much would you know? A lot more. This is because `dollar` is a more common word, and therefore appears in many more different contexts than the word `Jedi` does. A popular algorithm for this is called **TF/IDF**, which stands for "term frequency / inverse document frequency." The amount that a vector's entry contributes to the dot product is the frequency of that word in the page (*i.e.*, how many times `abstention` or a variant of it appears in that page) divided by that word's frequency appearing in documents (*i.e.*, what percentage of all Web pages that `abstention` appears on). Words like `dollar` will appear in a much higher percentage of Web pages, and thence be "discounted" more steeply when it comes to computing similarity to queries.

W2. Web search: Google

Now let's take a step back. All of the details in the previous section were devoted to one strategy: find Web pages whose *content* matches the user's search terms well. The entire purpose of a search engine (everyone thought before 1998) was to identify relevant documents for the user, and "relevant" meant "the words on the page are a good match for what the user typed."

When Google came on the scene in 1998, they of course did all that content-matching stuff too. But they added a critical second component to the criteria for ranking search results. In a way, I've always thought their new ingredient was kind of depressing, but in the end it turned out to be what the world really wanted. The key second ingredient was to factor in the **popularity** of a page, in addition to its content.

Simply put, Google realized that in addition to wanting pages that match their search terms, users also want pages that are well-known and in some sense authoritative. They want to be channeled towards the pages that everyone else already knows about and likes. I find this depressing because it seems to encourage a herd mentality, and to discourage the discovery of new information. But the fact of the matter is that when I type "`harry potter the sorcerers stone`" in a search box, most of the time I don't want to read the Web page of some random crazy Harry Potter fan from Greenland. Instead, I want the IMDB page from the movie, or J.K.Rowling's site that discusses her ideas, or the Wikipedia page describing the book's release and its reception. In a word, I want the popular websites.

That was Page's and Brin's first innovation: to factor popularity into search results, so that even if a big well-known website didn't match the search terms as well as a lesser-known website did, it would get funneled up to the top of the results list anyway.

W3. The PageRank algorithm

So their first innovation was to take into account a page's popularity at all. Their second one was in how to *determine* the popularity of a page. A good illustration here is to think of the drama on a middle school playground. Everyone knows that a school has popular kids, and not-so-popular kids. (I was one of the latter.) A first cut at measuring this could be expressed as follows:

First try: *"You're popular if a lot of kids like you."*

Now if we substitute Web pages for kids, this formula gives us some hope of quantifying the popularity of a Web page. All we have to do is figure out what one page "liking" another page really means. And I'll bet you can figure it out if you just think about it for a moment. The way page A can "like" page B – the way it can vouch for page B's awesomeness, or authoritativeness, or whatever – is simply to **link** to it. Most every Web page has embedded hyperlinks in it, so that when you click on a word or a button you're transported to another page. So we can measure a page's popularity by how many other pages have a link to it:

First try: *"A page is popular if lots of other pages link to it."*

WEB SEARCH

That simple idea is almost PageRank. Almost. But the killer feature of Google's algorithm was to add one little word to the middle school popularity contest. Here it is:

> PageRank: *"You're popular if a lot of **popular** kids like you."*

Or, expressed in terms of the Web:

> PageRank: *"A page is popular if lots of other **popular** pages link to it."*

Yeah, that does pretty much match my experience, I have to admit. If the dweebs and the losers like you, that doesn't say very much. But if kids who are themselves well-liked and admired by others express admiration for *you*, that's a gold-plated imprimatur.

W4. Calculating the PageRank vector

Now as true as the above definition of popularity rings, you may rightly object that it seems circular. We want to measure how popular Sam is. And we know that popular kids are liked by lots of popular kids...but how could we determine how popular Sam's admirers are themselves without getting in an infinite loop?

Eigenvectors will turn out to solve this problem for us. Like. Magic.

To get there, remember your graphs from *A Cool Brisk Walk* Chapter 5, or from p. 196 of this book. The World Wide Web is nothing other than a gigantic directed graph, where each vertex is a Web page and each edge is a hyperlink. Here's a tiny tiny example of one:

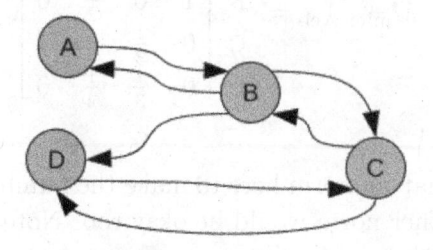

In this minuscule "Web" of just four pages, page A has a link to page B, page B has links to each of the other three, page C has links to B and D, and page D has only a link to page C.

Remember also from p. 200 that we can represent a graph by its adjacency matrix A. This square matrix has one row/column for each vertex of the graph, and a 1 in the positions with an edge from one vertex to another. In this case, the matrix is:

$$A_{\text{mini-Web}} = \begin{array}{c} \\ A \\ B \\ C \\ D \end{array} \begin{array}{c} \begin{array}{cccc} A & B & C & D \end{array} \\ \left[\begin{array}{cccc} 0 & 1 & 0 & 0 \\ 1 & 0 & 1 & 1 \\ 0 & 1 & 0 & 1 \\ 0 & 0 & 1 & 0 \end{array} \right] \end{array}.$$

(Run your eyeballs over that matrix, and compare it with the graph, before continuing.)

We're going to compute what's known as the **PageRank vector** for this graph. It will have one numeric entry for each Web page, which will represent the popularity of that page.

Here's how to do it.

First, we'll do some light bookkeeping on the $A_{\text{mini-Web}}$ matrix, by (1) taking its transpose and then (2) normalizing the columns. We'll call this revised matrix M:

$$M_{\text{mini-Web}} = \begin{array}{c} \\ A \\ B \\ C \\ D \end{array} \begin{array}{c} \begin{array}{cccc} A & B & C & D \end{array} \\ \left[\begin{array}{cccc} 0 & \frac{1}{3} & 0 & 0 \\ 1 & 0 & \frac{1}{2} & 0 \\ 0 & \frac{1}{3} & 0 & 1 \\ 0 & \frac{1}{3} & \frac{1}{2} & 0 \end{array} \right] \end{array}.$$

I used the Manhattan norm here to make the numbers easier on the eyes, but any other norm would be okay too. Note that the sum of each column is 1.

WEB SEARCH

Now here's how to interpret M. Each column corresponds to one page's "praise" for the other pages in the Web. And that page has a total of *one* "praise point" to spend on this praise. In the first column, we see that page A has put all its eggs in one basket: it's screaming loudly that page B, and only page B, is important. That's because in the graph, A has only one outgoing link (which is to B). In the second column, by contrast, page B has spread its praise equally across pages A, C, and D – since it has links to all three of those. Page C divvies up its praise between B and D, while D shouts loudly for C and only C.

The rationale behind normalizing the columns should now be apparent to you. It's the matchmaker leveling effect in action again. A page can have as many outgoing links as it wants, but the more it has, the less potent each one will be in determining popularity.

To get your head around PageRank, try to visualize a **random surfer** mindlessly clicking links in his browser as he surfs the Web. Imagine that this surfer started with some arbitrary page, and then he chose one of its links at random and clicked on it. Then he chose one of *that* page's links at random and clicked on it, and continued that process indefinitely. (You should try this at home – it's usually rather amusing where you end up after a minute or two, no matter what page you started on.)

The key question to ask is this: after the random surfer does his thing for a few hours, what's the probability that he lands on page A? What about B? C? D?

Let's work it out mathematically. We'll create a vector $\vec{p}$ that contains, for each page, the probability that the random surfer will be on that page. The process starts with a completely random page, remember, so we have a $\frac{1}{4}$ probability of starting on each:

$$\vec{p}_1 = \begin{bmatrix} .25 \\ .25 \\ .25 \\ .25 \end{bmatrix}.$$

The "1" subscript says that these are the probabilities for the *first* page the random surfer browses.

Okay, what's the probability that the *second* page he browses is each of the four?

If you remember your Law of Total Probability from *A Cool Brisk Walk*, you'll know that the probability of visiting page A second is:

Pr(page A second) = Pr(page A second | page A first) +
Pr(page A second | page B first) +
Pr(page A second | page C first) +
Pr(page A second | page D first).

In other words, there are four different ways that page A could be my second destination; namely, my first two pages could have been AA, BA, CA, or DA.

Do you see how to get the probability of this – and also the probability of landing on any of the other pages second – from the M matrix? It's a snap. All you do is matrix-vector multiplication! $\vec{p}_2$ is simply $M \cdot \vec{p}_1$.

$$\vec{p}_2 = M \cdot \vec{p}_1 = \begin{bmatrix} 0 & \frac{1}{3} & 0 & 0 \\ 1 & 0 & \frac{1}{2} & 0 \\ 0 & \frac{1}{3} & 0 & 1 \\ 0 & \frac{1}{3} & \frac{1}{2} & 0 \end{bmatrix} \cdot \begin{bmatrix} .25 \\ .25 \\ .25 \\ .25 \end{bmatrix} =$$

$$.25 \cdot \begin{bmatrix} 0 \\ 1 \\ 0 \\ 0 \end{bmatrix} + .25 \cdot \begin{bmatrix} .333 \\ 0 \\ .333 \\ .333 \end{bmatrix} + .25 \cdot \begin{bmatrix} 0 \\ .5 \\ 0 \\ .5 \end{bmatrix} + .25 \cdot \begin{bmatrix} 0 \\ 0 \\ 1 \\ 0 \end{bmatrix} = \begin{bmatrix} .083 \\ .375 \\ .333 \\ .208 \end{bmatrix}.$$

I'm using the "second way" of thinking about matrix-vector multiplication here (from p. 91) – a linear combination of M's columns. Since there's a $\frac{1}{4}$ chance of being on page A first, and page A always goes to page B, that means there's a .25 probability of starting the random surf with the sequence AB, and a 0 probability of starting with AA, AC, or AD. So when constructing our totals, we add .25 times [0 1 0 0]$^\mathsf{T}$.

There's also a $\frac{1}{4}$ probability of starting on page B. But if that happens, then there's a $\frac{1}{3}$ chance (each) of going to A, C, or D next. Put that together, and you see that there's a $\frac{1}{12}$ probability of starting with any of the BA, BC, or BD sequences, and a 0 probability of starting with BB. *Etc.* Repeat that process, and you get the $\vec{p}_2$ result shown above: a 37.5% chance of landing on page B second, nearly that high a chance (33.3%) of landing on page C second, and smaller likelihoods (8.3% and 20.8%, respectively) of landing on page A or D second.

What about how likely each page is to be *third* in the sequence? Just multiply by M again to get $\vec{p}_3$.

What about fourth? Just multiply by M again to get $\vec{p}_4$.

What about fifth? Just multiply by M again to get $\vec{p}_5$.

(...and so on ...)

And now for the finishing touch. What about the *long-term* likelihood of visiting each of the pages? In other words, after the random surfer has been doing his thing for a while, what do the probabilities settle down to?

What we're really asking for is $\vec{p}_\infty$. This would seem to require infinite multiplications to compute the value of $M^\infty \cdot \vec{p}_1$. But remember the magic of eigenvectors: if you keep multiplying M by *any* vector, it will be drawn to the dominant eigenvector like a moth to the flame. So we don't have to actually multiply infinitely many times, or even once; instead, we just take M's dominant eigenvector!

And that, my friends, is the PageRank vector. For the graph above, the dominant eigenvector turns out to be:

$$\vec{\mathbf{pagerank}}_{\text{mini-Web}} = \begin{bmatrix} .159 \\ .286 \\ .305 \\ .249 \end{bmatrix},$$

which announces with finality that C is officially the most popular page of the bunch, with a PageRank score of .305, and that the others are B, D, and A, in that order.

The PageRank algorithm vanquishes the circularity problem. We can safely define popular pages as "pages which lots of other popular pages link to" yet not get stuck in an infinite loop. All we need to do is calculate the dominant eigenvector of the modified adjacency matrix, and we magically obtain the popularity of every page in our Web.

Combining this popularity information with the relevancy information used by older search engines (p. 254) is how Google changed the world. It's why you can type any old thing into a search engine these days and in the blink of an eye get exactly the pages you were looking for. I search the Web many times every day, and I almost never need to go to even the *second* page of search results. The pages I want are invariably at the top of the list. Who knew that steering me towards popular pages would be exactly what I really wanted?

Answers to Markov chain puzzle from p. 250

Just by thinking about how we designed the probabilities, you can probably eyeball that sequence d is the most likely and sequence b the least likely. In sequence d, we have four sunny days in a row, followed by three cloudy days, and it is in fact true that both sunny days and cloudy days like to follow each other. In sequence b, though, we have four rainy days in a row which just isn't going to happen very often, since our probability of two consecutive rainy days is a mere .05.

Here's the precise numerical answers:

a. $\Pr(rainy_2 \mid sunny_1) \cdot \Pr(sunny_3 \mid rainy_2) \cdot \Pr(rainy_4 \mid sunny_3) \cdot \Pr(sunny_5 \mid rainy_4) \cdot \Pr(rainy_6 \mid sunny_5) \cdot \Pr(sunny_7 \mid rainy_6)$
= .1 · .4 · .1 · .4 · .1 · .4 = **.000064**

b. $\Pr(rainy_2 \mid sunny_1) \cdot \Pr(rainy_3 \mid rainy_2) \cdot \Pr(rainy_4 \mid rainy_3) \cdot \Pr(sunny_5 \mid rainy_4) \cdot \Pr(sunny_6 \mid sunny_5) \cdot \Pr(sunny_7 \mid sunny_6)$
= .1 · .05 · .05 · .4 · .7 · .7 = **.000049**

c. $\Pr(cloudy_2 \mid sunny_1) \cdot \Pr(sunny_3 \mid cloudy_2) \cdot \Pr(cloudy_4 \mid sunny_3) \cdot \Pr(sunny_5 \mid cloudy_4) \cdot \Pr(cloudy_6 \mid sunny_5) \cdot \Pr(sunny_7 \mid cloudy_6)$
= .2 · .3 · .2 · .3 · .2 · .3 = **.000064**

d. $\Pr(sunny_2 \mid sunny_1) \cdot \Pr(sunny_3 \mid sunny_2) \cdot \Pr(sunny_4 \mid sunny_3) \cdot \Pr(cloudy_5 \mid sunny_4) \cdot \Pr(cloudy_6 \mid cloudy_5) \cdot \Pr(cloudy_7 \mid cloudy_6)$
= .7 · .7 · .7 · .2 · .6 · .6 = **.024696**

Take special note that even though weeks a and b have the same number of rainy and sunny days, the order makes all the difference. Since rainy days don't like to follow each other, sequence a is more likely to occur than sequence b. By contrast, weeks c and d have the same number of sunny and cloudy days, but since those types of weather *do* like to follow each other, sequence d is far more likely.

Index

: (colon), 105
[] (boxies), 46, 103
"1-path", 206

aardvark, 255
additive inverse, 157
adjacency matrix, 199, 259
adjacent (vertices), 197
affine function, 3
"ah-ha!" moment, 21
Algebra, 1
"an algebra", 1, 19
Anaconda, 7
arange() function, 47, 77
.argmax(), 50
.argmin(), 50
argument, 74
array, 21, 46, 103
aspect ratio, 236
assignment (Python), 9
associative (operation), 154, 226, 251
associative array, 21
average() function, 75

backwards, 60
bag of words, 255
bake sale, 32, 92

basis, 69, 71, 94, 165, 224
Battlestar Galactica, 125
Biff, 27
bijective function, 133, 170
binary, 186
bit / byte, 236
block diagonal matrix, 99, 204
blue matrix, 170
BMI (body-mass index), 116
body (function), 74
Bond, James, 147
Bowser, 156
branching, 107
bridge, 212
Brin, Sergey, 254
brownies, 32, 92
bunny rabbit, 180
butterfly, 178

calculator, glorified, 7
"calling" a function, 75
Cartesian coordinates, 17
Cartesian plane, 13, 155
Cartesian product, 86
CGI movie effects, 124
change of basis, 72, 94, 165, 225
chess, 178

chocolate chip cookies, 32, 92
closure, 2
cnn.com, 254
code, 7
code word, 192, 193
codomain, 20, 86, 114, 133
Col. Mustard, 23
collectively exhaustive, 248
colon operator (NumPy), 105
colonial viper, 125
column vector, 84, 88, 151
commenting out code, 8
commutative, 23, 25, 154, 184
conditional probability, 245
connected (graph), 198
console window, 7
coordinate, 16
coordinate plane, 13
corrupted data, 187
cosine, 36
counter-clockwise, 13
covariance matrix, 229
CPSC 284, 199
credit card, 150
cross product, 24
"crow-flies" distance, 17, 35
.csv file, 104
cycle, 199
Cylon, 125

DAG (directed, acyclic graph), 199
debug, 7
def (Python), 74
default, 84
degree (of a graph vertex), 198
degree of freedom, 129
diagonal matrix, 97, 110

diagonal, of a matrix, 96, 157, 201
diagonalize (a matrix), 222
dictionary, 21
dimension, 11, 18, 70, 85, 103, 130
directed graph, 197, 198, 201
direction (of a vector), 13
disconnected (graph), 198
discrete-time system, 179
distributive, 23
domain, 20, 86, 114, 133
dominant eigenvector, 218, 238
domino basis, 71, 94, 165
.dot(), 51, 107, 172
dot product, 24, 25, 34, 36, 51
double-pipe sign ($\|\cdot\|$), 35
dweeb, 259

edge (graph), 196
editor window, 7
eigenbasis, 224
eigendecomposition, 222, 238
eigenvalue, 217
eigenvector, 217
element, 16
elephants, 6
else branch, 109, 111
error syndrome, 189
error-correcting code, 186
Euclidean distance, 35
Euclidean norm, 36, 52, 237
expectations, linear, 5

Facebook, 197
fat, saturated, 33
fecundity, 181
fern, 178

INDEX

Filbert, 27, 44, 254
first-order, 247
Fiver, 185
`for` loop, 76, 110
frame (of a video), 236
Fredericksburg, Virginia, 85
frequency, resonant, 211
Frobenius norm, 237
fudge, 32, 92
full-rank matrix, 131, 171
function, 3, 20, 21, 83, 86, 113
function (Python), 74

Get Out Of Jail Free card, 178
GIF file, 186
Google, 254
graph, 196, 259
gray scale, 236
guitar, 213

Hamming code, 186
Harry Potter, 255, 257
hash table, 21
hashtag, 8
Hazel, 185
Hermione, 73, 95, 165, 224
hippo butts, 120
horses, 134
hyperlink, 258

identity element, 157
identity matrix, 98, 118, 157, 164, 173
`if` statement, 107
in-degree, 198, 205
indentation (in Python), 74, 77, 107
independence, 246
index number, 16, 46, 85, 103

`Inf` (infinity), 52
information loss, 12
initial condition, 252
injective function, 133, 170
inner product, 152
inverse, 73, 95, 136, 157, 163, 165, 171, 225
`is_diagonal()`, 110
`is_square()`, 109
iteration, 76

Jezebel, 27, 91, 254
JPG file, 186

kernel, 125, 130, 136, 171
King of the World, 102, 163
Kylo Ren, 247

label, 19, 85
Law of Total Probability, 262
left-ness, 12
length (of a vector), 13
Leslie matrix, 180, 249
Letterman, David, 201
lifespan, 180
`linalg.eig()`, 231
`linalg.inv()`, 173
`linalg.norm()`, 52
`linalg.solve()`, 174
linear, 3
linear combination, 58, 67
linear expectations, 5
linear independence, 53, 63, 171
linear map, 114
linear operator, 117, 213, 250
linear transformation, 113
`linearCombo()`, 78
list, 21, 46
`loadtxt()` (NumPy), 48, 104

loop, 76
losing information, 12
lower-triangular, 97

machine, 113
magnitude (of a vector), 13
main diagonal, of a matrix, 96
Manhattan norm, 39, 260
Mario Kart, 124
Markov chain, 247
Markov property, 179, 247
Markov, Andrey, 247
`matchmaker.com`, 27, 28, 44, 91, 149, 254
mathematical object, 1
matrix (plural: matrices), 84
matrix multiplication, 173
matrix-vector multiplication, 107, 145, 160, 204
`.max()`, 50
McDonald's, 117
middle C, 213, 216
`.min()`, 50
mirror, 96
Miss Scarlet, 23
modularity, 74
modulo operator (mod), 186
Monopoly, 178, 245
mosquito, 14
MP3 file, 186
Mr. Green, 23
Mr. Right, 28, 44, 254
Mrs. Peacock, 23
Mrs. White, 23
multiplicative inverse, 157, 166
mutually exclusive, 248

`ndarray` (NumPy type), 46, 103
nested `for` loop, 110
network-based data, 196
nibble, 189
"no can do", 22, 23
"noisy channel", 187
`norm()` (from `linalg`), 52
norm (of a matrix), 237
norm (of a vector), 35, 52, 222
normalizing (a vector), 43, 223, 231, 254
nullity, 130, 171
nullspace, 125
NumPy, 7, 46, 103

Oakenshield, Thorin, 235
object, mathematical, 1
one-dimensional quantity, 11
order (of a graph), 197
origin, 3, 126
orthogonal, 30, 100
orthogonal matrix, 100, 163
orthonormal, 102
orthonormal basis, 164, 229
out-degree, 198, 205
outer product, 152, 235

Page, Larry, 254
PageRank vector, 260
partition, 204
path (through a graph), 197, 205
perpendicular, 30
piano, 213, 216
plain-text file, 48, 104
playground, 212
`plot_operator()`, 140

plotting, 78
point of origin, 13
polar coordinates, 17
popularity, 257
porcupine, 3
Potter, Harry, 255, 257
prerequisite, 199, 202
probability, 245
probability matrix, 249
Prof. Plum, 23
programming, 7
pylab library, 78, 138
`pylab.arrow()`, 138
`pylab.plot()`, 78
`pylab.xlim()/ylim()`, 78
Pythagorean Theorem, 17, 35
Python, 7

rabbit, 180
racehorses, 134
"radius", 17
`random.rand()` function, 48, 104
random surfer, 261
rank, 131
rank-deficient, 131, 171
rank-nullity theorem, 132
"reachable" vertex (graph), 198
reciprocal, 157, 166
Ren, Kylo, 247
resonant frequency, 211
`return` statement, 74, 109
reversible, 134, 170
Rice Krispie treats, 92
Richmond, Virginia, 85
right angle, 30
right-ness, 12
Ron, 71, 94, 165, 224

rotation matrix, 123, 127
`round_()` function, 49
row vector, 84, 88, 151
Rowling, J.K., 257

saturated fat, 33
scalar, 11
scalar-vector multiplication, 22, 51, 220
scale of measure, 11
scattershot, 225
scientific notation, 173
search engine, 254
set, 126
shopping list, 33
signal, 189
simulation, 179
simultaneous equations, 159
single-bit error, 194
singular matrix, 166, 171
singular value decomposition (SVD), 237, 238
size (of a graph), 197
slice, 49, 106
Slinky, 212
smooshing, 120, 127
Social Security Number, 133
span, 68
Spectral Theorem, 222, 229, 239
Spyder, 7
square matrix, 95, 109, 117
squishing, 120, 127
standard basis, 69, 71, 94, 165, 225
Starbuck, 125
Stark, Arya, 13
state, 245

state (of a system), 178
state vector, 178
stemming, 256
stochastic matrix, 249
stock price, 12, 116
stop list, 256
stretching, 119, 127
strongly connected (graph), 198
stupid dog tricks, 201
subdiagonal, 181
substitution matrix, 249
sucky matrix, 132
`.sum()`, 50
Supreme Leader Snoke, 247
surfer, 261
surjective function, 133, 170
survival rate, 181, 185
swing, 212
symmetric matrix, 95, 153, 164, 201, 229
system, 178, 245

Tacoma Narrows Bridge, 212
tail (of a vector), 13, 17, 35
taxicab norm, 39
tensor, 103
TF/IDF, 256
the Domino Game, 53
Thrace, Lt. Kara, 125
tip (of a vector), 13, 17, 35
transition matrix, 249
transpose, 88, 91, 152, 163, 191, 260
`.transpose()`, 107
traversing (a graph), 197
"trivial" solution, 64, 126, 128
`trunc()` function, 49
tuna fish, 12

Twitter, 197
`.txt` file, 48, 104

Ulam, Stanisław, 6
undirected graph, 197, 201
upper-triangular, 97, 202

variable (Python), 9
vector, 11, 12, 21, 83
vector addition, 22, 51
vector multiplication, 24, 51
vector space, 19, 68
vertex (graph), 196
video file, 186

Wal-Mart, 132
Washington, D.C., 85
Watership Down, 185
weakly connected (graph), 198
Web search, 254
Wegmans, 33
weighted graph, 197
`weights`, 50, 75, 107
Wendell, 27
whirlpool, 127
windshield wiper, 60
word count, 254

y-intercept, 3
$y = mx + b$, 3
Yahoo 254
yellow matrix, 170

zero vector, 125
`zeros()` function, 47, 104
zombie, 178
zoology, 255